THE CHURCH
IN
THE WORLD

THE CHURCH IN THE WORLD

OPPOSITION, TENSION, OR TRANSFORMATION?

Robert E. Webber

Academie Books Grand Rapids, Michigan
Zondervan Publishing House

THE CHURCH IN THE WORLD
Copyright © 1986 by The Zondervan Corporation
Grand Rapids, Michigan

ACADEMIE BOOKS
is an imprint of
Zondervan Publishing House
1415 Lake Drive S.E.
Grand Rapids, Michigan 49506

Library of Congress Cataloging in Publication Data
Webber, Robert.
    The church in the world.

    Bibliography: p.
    Includes index.
    1. Church and the world—History. I. Title.
BR115.W6W42   1985   261.1'09   85–22801
ISBN 0–310–36601–1

Designed by Louise Bauer
Edited by Joseph D. Allison

Printed in the United States of America

86 87 88 89 90 91 / 9 8 7 6 5 4 3 2 1

Dedicated to
MORRIS INCH, Ph.D.
on the Occasion of his Retirement
from Wheaton College, 1986
Esteemed Colleague and Chairperson
A Man of Scholarship, Christian Maturity
and Tempered Spirit

CONTENTS

INTRODUCTION

In the past twenty years a number of books have been written on the subject of church and society. Most of these books have been either calls to social action or treatments of specific social issues such as abortion, hunger, environmental issues, energy matters, the distribution of wealth, Christian political presence, and related issues.

The Church in the World differs from these books in that it is written especially for use as a classroom textbook. I envision this book as a text in college and seminary courses dealing with church and society issues. However, it has been written in such a way that it will be of interest to pastors as well as leaders and workers in the front line activities of social action; and it should be of interest to church study groups who wish to gain a better understanding of the role the church plays in local political and social issues.

The reader should be aware of the strengths and weaknesses that characterize this work. One strength is that it is comprehensive in scope. I have attempted to bring together in a single volume the most pertinent biblical, historical, theological, and contemporary information related to the church and world issue. The advantage of this approach is that the student is able to see the present historical moment with its particular issues in relation to an entire body of literature. Such a comprehensive perspective prevents one from having a myopic viewpoint. A second strength of *The Church in the World* is its biblical-theological emphasis. I have attempted to develop a perception of church and world that is rooted in a current scholarly consensus drawn both from biblical exegesis and theological reflection. The advantage of this approach is that the text of Scripture, far from being ignored, plays a central, decisive, and authoritative role in understanding the work of the church in the world. Third, a great deal of attention has been given to the relationship between church and world in various historical periods of the church. Such an understanding of how the church has related to the world in other cultures and under various circumstances prevents us from being ahistorical in our judgments today. Finally, *The Church in the World* is appropriately ecumenical. I have attempted to be even-handed in my assessment of contemporary viewpoints regarding the role of the church in the world. Therefore, the final section includes chapters on the World Council of Churches, contemporary Catholic views, the Religious Right, and the World Evangelical Fellowship.

There are also certain weaknesses in the methodology I have employed in *The Church in the World*. One obvious weakness is that each chapter is a summary of what could be a complete book. I have attempted to counter this problem by footnoting sources for further reading and by including an extensive bibliography for each section of the book. A second concern that some readers will have is that I do not treat specific current social, economic, political, and moral issues. Since the nature of the book is to provide a biblical, historical, and theological framework from which specific issues may be studied, the examination of these issues in detail would require another volume.

The overriding theme of *The Church in the World* is a christological vision of the church and the world. Christ, the victor over the powers of evil, will restore the created order in the consummation with the final defeat of evil powers. The church, now commissioned to proclaim this message, heralds the defeat of evil with its power to distort the spheres of creation, and thus provides hope for humanity and the world in the eschatological vision which it declares and by which it seeks to live.

In the process of writing a book there are many people known and unknown to whom thanks are due. I particularly wish to express my appreciation to the administration of Wheaton College for a sabbatical leave from teaching that enabled me to concentrate on this project and to the Aldeen Fund for supplying money for the typing of the manuscript in final form.

I also wish to acknowledge that parts of this book have drawn on previously published material in *The Secular Saint* and *Reshaping Evangelical Higher Education*. A special thanks is in order to Zondervan Publishing Company for releasing this material. Thanks also to my editors Stanley Gundry, Ed van der Maas, and Joseph D. Allison, for their helpful organizational suggestions and line editing; I especially wish to thank Mr. Allison in this regard. I also wish to express a word of appreciation to my colleague, Dr. Herbert Jacobsen, who read the manuscript in its early form and made valuable suggestions; to the Reverend Thomas W. Strieter, who provided counsel on the interpretation of Luther; and to Harry Genet, who provided me with materials on the history of the World Evangelical Fellowship. I would be remiss in not mentioning my appreciation to the librarians of the Billy Graham Library at Wheaton College for providing a much appreciated comfortable space for writing. And last but certainly not least, I wish to express my deepest appreciation to Jane Marston, secretary to the Bible and Religion Department, who has faithfully typed, retyped, and corrected this manuscript in its various stages.

ROBERT WEBBER
WHEATON COLLEGE

I

THE BIBLICAL BASIS

1

CHURCH AND WORLD

Since the sixties, evangelical Christianity has undergone some very significant changes. By far, the most extensive change and the one that has produced the widest controversy is the emergence of evangelical social concern. The shift has been away from an individualistic Christianity toward a Christianity that relates not only to the whole person, but to the whole of society as well.

We may define evangelical social concern as the application of the Christian world view to the political, legislative, economic, and moral life of society and individuals. It is a repudiation of Christian privatism and obscurantism, and a reclamation of the lordship of Christ over every aspect of life. It is an acknowledgment of the presence and permeation of evil in the structures of life, an attempt to reduce the influence of evil in society and an active promotion of justice and morality.

The purpose of this book is to provide the biblical, historical, and theological data needed to think constructively about evangelical social action in the contemporary world setting. While the ultimate source of our knowledge is Scripture, an investigation into the history of the church plays an important part in our interpretation of the biblical data. Because we Evangelicals assume that we are a phenomenon of the twentieth century, we tend to ignore the experience of the church that has gone before us. However, because the church has wrestled with problems similar in principle to those we wrestle with today, our study of their mistakes and triumphs will inform and guide the choices we make. Therefore, in this book a significant emphasis will be placed on the church in history, not as a way of negating biblical teaching on church and world, but as a way of getting at that teaching. Our study will begin with the primitive Christian community, with particular emphasis on its understanding of the powers of evil that are at work in the world. This concept of the powers, of their function in the world, of their defeat by Christ, and of the witness of the church to them is of central concern in early Christianity.

The most natural place to begin a study of the relationship between church and world is in the New Testament documents. The church emerged within the context of the Greco-Roman culture and was faced immediately with the problem of being a people organized into a distinct society within the world. Consequently, questions arose about the nature of the church, the nature of the world, and the relationship between them. But how are we to view these issues?

Since the New Testament documents are approached either with a naturalistic or supernaturalistic view, it is important to set forth some presuppositions at the outset of this work. I do not follow the school of thought that regards the New Testament conception of the powers of evil, the demonic, and the intervention of supernatural powers as mythological.[1]

My purpose is not to debate or explore the presupposition of a supernatural or naturalistic world view. Yet I do regard one's conviction toward this question as one of utmost importance. The person who takes a mythological view of the New Testament will inevitably interpret the present struggle between the church and the world today in one way, while one who assumes a supernatural world view will approach the church and world issue differently. The supernaturalist will regard the forces of evil as not only real, but having an ontological point of reference. Rather than interpreting the New Testament language as mythical and describing an existential experience only, the supernaturalist will view the battle between good and evil forces in a historical way, arguing that time, space, and history is the battleground, and that what the New Testament describes is in fact occurring now in the present.

My premise is that the New Testament world view is both normative and dynamic. It is normative in that it must be used to judge all of the views on church and world that have been propounded in the history of the church. It is dynamic in the sense that it continues to inform and shape the relation between church and world in every period of history, including the present. With this premise in mind, we turn first to an examination of the idea of the world in the New Testament, and second to the idea of the church.

THE WORLD

In the New Testament, the word for "the world" (*kosmos*) and the ideas associated with it appear to be used in ways that can be categorized under two headings: Sometimes *kosmos* is used in a general sense referring to creation and the world of people; other times *kosmos* is used to refer to spiritual agencies which are at work in the world. (See Appendix A.)

World as Creation and the World of People

The conviction that God created the world is accepted without question by all the New Testament writers.[2] Thus, the New Testament writers stand in continuity with the Old Testament teaching about the origin of creation. Consequently, no New Testament document contains a trace of Gnostic dualism with its rejection of the material order as evil. Nor is there a hint of the Neoplatonic concept of a demiurge, an emanation from the primal God who acts as fashioner of the world. Rather, the New Testament writers see the world as a result of the direct creative activity of God.

However, there is one unique feature of creational thought in the New Testament over against that of the Old Testament writers—namely, the christocentric concept of creation. Paul, for example, views Christ as the agent of creation in Colossians 1:16, "For by him all things were created: things in heaven and on earth, visible and invisible, whether thrones or powers or rulers or authorities; all things were created by him and for him." This conviction seems to be shared by the author of Hebrews when he refers to Christ as the one "through whom he made the universe" (1:2).[3]

Because of the biblical doctrine of creation, Christians do not reject the world. The world is good because God made it. Consequently, the Christian affirms life and affirms human vocations within life. According to the Christian doctrine of creation, there is nothing wrong with the world of physical material nature. Also, throughout Christian history, Christians have affirmed the order of creation and acknowledged that to be involved in the structures of existence—such as family, government, economics, and the like—is good. Biblical Christianity does not require men to withdraw from the world and from human vocation and activity. In short, it can be said that because God created the world through Christ and because God became human in Christ, affirming creation by the Incarnation, nothing in the world of God's creation can be regarded as profane.

The World of Adverse Powers

The second usage of the word *world* in the New Testament is not related to creation, but to the Fall. It describes a world of evil; and world of adverse spiritual powers that work through men and the orders of existence to produce hate, selfishness, greed, murder, violence, and perversion. This is the world that does not recognize Jesus (John 1:10) and hates Him (John 1:7). It is a system of evil that opposes God, Christ, the Spirit, the church, and Christian people (John 16:33). It is the world of sinister powers, against which the Christian must wrestle (Eph. 6:12). (See Appendix A.)

In Paul's letter to the Ephesians, he makes it clear that the Christian's struggle is not against flesh and blood, "but against the rulers, against the authorities, against the powers of this dark world and against the spiritual forces of evil in the heavenly realms" (Eph. 6:12). These spiritual forces work through the structures of God's good creation in such a way that those structures become idols which humans serve. (See Appendix C.) When this happens, mankind worships the creature rather than the Creator. Faith is placed in certain structures of existence, rather than in God the Creator and Redeemer of these structures.

Satan's work is to influence people in such a way that the true function of creation is brought to ruination. The New Testament gives examples of Satan's influence with regard to his power over people, nature, the course of events, the state, and religion. By examining these examples we can gain a better understanding of the principle that Satan may distort the structures of existence and hold people under the power of their perversion.

First, Satan's influence over people is frequently seen in the Gospel accounts of those who have been possessed by an evil spirit (see Matt. 8:28; Mark 1:23ff.; Luke 8:27ff.). The description of these people leaves one with the impression that their very humanity has been disfigured. Their physical appearance is usually contorted; their mental capacity is deranged; and their emotional state is in a frenzy. Here the work of Satan is to destroy the creaturely function of human beings, bringing them to ruination and destruction. Through human disfiguration, the image of God in man is distorted and changed into something other than God intended. A contemporary example is surely found among those who are possessed by evil.

Second, Satan can also turn the human perception of reality into something other than what it is, causing people to be deluded and misinformed regarding truth. For example, Paul recognizes the influence Satan has over the human perception of nature. He warns the Galatians against an astrological faith which trusts astral signs and the movements of heavenly bodies to predict the course of human events (Gal. 4:10). Such a distortion of creation is not only ancient, but modern. Those who read and depend on astral signs have twisted the meaning of the heavenly bodies, expressing faith in their movements and configurations. Satan uses this distortion to keep human beings from faith in the true God. This is true today of those who put faith in horoscope readings and the like.

Third, Satan may also have a deleterious effect on a structure of existence such as the course of events. In Paul's letter to the Thessalonians, he tells of his repeated attempts to see them and attributes to Satan the events that prevented him from coming: "For we wanted to come to you—certainly I, Paul, did, again and again—but Satan stopped us" (1 Thess. 2:18). Furthermore, according to Paul, the course of events in life frequently work against our relationship with

God. "Who shall separate us from the love of Christ?" asks Paul. "Shall trouble or hardship or persecution or famine or nakedness or danger or sword?" (Rom. 8:35). Apparently, Paul mentions this list because these matters *do* separate people from God. Satan uses these events to corrupt faith, to turn people away from truth, to distort their perception. Satan's power over a person's life even extends to his ability to put people in prison. John tells the Christians in Smyrna that "the devil will put some of you in prison to test you" (Rev. 2:10). The power of Satan to turn people against God through the natural course of events must not be underestimated. Surely today Satan brings disaster into people's lives as he did with Job, to turn them away from faith in God and His providential care over their lives.

Fourth, Satan's power to influence also extends to the state. John develops this theme in the Book of Revelation. Satan causes the anti-Christian state to be worshiped as an idol and "leads the whole world astray" (Rev. 12:9). In Revelation 13, we see that this satanic influence permeates all of life. Satan, through the state, slanders the name of God and exercises "authority over every tribe, people, language and nation" (Rev. 13:7). The state is worshiped as ultimate and all the inhabitants of the world are deceived (Rev. 13:14). The totalitarian state thus permeates everything and establishes itself everywhere. Here again, Satan has distorted a structure of existence, the state—which is good in and of itself—and turned it into an evil force. The power that Satan exercises through the state is demonic, for it not only distorts the purpose of the state, but sets the state up as something to believe in. Those who believe in the state as the ultimate authority are prevented from having faith in the living God. Even today there are those who would find their salvation in the power and strength of the state, as those who place their trust in communism or in American military superiority.

Finally, Satan even exercises an influence within the structures of religion. This claim is substantiated by the words of Jesus to the religious leaders of this time. He told them, "You belong to your father, the devil, and you want to carry out your father's desire" (John 8:44). John goes so far as to say, "I know the slander of those who say they are Jews and are not, but are a synagogue of Satan" (Rev. 2:9). Paul argues that the law, when it is perverted, can become distorted. "I found," he writes to the Romans, "that the very commandment that was intended to bring life actually brought death." In the next verse he claims it was sin (the power of the evil one) which "deceived me, and through the commandment put me to death" (Rom. 7:10–11).

In similar fashion, Satan exploits the Christian faith. He appoints "false prophets" who are deceitful workmen, masquerading as apostles of Christ. "And no wonder, for Satan himself masquerades as an angel of light" (2 Cor. 11:13–14). In Paul's instructions to Timothy, he tells him that "some will abandon the faith and follow deceiving spirits and things taught by demons" (1 Tim. 4:1). John warns his readers in similar fashion, cautioning them to "test the spirits to see whether they are from God, because many false prophets have gone out into the world" (1 John 4:1). James tells his readers that if they "harbor bitter envy and selfish ambition" they are "earthly, unspiritual, of the devil" (James 3:14–15). There is no area of life, no structure of existence that is immune from the influence of Satan. Like the great deceiver that he is, Satan seeks to corrupt the structures of existence by turning them into instruments of evil, perverting their true purpose and diverting faith from the living God. Even the structure of religion is susceptible to demonic deception.

In sum, if we are to understand the function of the church in the world, it is necessary to distinguish between the two biblical usages of the word *world*. For the church relates in one way to the creation and in another way to the fallen powers and their sinister influence within the creation.

THE CHURCH

Space does not permit an exhaustive study of the New Testament teaching on the church.[4] Since the amount of material on ecclesiology is voluminous, and since matters such as organization, officers, gifts and the like are not directly related to the subject at hand, discussion of the church will be limited to three New Testament insights: (1) The church is indissolubly linked with Jesus Christ and His saving event. (2) The church is united with the exalted Lord. (3) The church is an eschatological community.

The Church Is Indissolubly Linked With Jesus Christ and His Saving Event.

The essential relationship between Christ and His work on the cross is proclaimed by Paul in His farewell speech to the Ephesian elders: "Keep watch over yourselves and all the flock of which the Holy Spirit has made you overseers. Be shepherds of the church of God, which he bought with His own blood" (Acts 20:28). Here Paul strikes on a theme that is everywhere present in the New Testament. It is the idea that in the old covenant God acquired a people for Himself by delivering them from Egypt. Now God acquires a new people for Himself in a new covenant ratified by His blood. Now all who have been redeemed by Jesus Christ have become God's own people so that Paul can refer to them as churches that are "in Christ" or "of Christ" (Rom. 16:16; 1 Thess. 1:1; 2 Thess. 1:1; Gal. 1:22).

To say that the church is "in Christ" is to root the church in redemption history, a concern that is predominant in Luke and Paul. Luke explains in the infancy narratives that the promises given to Israel are fulfilled in Jesus and the church (Luke 1:32ff., 54–55, 68–75; 2:25–32, 38). The age of the church which is the age of fulfillment was announced by the prophet Joel and initiated at Pentecost (Acts 2:16–21). But the creation of the church also came as a result of Jesus' promise to send the disciples a "power from on high" (Luke 24:49). Luke points out that the church is connected with the ancient promises, the saving event of Christ, and receives the present power of the living Christ through the Holy Spirit. (See Appendix B.)

The Church Is United With the Exalted Lord.

Allusion has already been made in the preceding section to the relationship of the church with its exalted Lord. This heavenly dimension of the church is expanded particularly in the epistles to the Ephesians and the Colossians (Eph. 1:10, 23; Col. 1:17–20, 2:19). The tension between the heavenly and earthly existence of the church becomes apparent through this image. In Ephesians 2:6, Paul speaks of the church as seated "with him in the heavenly realms." In Colossians 1:13, he says, "He has rescued us from the dominion of darkness and brought us into the kingdom of the Son he loves." Therefore, according to Paul, "our citizenship is in heaven" (Phil. 3:20).[5]

If the true location of the church is in heaven, then one must ask about the relationship of the church to the world. Peter finds an especially fitting metaphor to describe the church's place in the world: It is an "alien and stranger" (1 Peter 1:1, 2:11; cf. Heb. 11:13; 2 Cor. 5:6). The motif of the church as "alien" was surely intensified by the persecution of Christians by Nero, already underway when Peter wrote this epistle. Then, as now, the world which is ruled by the diabolical powers under God sets itself against the church so that the church's heavenly nature is realized more intensely. But, as John envisioned in the Apocalypse, the church in Christ will be victorious. Because of this hope, the church on earth may be described as an eschatological community.

The Church Is an Eschatological Community.

We have already seen that the church is rooted in the saving event of Jesus (Heb. 9:11–28), yet must prove itself in its earthly journey (Heb. 10:32–36). In this tension, the church realizes that "here we do not have an enduring city, but we are looking for the city that is to come" (Heb. 13:14). The church looks back to the Cross from which it originated, yet looks to the future consummation as its destination. In its pilgrimage and sojourn here on earth, it is therefore supremely an eschatological community. The church lives in expectation of the end (Mark 13:34–37; Luke 12:40; 1 Thess. 1:3; 5:6) yet continues to do the work of Christ (John 15:1–6), gathers together those who belong to God (John 10:14–16), and battles the world which is hostile to it (John 16:33; 1 John 5:4–5).

This eschatological expectation of the church cannot be properly understood apart from its association with the kingdom of God.[6] According to Paul, Christ must "reign until he has put all his enemies under his feet" (1 Cor. 15:25). "The end will come, when he hands over the kingdom to God the Father after he has destroyed all dominion, authority and power" (1 Cor. 15:24).

Since the kingdom and not the church is the eschatological goal of the Father, we must ask how the eschatological anticipation of the church is related to the kingdom.

First, the church is the servant of the kingdom. In its

work here on earth, it has been given heavenly power over the powers of evil which Christ will destroy at His consummation. It has the power to forgive sins—that is, to declare in the name of Christ that a penitent sinner is forgiven (Matt. 18:18; Mark 2:10; John 20:23); it may exercise power over the evil spirits (Mark 3:15; 6:7); it has power to teach with authority (Mark 1:22, 27; Matt. 28:20) and through these means it exercises Christ's power to break the rule of Satan and to establish the reign of God, the presence of His kingdom (Luke 11:20; Matt. 12:26). Because Jesus has been exalted yet rules through the church, the church's power to set up the kingdom bears a cosmic proportion. Christ has sent His church to all nations to call people into His church and under His rule (Acts 1:8). In its missiological dimension, the church is therefore a servant of the kingdom, calling people into repentance, conversion, and baptism into Christ.

In its inner life, particularly in its worship, the church witnesses to the coming kingdom. The chief act of worship, the celebration of the Lord's Supper, is a revelation of the kingdom to come. Jesus Himself said, "I will not drink again of the fruit of the vine until that day when I drink it anew in the kingdom of God" (Mark 14:25). In the Last Supper, Jesus emphasized that His blood was the blood of the new covenant through which people will share in His kingdom. An indispensable element of this covenant is the church, the people of the blood, who celebrate not only the past event of the Cross but the future event of the consummation. As Paul stated to the Corinthian community, "Whenever you eat this bread and drink this cup, you proclaim the Lord's death until he comes" (1 Cor. 11:26). Communion is a proclamation, a witness to the people of God that they are connected to the Cross and the consummation. Further, it is an empowerment to do the work of the eschatological community, to proclaim the ultimate rule of God and to live in its expectation.

The church is finally merged into the kingdom in the eschaton. In the new heavens and the new earth, it no longer has an existence separate from the kingdom. It is no longer characterized as a group of "aliens and strangers," for it enters into its sabbath rest. The angel told John, "No longer will there be any curse. . . . And they will reign forever and ever" (Rev. 22:3, 5). When in the end all the enemies of God have been destroyed, when their power to subvert the creation and turn it against its Creator has ceased, when the struggle of the church against the powers and principalities is ended and God rules over all, there will be no need of the church. For His kingdom will prevail. This vision of the future is captured in the imagery of the church as the heavenly bride, the wife of the Lamb (Rev. 21:9).

THE CHURCH IN THE WORLD

In sum, the quest to understand the relationship between the church and the world does well to begin with an understanding of the various uses of the word, *world*. On the one hand, the Bible uses the word in a very positive sense, referring to the natural creation and to the world of people. Therefore, we are to affirm the world as God's creation and to work actively in it as God's agents, caring for it and tending to it even as He instructed our first parents "to work it and take care of it" (Gen. 2:15), to subdue it and rule in it (Gen. 1:28). However, there is another "world," not the natural creation but a supernatural world of evil powers. This is the world of evil that works in those who are disobedient (Eph. 2:2). This is the world with which the Christian and the church are in continual conflict (Eph. 6:12).

When considerations arise about the relationship of the church to the world, one must distinguish between the relationship of the church to creation and the relationship of the church to the powers of evil. The church affirms creation but confronts the world of evil. The church affirms creation because God created it and re-created it in Jesus Christ. But the church confronts the powers of evil working in the creation because the church is linked to Christ in His earthly saving event and His exaltation over all the powers of evil. However, since the church is also here on earth, bound to time and space, it is supremely characterized by its eschatological hope for the ultimate destruction of all powers of evil and the subsequent formation of the new heavens and the new earth.

Keeping in mind its past (the Christ event) and its future (the consummation), the church now sustains a twofold ministry to the world: It witnesses to the dethronement of evil powers and acts as a responsible agent bringing the creation under the lordship of Christ. This dual responsibility of the church to the world will be made more clear in the next chapter.

2

THE POWERS AND THE WORLD

Since World War II, a number of theologians have become increasingly aware of the need to develop an understanding of the world which gives proper attention to the powers of evil.[1] The event which, more than any other, has succeeded in refocusing attention on these powers was the inhuman and incomprehensible holocaust of six million Jews under Hitler's Third Reich. Other instances of brutality against humanity such as the slaughtering of millions of innocent people in the communist revolutions of Russia and China, the systematic elimination of the Armenians, the current unconscionable abortions of unborn infants, as well as the possible scenario of the human race annihilated through nuclear war, make the evil powers a matter of immediate concern.

It is the purpose of this chapter to systematize the biblical emphasis on evil powers and thus provide a theological interpretation of the New Testament use of the word *powers*. My argument is that Paul uses the word *power* in two ways. First, the word *power* sometimes refers to the structures of creation which guide and control our lives, such as the power of the family, the state, educational institutions, and even the communications media. Second, the word *power* most frequently refers to the adverse spiritual powers that work through the structures of creation, turning men into instruments of evil. (See Appendix C.)

CHANNELS THROUGH WHICH THE POWER OF EVIL WORKS IN THE WORLD

The relationship between demonic influence and the worldly powers is made clear by Paul in 1 Corinthians 2:8: "None of the rulers of this age understood it, for if they had, they would not have crucified the Lord of glory." The link between demonic influence and the structures of existence is set forth in the phrase, "the rulers of this age."[2] The term *rulers* does not refer to those in power, but to super-earthly realities identical with the powers of which Paul speaks elsewhere (Rom. 8:38; Gal. 4:1–11; Col. 1:14–20, 2:15). Although these powers are not earthly persons, they work through persons and systems. It is true that Jesus was crucified by high priests and scribes, who acted together with Herod and Pilate. Yet these men worked in concert with a demonic power, exercised through the Roman state and a misguided Jewish piety, in order to kill Jesus. Demonic power worked through the structure of state and religion to accomplish its diabolical end.

This link between the demonic and the structures that rule over life is dramatically stated by Paul in Ephesians 2:1–3: "As for you, you were dead in your transgressions and sins, in which you used to live when you followed the ways of the world and of the ruler of the kingdom of the air, the spirit who is now at work in those who are disobedient. All of us also lived among them at one time, gratifying the cravings of our sinful nature and following its desires and thoughts." Here the "ruler" is Satan and the "kingdom" is the power. In Paul's cosmology, the earth is ruled by the powers of the "air" which are subject to Satan's influence. Satan works through the structures of existence to deceive and to lead astray, so that those who are under the powers of evil act out their commitment to evil through the various structures of existence such as the state, economics, family life, and work.

Paul indicates that Satan is "the ruler of the kingdom of the air, the spirit who is now at work in those who are disobedient" (v. 2). The term *air* has reference to the general spiritual climate which influences people, perhaps even a culture of people. We acknowledge this notion in everyday speech when we say, "Something is in the air." The term can be used in the negative, indicating an oppressive atmosphere, or in the positive, emphasizing a sense of freedom and joy. Paul's point is that evil comes from a spirit, the power of which is felt in the environment. It "is at work," Paul states, "in those who are disobedient." Specifically how this spiritual atmosphere works is described in greater detail by the New Testament writers.

First, the "spirit" works as a destroyer of that which is good. In 1 Corinthians, Paul makes reference to the "destroying angel" (1 Cor. 10:10). John speaks of the Devil as a "murderer from the beginning" (John 8:44), and the writer of Hebrews claims the Devil "holds the power of death" (Heb. 2:14). The point is that Satan's intent in the world is to destroy God's creation. He is not satisfied to destroy people only. He wants to destroy the total work of God's hands—including the proper use of the structures of existence. His reign is that of chaos, disintegration, and death. He is an untiring worker against God, seeking with malicious intent to bring God's work of creation to ruination. Satan's spiritual battle against God has clear and definite repercussions in the physical world. He loves to see hate, greed, lust, murder, envy, immorality, and violence of every sort expressed through the very structures of existence that were originally created to guard and preserve order, morality, love, and peace. His is a mission of destruction.

For this reason, it is Satan's intention to lead people into temptation. Matthew, in describing the temptations of Jesus, speaks of "the tempter" who came to Him (Matt. 4:3). Paul uses the same term to describe the one who tempts the Christians at Thessalonica (1 Thess. 3:5). And John speaks of "the hour of trial that is going to come upon the whole world to test those who live on the earth" (Rev. 3:10). It is naive to assume that temptation and ensuing sin is a matter pertaining only to the individual. Sin of all sorts always has a social dimension to a lesser or greater degree. Because sin deifies the created orders of existence, causing their perversion and distortion, it may take the form of an act of aggression against another person or the twisting of a relationship in some other way. For example, to ascribe ultimate allegiance to national honor in blind patriotism is as much the result of satanic activity as sexual immorality. To interpret religion as though it can be reduced to a mere function of the psyche is as sinful as greed. To pervert morality, making all of God's law subject to human discretion, is a malicious affront to the character of God. Thus Satan draws us into the temptation to distort reality, persuading us that a lie is truth and perverting our use of the structures of existence which God created for the common good and social stability.

Further, the demonic spirit works sin in those who are disobedient through falsehood. John describes Satan as one who is a "liar and the father of lies" (John 8:44). Indeed, Paul speaks of Satan as one who "masquerades as an angel of light" (2 Cor. 11:14). In this role, Satan deceives and leads people astray so that a true perception of reality is unattainable. To make one act as though the state is ultimate or to believe that history is run by ironclad economic laws (as in Marxism) is to delude people into a false perception of that which is ultimate. God, not His created order, is ultimate. It is to Him we owe our allegiance and not to some political or economic order.

These examples of Satan's power illustrate the biblical principle that *Satan works through the structures of society to distort, pervert, and disfigure that which is good.* No part of the created order can escape the influence and power of Satan.

Finally, it must be pointed out that this aspect of demonic power was very much a part of the experience of the early church.

THE CONCEPT OF THE DEMONIC IN THE PRIMITIVE CHRISTIAN COMMUNITY

The awareness of evil powers in society was not a new discovery for the New Testament church. Demonic consciousness lies within the Hebrew faith in which Christianity is rooted. Job and the prophets (especially Isaiah, Jeremiah, Hosea, and Daniel) perceived that the demonic is actively at work through social, political, and economic structures. Consequently, the keen sensitivity to demonic activity among the New Testament writers stands in the tradition of an Old Testament perception of the permeating presence of evil in society.[3]

This sense of the demonic is reflected by Luke. "Crowds," he tells his readers, "gathered also from the towns around Jerusalem, bringing their sick and those tormented by evil spirits, and all of them were healed" (Acts 5:16; cf. 8:7). We meet the same overwhelming power of the demonic in the accounts of the missionary journeys of Paul. In Paphos, Paul confronted Elymas the sorcerer, who had been disturbing his ministry, with the words, "You are a child of the devil" (Acts 13:10). In Philippi, a girl who "had a spirit" followed Paul about town, apparently making a nuisance of herself and standing in the way of the Holy Spirit's ministry. Paul commanded the evil spirit to leave her (Acts 16:16–18). Luke records "extraordinary miracles" were accomplished through Paul in Corinth, where "illnesses were cured and the evil spirits left them" (Acts 19:11–12). Before Agrippa, Paul testified about his encounter with Jesus on the Damascus road, where Jesus told him, "I am sending you . . . to open their eyes and turn them from darkness to light, and *from the power of Satan to God*" (Acts 26:17–18, italics added).

This keen sense of the demonic is also an underlying theme in the Epistles. As we noted earlier, Paul tells the Christians at Ephesus that they used to follow "the ruler of the kingdom of the air, the spirit who is now at work in those who are disobedient" (Eph. 2:2); he reminds them that their present struggle is "not against flesh and blood, but against the rulers, against the authorities, against the powers of this dark world and against the spiritual forces of evil in the heavenly realms" (Eph. 6:12). See also Romans 16:20; 1 Corinthians 2:6, 8, 12; 2 Corinthians 4:4, 12:7; Ephesians 1:21, 3:10, 4:27, 6:16; Colossians 2:8, 10, 15, 18, 20; 2 Thessalonians 3:3; 2 Timothy 2:26.

This strong sense of the demonic was not unique to Paul; it was articulated by all the other New Testament writers as well. Two of the most popularized statements come from Peter and John. Peter warns his readers that "your enemy the devil prowls around like a roaring lion looking for someone to devour" (1 Peter 5:8). And John sternly warns that "he who does what is sinful is of the devil" (1 John 3:8; cf. 2 Peter 2:4, 10; 1 John 3:10, 4:1, 3, 6).

In Revelation, John speaks often and pointedly of the demonic. The church in Smyrna is "a synagogue of Satan" (2:9); the church in Pergamum lives "where Satan has his throne" (2:13); mankind not killed by the plagues still do not stop "worshiping demons" (9:20). In chapter twelve, the great dragon is identified as "that ancient serpent called the devil or Satan, who leads the whole world astray" (v. 9); this dragon gives "the beast his power and his throne and great authority" (13:2). In chapter sixteen, John observes that evil spirits come out of the mouth of the beast; he identifies them as "spirits of demons" who influence the "whole world, to gather them for the battle on the great day of God Almighty" (v. 14). But then "another angel" comes down from heaven with "great authority" to shout "Fallen! Fallen is Babylon the Great! She has become a home for demons and a haunt for every evil spirit" (18:1–2). Finally, this angel seizes "the dragon, that ancient serpent, who is the devil, or Satan, and bound him for a thousand years" (20:2).

These passages as well as others (James 2:19, 4:17; Jude 6, 8) leave one with the impression that the early Christian church was clearly aware of the presence and pervasive power of the demonic in the life of the world. These New Testament examples of the demonic compel one to conclude that a viable New Testament theology of society must acknowledge the presence and power of the demonic, acting through the social structure and fabric of human existence.[4]

CONCLUSION

It was the stated purpose of this section to investigate the Pauline usage of the word *powers* and to assess the importance of his concept for our understanding of the world. We conclude first that the creation consists not only of the physical realm of nature but of those cultural institutions which regulate human existence in the world. These include the reality of the state, economics, the family, ideas, social rules and regulations, as well as natural perimeters of space, time, life, death, and the like. These structures of existence are sometimes referred to as *powers* because they order human life and social institutions.

Second, because of the Fall, satanic and demonic powers seek to distort God's good creation by causing people to put to perversive use the structures of existence ("powers"). For example, the state and religion became the instruments of evil when wicked men through the state crucified Jesus Christ. In this and other numerous ways, God's good creation has been distorted and turned into an instrument through which Satan's opposition to God is expressed.

Assuming that the Pauline world view is still viable in

the twentieth century, we need to recognize the powers of evil working through the structures of existence. However, since the structures of existence are not evil within themselves, we may consider how the influence of good may be expressed through these structures as well. As Hendrik Berkhof has written, "The believers' combat is never to strive against the orders, but rather to battle for God's intention for them and against their corruption."[5]

In Parts II and III of this book, the relationship between church and world in the ancient, medieval, modern, and contemporary eras will be evaluated by the conclusions we have drawn from the biblical text. Finally, in Part IV, a christological view of church and world for our time will be articulated.

3

CHRIST, THE CHURCH, AND THE POWERS

The argument of this chapter is that Christ, who is the victor over the powers of evil, confronts the powers of evil that work in the world, through the church. The church, which is the locus of His continuing action, thus witnesses to the order and design that God has for His creation.

In the New Testament, the church appears as an extension of Christ (John 15:5–8; Eph. 2:19–22). Christ remains present in and to the world through the church, which is His body (Eph. 5:23–33), the people whom He will present to the Father as the spotless bride (Rev. 21:2, 9; 22:17). One cannot think adequately about the church apart from its christological source, its soteriological function, and its eschatological anticipation. Consequently, to speak about the relationship between Christ, the church, and the powers is to bring together a fundamental cluster of theological ideas with specific bearing on the issue of church and world.

By the word *church* I do not have in mind a particular denomination. Rather I mean the people of God, the body of Christ. These are the people from every denomination, every culture, every nation that confess "Jesus is Lord" (Rom. 10:8–9). This is not an aggregate of individuals, but a corporate body of people who constitute a unique society within the societies of the world. Their allegiance to Christ as the head of the church and to the members of the universal church as a household of faith transcends boundaries of nation, culture, and color. This is the universal communion of Christians membered together through faith in Christ, characterized by earthly government, Scripture and creeds, worship, sacraments, and a commitment to serve in the world.

Because it is the purpose of these pages to focus on the relationship between the church and the powers, it is my concern to show that Christ manifests His victory over the powers through the church. Consequently, a biblical view of the relationship between church and world must take into account how Christ continues to work through the church to confront the demonic perversions exercised through the structures of existence. This study will consist of two parts. First, it will examine the biblical data regarding Christ's victory over the demonic powers; and second, it will illustrate those ways in which Christ's victory over the powers continues to be expressed through the church.

CHRIST AND THE POWERS

Christ Has Bound Satan
and All Demonic Powers.

Christ makes the claim to have bound Satan in a confrontation between Himself and the Pharisees (Matt. 12:22–29). The occasion for the confrontation was the healing of a blind and mute man who was possessed by demons (v. 22). According to the Pharisees' interpretation, "it is only by Beelzebub, the prince of demons, that this fellow drives out demons" (v. 24). Rather than seeing Jesus as one who had power over the demonic, they saw Him as subject to and even as an agent of the demonic. But Jesus, showing them the absurdity of this conclusion, argued that "if Satan drives out Satan, he is divided against himself" (v. 26). More importantly, Jesus categorically stated, "How can anyone enter a strong man's house and carry off his possessions unless he first ties up the strong man?" (Matt. 12:29).[1]

The point made by Jesus is that He has power over the demonic because He has already entered into the domain of evil and found its source. The event in the life of Christ where this "binding" most likely occurred is the temptation

(Matt. 4:1–11). Generally, exegetes are united in their recognition that the temptation of Jesus by Satan was not a test of His moral character but of His messianic calling.[2] This messianic interpretation asserts that in the temptation Satan attempted to divert Jesus from the work His Father had called him to do, offering Him the kingdom of the world if He would bow down and worship him. Jesus' final answer was, "Away from me, Satan! For it is written: 'worship the Lord your God and serve him only' " (v. 10). Christ's refusal to bow to Satan signaled an important moment in the work of overcoming the power of Satan. Christ's rejection of Satan's power and affirmation of His service to God alone reversed the trend initiated by Adam when he chose Satan over God in the garden. Just as Adam was seduced by the word of Satan and brought the whole human race under his influence, so Jesus broke the power of that seduction and set in motion the chain of earthly events which would ultimately and conclusively destroy the power of Satan. Thus Paul writing to the Romans was able to say, "For just as through the disobedience of the one man the many were made sinners, so also through the obedience of the one man the many will be made righteous" (Rom. 5:19).

In the temptation Satan had met his match, the end of his free rein over the world had begun. As Martin Luther wrote in his hymn, "A Mighty Fortress Is Our God," his doom was sure. It is in this light that Christ's power over the demonic is to be understood. In the Old Testament none of the prophets of God, nor His priests, nor kings had ultimate power over evil. But now the son of God, who has come to enter into battle with Satan and to destroy him (Gen. 3:15), begins his earthly ministry with a demonstration of his power over Satan.

The Gospel writers pointedly accent the power of Jesus over Satan to their readers. Matthew saw that the power of Jesus over evil was in fulfillment of the Old Testament prophecies (Matt. 8:16–17) and came as a result of the "Spirit of God" (12:28). Mark and Luke also acknowledged that Jesus had power, even authority over evil (Mark 1:21–28; Luke 9:37–43). The exercising of Christ's power over Satan had the effect of restoring to wholeness a part of God's creation that had become demented, twisted, distorted, and corrupted by Satan. When Jesus cast out demons, healed the blind, made the lame to walk, restored health, and raised the dead, He demonstrated that His purpose was to restore, renew, and recreate His universe. In order to recreate the creation, it was first necessary for Christ to dethrone that power which was distorting the creation. Evil was perverting the purposes of the structures of existence (which were created to provide order and meaning to the world), so they had to be dethroned in order to set the creation free from "its bondage to decay" (Rom. 8:21). This was accomplished by the death and resurrection of Jesus Christ.

Through the Death and Resurrection of Jesus Christ, the Power of Satan Has Been Dethroned.

In the previous pages, I have asserted that one of the purposes of Christ's life, death, and resurrection was to destroy the power and influence of the evil one and to create anew His Father's creation. Can this be substantiated by the words of Jesus? Jesus announced this purpose to a crowd near the close of His life. According to John, Jesus had been talking of His impending death and called upon His Father to glorify His name when a voice came from heaven, saying, "I have glorified it, and will glorify it again" (John 12:28). Jesus told the crowd, "This voice was for your benefit, not mine. Now is the time for judgment on this world; *now the prince of this world will be driven out*" (vv. 30–31, italics added).[3]

Paul expands the idea of Christ's victory over Satan in his letter to the Colossian people. He writes that Christ's death and resurrection had "disarmed" the powers and authorities and "made a public spectacle of them, triumphing over them by the cross" (Col. 2:15).[4]

According to Paul, the death and resurrection of Christ has "disarmed" the powers and authorities. The force of the word *disarm* is that of "taking away," like stripping a soldier of his guns, putting him in a position of vulnerability. So Christ's death has had the effect of exposing the deception that Satan exercises through the structures of existence. Christ is seen as Lord, not only over death, but over all other evil influences which seek to distort our lives. The illusion that life or death, manmade religious observances, or human social regulations are ultimate is now exposed for the lie it is. Likewise all other aspects of the created order which people elevate to positions of ultimate authority are stripped of their power to deceive. Now people can be free from these illusions. It is no longer necessary to be bound by the power of a false understanding of the created order. Faith in Jesus Christ, who is ultimate ruler over all of life, can break the twisting of political, economic, social, and moral structures into secular salvations. Because these secular salvations are disarmed, they can no longer exercise ultimate power in our life system and act as gods over our lives.

Thus, the Christian does not see earthly political power as the means of ushering in a kingdom of peace and brotherhood; the Christian is not committed to a particular economic system as though it will establish prosperity for all people; the Christian is not characterized by a nationalistic fervor which claims God to be on its side; the Christian does not seek to impose moral standards on society with the assumption that moral externalism is an end in itself. These are illusions from which Christ has set His people free.

In the Cross, Christ made a "public spectacle" of the false use of the powers. He made clear the true nature of the powers and authorities. By bringing to light their true nature, He has given us both a negative and positive understanding of them. On the negative side they are seen for what they are, "weak and miserable principles" (Gal. 4:9). We realize that the powers have no ability to save, they are not ultimate, they are not the integrating principle of life. On the positive side, we know that the powers are God's creation which serve as agents to provide order, guidance, and meaning. The false ultimate authority attributed to them has been made visible by the Cross, so that their true meaning is understood by those who live under the lordship of Christ.

Christ has "triumphed" over the pretentiousness attributed to the powers by their satanic perversion. In the Cross, he defeats the strangulating grip they hold over those who believe in them. Men and women, having been set free to see the structures of existence for what they are, no longer need to fear the tyranny of their falsehood. Christ has so utterly destroyed Satan's power of illusion which he exercises through them that the fear of the demonic powers is gone for those who believe. Those who perceive the true nature of the structures of existence are free to function within them, regarding them as agents to enhance life rather than tyrants over life.

For this reason, the Christian can take a positive view of the state, economics, education, law, and other structures. The Christian should see these as expressions of God's goodness toward us; they are here for our good, to prevent chaos and to provide justice, equity, and peace. Christians should not fall down before a political system and worship it as an idol; they do not believe the political process can provide salvation from the crises of life. Nevertheless Christians should believe that believers working within the political system can, through that system, act with compassion toward human need and work toward understanding between the nations and peoples of the earth. Yet this does not seem to be the case today. It appears that many people, even Christians, still give their allegiance to the "isms." It appears that the primitive Christian community was more aware of the implication of Christ's victory over sin and death than many contemporary Christians. We need to renew the primitive church's emphasis on what it means to wrestle with the powers (Eph. 6:12) and to be free from the distortions they create (Rom. 8:38–39; Gal. 4:8–9; Col. 2:8). How can we as Christians fight the powers when we succumb to them by entering into alliances with political and economic systems? We, of all people on the earth, must be free from these unholy alliances in order to be prophetic about every system, every institution, every "ism," and every ideology that purports to offer salvation from the crises of the world. We serve a different God, we speak a new language, we offer a new hope. Our hope is not in America, not in military might, not in the free enterprise system, not in socialism. Our hope is in God, who in Jesus Christ has dealt a decisive blow to evil, who in the consummation will utterly and finally destroy all evil influences, putting them away forever.

In the Consummation, Satan's Influence Over the Powers Will Be Utterly Destroyed.

Although the influence of Satan, which he exercises through the powers, has been overcome through the life, death, and resurrection of Christ, the final blow to Satan will not occur until the consummation of Christ's work in His second coming. Even though Jesus spoke of an "eternal fire prepared for the devil and his angels" (Matt. 25:41), a more elaborate development of the idea of Satan's ultimate destruction occurs in the thought of the early church. In Paul's classic statement on the power of the resurrection over death (and the disintegration of the created order implied in the symbol of death), he reminds his readers that the end will come "after he has destroyed all dominion, authority and power. For he must reign until he has put all his enemies under his feet" (1 Cor. 15:24–25).[5] The apostle John, in his apocalyptic vision of the end times, declares that "the devil, who deceived them, was thrown into the lake of burning sulfur, where the beast and the false prophet had been thrown" (Rev. 20:10). This chorus of voices affirms the total destruction of Satanic forces and assures us that the work of Christ which we have seen linked to the temptation (the binding of Satan) and the Cross (the overcoming of Satan) is concluded by the consummation (the final defeat of Satan).

When the final defeat of Satan occurs, the influence and power he holds over the structures of creation will come to an end. Then the creation, which was "subjected to frustration" and brought under a "bondage to decay," will be "liberated" and "brought into the glorious freedom of the children of God" (Rom. 8:20–21). This means that the influence of Satan over the structures which guide and hold our lives together will be dismantled. The illusion of hope and salvation which they hold for people will be completely exposed and their true nature and function in the world will be more fully revealed.

Between the Resurrection and the Consummation the Power of Satan Is Limited.

It would be naive to conclude that Satan no longer has power in the social order. He is still the master of deception. He still blinds the eyes of people to the truth about creation. He still masterminds faith in false gods and creates messianic illusions which people follow to their own destruction. Yet his influence is limited, for Jesus has overcome him. "In this world you will have trouble," said Jesus, "But take heart! I have overcome the world" (John 16:33). In his first epistle, John interprets this saying of Jesus to describe those who believe in Him as overcomers. "For everyone born of God overcomes the world. This is the victory that has overcome the world, even our faith. Who is it that overcomes the world? Only he who believes that Jesus is the Son of God" (1 John 5:4–5).

Yet the overcoming is still not an established reality, as Paul indicates when he uses two words that mean "coming to nothing" and "expectation." The first word is used in his First Epistle to the Corinthians: "We do, however, speak a message of wisdom among the mature, but not the wisdom of this age or of the rulers of this age, who are *coming to nothing*" (1 Cor. 2:6). The force of the word translated "coming to nothing" is "being put out of action." In the military sense, it means the war is over; now the cleaning up of the final matters must occur. Guerrilla pockets may still exist, confrontation may still occur here and there; but the tide has been turned, the oppressor has been definitely routed, and it is only a matter of time till the end.

The second word, "expectation," describes the state of those who are to be released from the ravages of war. Paul uses this word in the Epistle to the Romans: "The creation waits in eager expectation for the sons of God to be revealed" (Rom. 8:19). This passage suggests a cosmic victory over a cosmic bondage. Satan has brought the entire creation under his dominion and influence, but that pervasive power has been so thoroughly broken that the entire creation—all the structures of existence—now experience an expectation of their release.[6]

These passages point to the importance of preaching as the means by which Satan continues to be exposed to his defeat. For it is through faith in Jesus Christ (as the one who has defeated Satan and all his attempts to distort the creation) that the extent of Satan's activity is limited. Satan may continue to deceive some, perhaps many, but not all. Preaching Christ continually unmasks the power of Satan, for faith in Christ opens a person's eyes to the reality of Satan's deception. Whenever anyone believes in Christ, the limitation of Satan's power is unmasked.

The Structures of Existence Are Ultimately Reconciled to God.

It is a comfort to know that the contest between Satan and Christ will have an end even as it had a beginning. Furthermore, as Paul states, the course of this cosmic conflict is under "the mystery of his will" and "according to his good pleasure." The will and pleasure of God are being fulfilled in Christ, whose purpose it is "to bring all things in heaven and on earth together under one head, even Christ" (Eph. 1:9–10). Paul mentions this same theme in his letter to the Corinthians, telling them that God has put "everything under him [Jesus Christ], so that God may be all in all" (15:28). For Paul, this means nothing less than the re-creation of the entire universe, including the structures of existence. Restoration of the structures is made more clear in his letter to the Colossians, when he tells his readers that it is God's purpose through Christ "to reconcile to himself all things, whether things on earth or things in heaven, by making peace through his blood, shed on the cross" (Col. 1:20).

In these passages, Paul does not imply that Satan and the fallen hosts which represent the demonic in this world will be reconciled to God. They are defeated and cast into the lake of fire (Rev. 20:10). What is redeemed, restored, and re-created is God's work of creation. The structures, not being evil in themselves, are released from the influence of the demonic that has caused them to be used in a perverted manner. They are set free from the illusion of ultimate authority in which they have been perceived by people. They will no longer lead people away from God. Rather, they will function according to God's original intention for them— providing stability and meaning, ordering life, and glorifying God by pointing to Him as ultimate. In this sense, the new heavens and the new earth will be as a restored paradise— the world as it was before the Fall and beyond.

THE CHURCH AND THE POWERS

The Victory of Christ Over the Demonic Is Made Present Through the Church.

In Paul's letter to the Ephesians, he asserts that Christ has now been exalted above "all rule and authority." This assertion implies the exaltation of Christ over the powers. It indicates that the right meaning of the structures of existence can be realized by those who are in Christ. For them, the world has been set in order. Therefore, the structures of existence, through which God rules in creation, can be seen and understood *under Christ*.

This position of Christ over everything is for the sake of the church (Eph. 1:22); it is the church which now enjoys the privilege of perceiving creation and its structures rightly. The church exalts Christ as its Lord and no longer believes life and death or religious observances or the state to be ultimate. The church "which is his body, the fullness of him who fills everything in every way" (Eph. 1:23) is character- ized by its ability to expose the illusions, the false gods, and the demons of life for what they are.

For this reason, the church may be regarded as the agent of God's power in the world.[7] It is the people in whom God's victory over sin, death, and the dominion of the Devil resides; because the church is inseparably linked with Christ and His historic work on the Cross, through which evil was defeated. The power of this defeat is made present to the world in the faith experiences of the church. Because of faith the "veil is taken away" (2 Cor. 3:16). The "god of this age" who has "blinded the minds of unbelievers" (2 Cor. 4:4) is defeated in his attempt to confuse and distort. For God has "made his light to shine in our hearts to give us the light of the knowledge of the glory of God in the face of Christ" (2 Cor. 4:6). This same Jesus "who has destroyed death" has also "brought life and immortality to light through the gospel" (2 Tim. 1:10). Paul aptly calls this change an enlightening of the "eyes of your heart" (Eph. 1:18). That is, faith in Christ saves people from an "enslavement" to the perverted use of the structures of existence (Gal. 4:9).

This idea—that Christ frees His people from the illusion of the powers—is developed by the early church fathers. The Fathers frequently speak of salvation as an "enlighten- ment" or an "illumination." Speaking of baptism, Justin Martyr says, "This washing is called illumination, since those who learn these things are illumined within."[8] The content of this illumination may very well be the recognition that Satan has been defeated and has no ultimate hold over those who believe in Jesus. The emphasis of the early church fathers on the destruction of Satan, his continued limitation, and the enlightenment of the righteous suggest that these ideas are connected in the thought of the early church fathers. Faith in Jesus Christ's victory over the evil one gives the believer a new view of life.

This new view of life belongs to the church because Christ, the head of the church, is inseparably linked with it.

His power over sin, death, and the dominion of the Devil now belongs to the church, not only by virtue of the church's understanding but by way of its action. The church acts in the name of Christ to witness through prayer, preaching, baptism, communion, lifestyle, and other means proclaiming that Satan is now doomed. The church is a corporate body of people who know Satan as a deceiver and liar. He has no ultimate power over them and their lives. Consequently, the church is a threat to Satan. He hates the church and wants to destroy it, for he cannot bear its power to expose his defeat nor its ability to free people from the distortions of reality in which they are entrapped.

The Power of Satan Against the Church

Because the church is the means through which Christ continues to be present in and to the world, the efforts of Satan are now directed against the church. Such efforts are recognized in the writings of the New Testament. Paul believes Satan has hindered him from going to Thessalonica (1 Thess. 2:18). Satan is the reason why Christians apostasize and fall away from the faith (Rev. 2:10). He produces heresy within the church and causes people to go after false doctrine (2 Cor. 11:3ff.; Col. 2:18ff.; 1 Tim. 4:1; 2 Tim. 2:26; 1 John 4:1ff.). Satan also brings Christian people under the power of the demonic (1 Cor. 12:2).

Satan has declared war on the church because he is threatened by the church's faith in Jesus Christ and his victory over sin, death, and the dominion of the Devil. This faith in Christ exposes Satan's defeat and points to the ultimate victory of Christ over Satan in the consummation. Therefore, to bring individual Christians under his power or to cause a part of the church to fall away from faith represents a temporary victory for Satan.

Satan's battle with the church may also occur in relationship to the structures of existence. Satan may tempt the church to accomplish its work in the world through a means other than its calling. For example, Satan delights in the church's entering into political and economic alliances and holding up these systems as saviors to bring about peace or world stability. Whenever Satan can move people to have faith in the structures of existence—political, economic, moral, national, medical, scientific, or others—Satan has

succeeded in shifting faith from Jesus Christ to something
that Christ has created. Satan loves to have people rest their
faith in a throne or power or ruler or authority whose use has
been twisted and perverted from its original intention.
Instead of providing order for life, such a structure of
existence now assumes for the believer a messianic quality
and functions as savior. For example, when science is made
the integrating principle of life and is treated as though its
technological products will eventually eradicate disease,
hunger, or pollution and establish prosperity and health for
all, science is no longer seen as the servant of the people but
the savior of the world. Consequently, faith in science as the
ultimate reality, being a perversion of its true character,
becomes demonic. When people of the church are drawn
into faith in science or belief in any other structure of
existence, Satan has succeeded in spoiling the Christian
witness that Christ is the only means through which the
salvation of the world will occur.

The Church as Witness

It is important to recognize that not even the church will
bring in the kingdom of Christ; only Christ will accomplish
that. But the church is a witness to the kingdom and thus an
instrument in the service of the kingdom.

This witness of the church to the kingdom of Christ has
at least two dimensions. On the one hand, the church
exposes evil; and on the other hand, it bears a responsibility
to act as an agent of reconciliation. The church is like a two-
edged sword, cutting both ways.

The work of the church in exposing evil is set forth by
Paul in the letter addressed to the Ephesians. He tells them
that God's intent through Christ is that "now, through the
church, the manifold wisdom of God should be made known
to the rulers and authorities in the heavenly realms" (Eph.
3:10). Through the church the continual unmasking of the
powers is to take place. As we have seen, Jesus has
"disarmed" the powers, made a "public spectacle" of them,
and "triumphed" over them (Col. 2:15); this is an accomplished work which took place with His crucifixion and
resurrection. But only the church knows what has happened
to the powers. Through the Cross, the church perceives the
twisting and distortion of the powers through the demonic

influence of Satan. Therefore, the calling of the church is to continually unmask the pretentions of the powers so that they can be seen for the weak and beggarly elements they are. This unique position is given to the church because it constitutes the people who are "heirs of God and co-heirs with Christ" who have shared "in his sufferings" in order that they "may also share in his glory" (Rom. 8:17). This glory of God, which recreates His universe through its ultimate release from demonic control through the powers (Rom. 8:18–25), is now to be experienced in the church (2 Cor. 3:13–18), whose very existence in the world is a testimony to the defeat of Satan.

Faith is the means through which this victory over the world becomes apparent. As John wrote, "Everyone born of God overcomes the world. This is the victory that has overcome the world, even our faith" (1 John 5:4). For faith in Jesus Christ excludes faith in the false use of the structures of existence. Not to have ultimate faith in science, reason, the state, economic systems, or nationalism already witnesses against the false pretentions of the powers and exposes the error of their messianic claims.

Faith repeats the obedience of the Son to the Father and applies the victory of Christ over sin, death, and the dominion of the Devil again and again. When faith is exercised, the believer experiences the power of Christ over sin. Christ now lives within and through the believer (Phil. 2:1–11) providing victory over sin (1 Cor. 15:57). In this way, the church witnesses to the defeat of Satan.

On the other hand, the church acts as an agent of reconciliation. It complies with Paul's injunction to no longer conform "to the pattern of this world, but be transformed by the renewing of your mind" (Rom. 12:2). Because the church is in the process of being transformed, it has a transforming effect on the social order. It is not only called to expose the demonic influence exercised through the structures of existence, but to function in respect to those structures of existence in such a way that their true nature is revealed. In this way, each structure of existence can be seen in the light of its original purpose; the structure is no longer set up as the ultimate reality of life, nor is slavish obedience to it demanded. Rather, it functions to order life and provides the context in which life is lived. For example, messianic nationalism perverts the true meaning of national identity by demanding absolute obedience and allegiance, and regarding this perverted patriotism as an integrating principle of life. In this way, nationalism becomes evil. The Christian alternative is to acknowledge one's national identity, pray for rulers, pay taxes, and affirm a patriotism that puts the state or nation in its proper relationship to the ultimate authority of God.

CONCLUSION

The purpose of the preceding pages has been to investigate the relationship between the church and Christ's victory over sin and the dominion of the Devil. A summary of this relationship is as follows:

Christ bound Satan at the time of the temptation, defeated him in the Cross and the resurrection, and will destroy him and his power to deceive through the structures of existence in the consummation of this age. In this present time, between the resurrection and the consummation, Satan remains free to continue his work against God by continuing to distort our perception of the structures of existence. Because the church is the extension of Christ, it is the agent through which Christ's victory over Satan is proclaimed. Therefore, Satan fights the church; nevertheless, the church must continue to expose evil through the preaching of Christian faith, calling upon its members to act within the created order in such a way that the structures of existence will be seen subordinate to God, and not as gods which are to be served.

A summary of the conclusions we have drawn from the biblical text is in order:

First, the word *world* is used in two different ways: Sometimes the word refers to the creation; sometimes it refers to adverse spiritual powers. The word *powers* is also used in two different ways: It may refer to the spiritual powers of evil or to the powers which we have called "the structures of existence." The Bible's various uses of the words *world* and *powers* lead us to a theological world view which affirms that the powers of evil work in and through the structures of existence to distort and pervert the use of God's good creation toward evil ends. This view of evil affirms its structural or institutional nature, as well as its spiritual source.

Second, we have argued that the biblical meaning of the *church* cannot be separated from Christ. Christ who has conquered the evil one by His incarnation, death, and resurrection has appointed the church—which is in insepa- rable union with Him in His saving event and His present exalted state—to be the eschatological community in the world, which witnesses to the defeat of both personal and corporate evil. Thus, from a New Testament perspective, the relationship of the church to the world is christological. The church relates to the world as an extension of the Incarna- tion; a continued presence of Christ in the world under the lordship of the exalted Christ; a presence of the Christ who has conquered the powers of evil that work through the structures of existence to distort God's creative work.

Finally, in view of the Incarnation, the church may be seen as the servant of the world; but in view of the lordship of Christ over the powers, the church may be seen as master of the world. This tension between the church as both servant and master of the world has not always been kept in balance.

II

THE HISTORICAL BACKGROUND

A. Church and World in Early and Medieval Thought

4

THE CHURCH OF THE CATACOMBS

Those who would know the present and the future must understand the past. Both the church and the world in which the church unfolds are so complex that simplistic slogans and quickly assembled models of church and world are to be shunned. Consequently, in this section we will seek to gain a perspective on church and world through a study of the church throughout history. Obviously, volumes could be written detailing the relation that the church has sustained with particular cultures in specific historical times. However, since a detailed study is not necessary for the purposes of this book, we will survey the relationship between the church and the world in the major periods of Western history only. These periods of history conveniently break down into the following sections:

The pre-Constantinian period, ending about A.D. 311;

The Constantinian period, which came to an end after the fall of Rome in A.D. 410;

The medieval period, which stretches from the fall of Rome to the beginning of the Reformation and Renaissance of the fifteenth and sixteenth centuries (600–1500); and

The modern period, which dates from the Reformation to the present.

In this section we will deal with the first of these periods, the church of the second and third century, prior to Constantine.

The world of the church during its first three centuries was the Roman Empire, which from the beginning took a hostile stance toward the church. In the response of the church to the empire we see irreconcilable differences between the church with Christ as Lord and the state with the emperor as lord; and here we gain the keenest insight into the continuing conflict between Christ and the adverse spiritual forces which are at work through the structures of existence in the Roman world.

CHURCH–STATE TENSION

The Roman state dominated the religions of the empire. The purpose of religion was to serve the state; that is, it was believed that as long as the gods were pleased with the worship of the people, they would bless the Roman Empire. The Romans attributed the peace and prosperity of their empire to the gods and encouraged their people to be religious.

Religion was in the hands of the Roman senate, and only those gods that had been approved by the senate could be worshiped. Nevertheless, as the empire expanded and people from all over the Mediterranean moved to Rome, the diversity of religions increased greatly. In order to give some kind of unity to all these religions, the Romans instituted a new cult centered in the person of the emperor. Everyone was required to recognize the emperor as deity, though he was not considered a god. *Deity* was defined as "the giver of good things." The Romans were to give honor and praise to the emperor as the *symbol* of the gods who gave prosperity to Rome and made it great. Consequently, the names of most of the traditional gods of Rome were attached to the emperor cult.

The circumstances, then, in which Christianity was born and grew were rather difficult. The state was in itself a religion; and in order to participate in the state, one needed to recognize its religious character, especially as symbolized in the emperor. This the Christian could not do. The natural result was an increasing tension between church and state.[1]

Several factors heightened the tension between church and state. For one thing, Christianity began as a Jewish movement. Since the Jews were already out of favor with the Romans, it was natural for Romans to transfer hatred from the Jew to Jewish Christians. Furthermore, like the Jews, the Christians were unable to produce an image of their God; and, like the Jews, they denied the existence of all gods except their own. The Romans concluded from this that Christians were "atheists." Furthermore, it was rumored that Christian worship consisted of some form of cannibalism, for they ate the "body" and the "blood" of the "son." The gossip in Rome was that Christians met in secret, butchered babies, ate their flesh, drank their blood, and ended their meeting with orgies. The Romans concluded from this that Christians were immoral. Another severe problem was related to the Christians' anticipation of the coming kingdom of Christ and His rule over the world. These apocalyptic hopes anticipated the destruction of all empires, the downfall of Rome, and the setting up of Christ's kingdom. News of this sort struck fear into the hearts of the Roman rulers, and caused the Romans to look on Christians as political anarchists. Because of these attitudes, the Christians hardly had a chance with the Roman state. Without a chance to receive a hearing they were judged to be atheists, immoralists, and political anarchists.

Persecution against the Christians began in the first century under Nero, and by the turn of the century had spread to other parts of the Roman Empire. But the persecutions were sporadic and local until the third century. Then several factors prompted a more systematic attempt to rid the empire of the Christians. For one thing, the fortunes of the empire were at low tide; and since the worship of the gods was regarded as integral to the continued prosperity of the state, it was thought that the gods were displeased and that their displeasure was expressed in the declining prosperity and stability of the Roman Empire. The widespread popularity of Christianity among the people made it suspect. Perhaps the gods were unhappy with the negative influence of these atheistic, immoral persons. Given these conditions and the fact that Christians supported the coming kingdom of Christ, the intensified persecution against them is understandable.

The Attitude of the Church Toward the State

The development of the church's attitude toward the state was related to the church's eschatology. It was the general consensus of Christians that the present world order would be completely destroyed by fire in the end times. In this sense, the early church was informed by the vision of Peter, who said they should "look forward to the day of God and speed its coming. That day will bring about the destruction of the heavens by fire, and the elements will melt in the heat" (2 Peter 3:12). But the church also looked forward to a restored paradise. In the tradition of Paul's teaching, the believers anticipated that "the creation itself will be liberated from its bondage to decay and brought into the glorious freedom of the children of God" (Rom. 8:21). Irenaeus summed up the consensus that it was neither the substance nor the essence of creation that would pass away but the *fashion* of the world: "But when this [present] fashion [of things] passes away, and man has been renewed, and flourishes in an incorruptible state, so as to preclude the possibility of becoming old, [then] there shall be the new heaven and the new earth, in which the new man shall remain, always holding fresh converse with God."[2]

This eschatological vision, coupled with a strong conviction that Christ's return was in the near future, fixed the Christians' vision of a perfect society in the future. The idea that the perfect kingdom of God could be realized on earth was quite foreign to the ancient Christian mind.

Nevertheless, Christian loyalty to the vision of the future kingdom of God did not mean that Christians were anarchists or disloyal to the state. The Fathers made it very clear that Christians did not have the right to rebel against the government. Christians, according to Justin, were taught civil obedience by Christ and were therefore to be accounted among the best citizens: "And everywhere we, more readily than all men, endeavor to pay to those appointed by you the taxes both ordinary and extraordinary."[3] Therefore, Justin continued, "to God alone we render worship, but in other things we gladly serve you, acknowledging you as kings and rulers of men, and praying that with your kingly power you be found to possess also sound judgment."[4] Likewise, Tertullian made it clear that Christians refused to worship the emperor because he was not God, but Christians were nonetheless loyal to the emperor.

The charge that Christians were immoral was also refuted with the assertion that the morality of Christians strengthened the fabric of Roman society. Theophilus, in his *Letter to Autolycus*, reminded him that with the Christians "temperance dwells, self-restraint is practiced, monogamy is observed, chastity is guarded, iniquity exterminated, sin extirpated, righteousness exercised, law administered, worship performed, God acknowledged."[5] The philosopher Aristides wrote that "they do not commit adultery nor fornication, nor bear false witness, nor covet the things of others. . . . They are eager to do good to their enemies; they are gentle and easy to be entreated. . . . [They] live holy and just lives, as the Lord enjoined upon them."[6]

Although the early Christians were unwilling to participate in the government, they believed that it functioned by divine sanction. They stood in the tradition of Paul, who wrote that "everyone must submit himself to the governing authorities" (Rom. 13:1 RSV), and of Peter, who likewise insisted that Christians "submit yourselves for the Lord's sake to every authority instituted among men: whether to the king, as the supreme authority, or to governors, who are sent by him to punish those who do wrong and to commend those who do right" (1 Peter 2:13–14).

Irenaeus summed up the general attitude in his work *Against Heresies*. He wrote that it was God who has "appointed the kingdoms of this world" and that "God imposed upon mankind the fear of man, as they did not acknowledge the fear of God, in order that, being subjected to the authority of men, and kept under restraint by their laws, they might attain to some degree of justice, and exercise mutual forbearance through dread of the sword."[7]

Although the government has a divine function, the early Christians nevertheless looked on government as a "human institution." Government was instituted as a result of the Fall. Consequently, it would not be needed in the new heavens and the new earth. The important feature of this conviction is that the early Christians did not assume that the government could become Christian. For that reason they, like their spiritual ancestors, were "looking forward to the city with foundations, whose architect and builder is God" (Heb. 11:10).

Christians as Aliens and Sojourners

From the very beginnings of the church, Christians recognized that they were part of society but that they were to be different. The *Didache*, the earliest Christian manual of behavior, begins by saying, "There are two ways, one of life and one of death; and between the two ways there is a great difference."[8] There follows a detailed description of how the Christian is to live, what he is to do and what he is to refrain from doing. These prescriptions are most revealing because they show that Christian obedience must take shape in respect to society and societal norms. This document is only one of many that give us insight into Christian living. Let us look briefly at some of the major concerns of these early documents.

In the first place, Christians generally refused to be involved in civil government. Government officials and workers in the New Testament period became Christians and apparently stayed in these positions.[9] But by the end of the second century, involvement in the military and civil service was avoided. Hippolytus, for example, indicates that a person who is in military service and becomes a Christian may remain, but "if a catechumen or a believer seeks to become a soldier, they must be rejected, for they have despised God."[10] A similar attitude was taken toward civil service. Hippolytus insists that a "civic magistrate that wears the purple must resign or be rejected [from the church]."[11] (Judges were continually expected to pronounce and inflict capital punishment. They were also involved in the support of emperor-worship.) Tertullian summarized the attitude of the early church by insisting that "there is no agreement between the divine and the human sacrament [oath], the standard of Christ and the standard of the devil, the camp of light and the camp of darkness. One soul cannot be due to two *masters* —God and Caesar."[12]

The early Christians also took a very negative view of Roman entertainment. Again, Hippolytus gives evidence of this in the screening of those who desire to become catechumens (converts in preparation for baptism and full membership in the church). He wrote that actors, chariot-eers, gladiators, or persons involved in any way with gladiatorial exhibitions must "desist or be rejected." Tertullian warned against shows in his work *On Shows*. After describing idolatry's permeation of the circus and other shows, he insists that "we lapse from God . . . by touching and tainting ourselves with the world's sins." For that reason, a Christian makes a break with his Maker by "going as a spectator to the circus and theatre," for "the polluted things pollute us."[13] Athenagoras warns against the shows because "to see a man put to death is much the same as killing him."[14]

The attitude of early Christians toward society was only partly negative. In many other ways, they exerted a strong positive influence on society by their concern for upright living. Even a pagan critic like Lucian observed, "It is incredible to see the ardor with which the people of that religion help each other in their wants. They spare nothing. Their first legislator [Jesus] has put into their heads that they are all brethren."[15]

To begin with, Christians were willing to share their wealth. Their attitude toward possessions evidenced itself in Jerusalem, where "no one claimed that any of his possessions was his own, but they shared everything they had. . . . There were no needy persons among them. For from time to time those who owned lands or houses sold them, brought the money from the sales and put it at the apostles' feet, and it was distributed to anyone as he had need" (Acts 4:32–35). This attitude continued in the early church. While there is little evidence that the churches actually banded themselves together in shared economic communities, there is much evidence that they continued to care for the needs of the brethren. Justin Martyr wrote, "We who valued above all things the acquisition of wealth and possessions, now bring what we have into a common stock, and communicate to every one in need."[16] Indeed, Martin Hengel in his work *Property and Riches in the Early Church* argues that "this idea that private property is a root of human dissension goes through the social admonitions of the fathers of the early church like a scarlet thread. The struggle for individual possessions destroys the original good order of the world, as all had an equal share in God's gifts."[17] There is also evidence that each congregation had a common fund to which all contributed for the benefit of the needy.

The Christian spirit of hospitality evidenced itself in the attitude taken toward the sick, the poor, and the homeless. The classical world had displayed very little concern for the needy. Plato, for example, thought that allowing the poor to die would shorten their misery. Ancient society even allowed orphans to be raised for prostitution. Christians, by contrast, were concerned about the poor, were active in hospitality to the stranger, and set about caring for orphans and castaway children. Aristides described this social awareness as follows:

> Falsehood is not found among them; and they love one another, and from widows they do not turn away their esteem; and they deliver the orphan from him who treats him harshly. And he who has gives to him who has not, without boasting. And when they see a stranger, they take him into their homes and rejoice over him as a very brother; for they do not call them brethren after the flesh, but brethren after the spirit and in God. And whenever one of their poor passes from the world, each one of them according to his ability gives heed to him and carefully sees to his burial. And if they hear that one of their number is imprisoned or afflicted on account of the name of their Messiah, all of them anxiously minister to his necessity, and if it is possible to redeem him they set him free. And if there is among them any that is poor and needy, and if they have no spare food, they fast two or three days in order to supply the needy their lack of food.[18]

Christians also took a more humane approach toward slavery. Most slaves were originally captured soldiers whose owners had complete control over their lives. In the second century, a series of laws made conditions for slaves more tolerable. They were able to accumulate enough wealth to buy their own freedom. Historical evidence shows that Christians also owned slaves but regarded them in a kindly way: Paul admonished Philemon to take Onesimus back, not as a slave but as a beloved brother (Philem. 16). Aristides informs us that "if one or another of them have bondmen and bondwomen or children, through love towards them they persuade them to become Christians, and when they have done so, they call them brethren without distinction."[19] We know that the church encouraged the release of slaves, that there was a liturgy for this, and that it was not infrequent for a slave owner to set a number of slaves free on the day of his baptism. Christian slaves were also active in the church, and one of them, Collistus, became bishop of Rome in A.D. 220.

Christians also had a positive effect on society through their emphasis on sexual morality and stable marriages. At a time when moral laxity was high and the family structure was breaking down, the Christian church insisted on high moral standards. As the author of the *Letter to Diognetus* said, "They marry, like everyone else. . . . They share their board with each other, but not their marriage bed."[20]

COMPARISON WITH
THE NEW TESTAMENT CHURCH

We may now ask: How does the attitude of the pre-Constantinian church toward the world compare with that of the New Testament church? Several observations may be made.

First, the church of the early centuries continued to affirm the basic goodness of the world through its doctrine of creation. During the latter half of the second century, the church became embroiled in a life-or-death controversy with the Gnostics over, among other things, the origin of creation. For the Gnostics, creation was intrinsically evil, having been created by Jahweh, the evil God. Orthodox Christians, rejecting this metaphysical dualism, world came into existence by God, "Father Almighty, the Creator of heaven and earth and sea and all that is in them."[21] Furthermore, in the sacramental consciousness of the early church, the material creation was viewed as a means through which God acts to encounter the human person. So Tertullian could write against the Gnostics "that the material substance which governs terrestrial life acts as agent likewise in the celestial."[22]

Next, the early church fathers appear supremely aware of the ability of spiritual forces, both good and bad, to work through the structures of existence and to influence the direction of people.[23] According to Irenaeus, "The devil . . . an apostate angel, is able as he was in the beginning, to lead astray and to deceive."[24] Tertullian claims "the business [of the fallen angels, who are the demons], is to corrupt mankind."[25] Origen, discussing free choice, reminds his readers that "while we make our own decisions, some powers may perhaps impel us to sin, and others help us to salvation."[26] More specifically, Origen states "To every man there are two attending angels . . . if . . . the thoughts of our heart be turned to evil, an angel of the devil is speaking to us."[27]

Finally, the notion that Christ by His death and resurrection has put down the evil one is found specifically in the liturgy of the church, the heart of the church's continuing experience with the risen Lord. In the *Didache* the celebrant prays, "Remember, Lord, your church, to save it from all evil and to make it perfect by your love. Make it holy, and gather it together from the four winds into your kingdom which you have made ready for it. For yours is the power and the glory forever."[28] In this brief prayer the Christian is reminded that evil is overcome, the church is gathered from around the world, and the kingdom is achieved because the ultimate power belongs to God. These same themes are accented in the earliest extant eucharistic prayer, by Hippolytus of the third century. This prayer refers to the death of Christ as the means through which "he might release from suffering those who have believed in you" and the occasion in which "he might destroy death, and break the bonds of the Devil, and tread down hell."[29]

This power of Christ to overcome the evil one is expressed by the early church in the baptismal liturgy where considerable attention is paid to the exorcism of evil. Hippolytus, writing about the role of bishop in baptism, declares: "And laying his hand on them he shall exorcise every evil spirit to flee away from them."[30] Later, the candidate for baptism says before going into the waters of baptism, "I renounce thee, Satan, and all thy service and all thy works," after which the candidate is anointed with the oil of exorcism accompanied by the words, "Let all evil spirits depart far from thee."[31]

CONCLUSION

We conclude that the New Testament consciousness of adverse powers at work in the world was very much alive in the experience of the pre-Constantinian Christian. Consequently, where the powers were in strong evidence—particularly in the state and in state-related vocations—the Christian generally exercised the option of discreet separation. By belonging to the church, a counter society, the Christians exercised through prayer and righteous living a stabilizing influence in the world. They were, as Peter had said earlier, "aliens and strangers" in a foreign land. Their eschatological vision of the coming kingdom meant that their ultimate citizenship was in the celestial city, in the "Jerusalem" which is above. This paradoxical relationship to the world is captured by the anonymous author of the second-century *Letter to Diognetus*:

> Christians cannot be distinguished from the rest of the human race by country or language or customs. They do not live in cities of their own; they do not use a peculiar form of speech; they do not follow an eccentric manner of life. . . . They live in their own countries, but only as aliens. They have a share in everything as citizens, and endure everything as foreigners. . . . They busy themselves on earth, but their citizenship is in heaven.[32]

A good summary of the relationship of the church to the world in this era is provided by the same author. "What the soul is in the body," he says, "that Christians are in the world. The soul is dispersed through all the members of the body, and Christians are scattered through all the cities of the world. The soul dwells in the body, but does not belong to the body, and Christians dwell in the world but do not belong to the world."[33]

In sum, the pre-Nicene church appears sensitive to the power of evil working through the power which human institutions, particularly the state, may exercise over them. These Christians seemed "dutifully obedient" to the structure powers, but "creatively resistant" to the evil exercised through them. They belonged not to the world but to another society, the church, which leaned into the future, patiently expecting the consummation of time. From this stance, the early Christians acted as servants of the world in full expectation of the day Christ would come as Master and Lord of the universe.

5

THE CONSTANTINIAN CHURCH

The period of history known as the Constantinian era represents a complete shift in the relationship between the church and the world. During the latter days of the pre-Constantinian period, the emperor Diocletian attempted to wipe out the Christian church. Decree after decree was issued against the Christians in an attempt to rid the world of them.

However, a complete reversal was taken by Constantine who, after his conversion to Christianity, issued the Decree of Toleration in 311 and the Edict of Milan in 313. The significance of these edicts for the relation between church and state is put this way by Charles Norris Cochrane: "By admitting the victory of Christianity over the secular order, it brought to a sudden and unexpected end the phase of opposition between the two; and by demonstrating, as nothing else could have done, the utter bankruptcy of the ancient religio-political idea, it pointed the way to a development of fresh relationships between the empire and church."[1]

The Edict of Milan introduced four favorable new provisions for the Christian church. First, it guaranteed Christians the right to profess the faith; second, it guaranteed them the right to gather for worship without fear of reprisal; third, it called for the restitution of buildings and land that had been confiscated from the church; and fourth, it recognized the corporate nature of the church by allowing it to hold property.[2]

This change in the state's attitude toward the church resulted in the principle of toleration toward all religions (changed by Theodosius in 378 when, by decree, Christianity became the only religion tolerated in the empire). This neutrality toward all religions actually made it possible for Christians to think in terms of a Christian social philosophy. It was out of this context, then, that a new idea was born: a Christian commonwealth. In the commonwealth, church and state would be no longer antithetical but complementary. This idea and the reality of it was not born or realized overnight. But it already began to be foreshadowed in the favorable disposition of the state toward the church.

The State Favors the Church

Even though the Edict of Milan promulgated a separation of church and state powers, Constantine's personal religion was rapidly becoming the religion of the state. Before long it was evident that Constantine sought to help the church in two ways. First, he issued a series of decrees that led to the full legal equality of Christianity, and second, he supported the church politically.

His concern to give the church full equality was first expressed in his decree to Anulinus, proconsul of Africa, in 313. In this decree he ordered the restoration of all church property. "Make haste," he wrote, "to have restored to them with all speed all things before belonging to them by right, whether gardens or buildings or whatever they may be."[3] In another decree written in the same year to Calcilian, bishop of Carthage, he arranged for the payment of a sum of money to the church and indicated that, should it not be enough, more was available.[4] Another unprecedented move occurred the next year, when bishops met at a synod at Arles. Many of these bishops who had suffered in the persecutions only a few years before were escorted to the synod by the chariot teams of Constantine. This was a privilege that, prior to this time, was granted only to imperial messengers and high government officials. Furthermore, Constantine issued certain edicts that gave the clergy authority in public matters.

One edict gave the bishops equal authority with the magistrates. Another put the manumission—that is, the freeing—of slaves by the church on an equal basis with manumission by the magistrate.

Constantine also favored the church politically. In 321 he declared that Sunday was an official day of rest. The only exception to this was to be made for the farmer who needed to look after his crops. Furthermore, Constantine brought numerous Christians into positions of authority in government. Previously, Christians had refused to participate in the government because to do so would have involved them in pagan festivals and sacrifice. But now all this had changed, and the government was filled with Christians on every level. Constantine was busily shaping the Roman Empire into a Christian world empire. He paid particular attention to the city of Rome and attempted to make it the Christian capital of the world by putting Christians in responsible positions and by providing money for the construction of churches.[5]

All of this, of course, had an effect on the church and on its attitude toward the state.

The Church Favors the State

The church, which only a few years before had faced the possibility of extinction by imperial persecution, now faced the possibility of creating a Christian empire because of the conversion of Constantine. The unexpected triumph of the church was viewed as evidence of the hand of God. And it shifted attention away from a preoccupation with the future kingdom in heaven to the possible expression of that kingdom on earth. The promise of the dominion of Christ over the world was at hand.

The great church historian Eusebius, who was a personal friend of Constantine and his chief adviser during the Nicene Council, expresses this vision of a Christian society. In his *Oration*, he speaks of the changes in the Roman Empire as a result of Constantine's conversion:

> Discourse and precepts, and exhortations to a virtuous and holy life, are proclaimed in the ears of all nations. Nay, the emperor himself proclaims them: and it is indeed a marvel that this mighty prince, raising his voice in the

hearing of all the world, like an interpreter of the almighty Sovereign's will, invites his subjects in every country to the knowledge of the true God.[6]

Even more than Eusebius, the philosopher-theologian Lactantius provides a clue to the spirit of the Constantinian age. In his celebrated *Divine Institutes*, he looks back to a bygone era of peace, prosperity, and brotherhood that was lost when the worship of the true God was taken away. After that men "began to contend with one another, and to plot, and to acquire for themselves glory from the shedding of human blood."[7] Lactantius cites lust as the source of all the evils of society, such as the motivation of private gain, slavery, the selfish acquisition of goods, unjust laws, tyranny, and violence. But in due time, he contends, "God, as a most indulgent parent, when the last time approached, sent a messenger to bring back that old age, and justice which had been put to flight, that the human race might not be agitated by very great and perpetual errors."[8]

What Lactantius appears to envision is not so much a world that has been transformed by the gospel as a society that identifies itself with moral, social, and political goodness. His religion is an innocuous Christianity that calls on people to suppress their evil desires and to return to the goodness of the original man. It is more a curious blend of pagan humanitarianism and Christian appearances than a thoroughgoing application of kingdom preaching to the ills of society. As Cochrane states, "It clearly forecasts that era of 'godly and righteous' legislation, of generous but not excessive reform, which was to be the net contribution of Constantinianism to the Kingdom of God."[9]

The point is that under Constantine the church was unable to effect a real transformation of society. What did occur was little more than the amelioration of certain societal ills along with the projection of a society that would, at least in external form, look more and more like the kingdom Jesus proclaimed. What this meant for the church in the world we will consider next.

THE CHURCH DURING THE CONSTANTINIAN ERA

The significance of the shift that occurred in the church between the third and fourth centuries cannot be overemphasized. From the church against the state to the church for the state—that is indeed a long distance. It represents two completely different conceptions of the Christian and the church in the world. Not surprisingly, this situation had both negative and positive effects on the church.

In the first place, the church became a wealthy institution. In the past, the clergy had been involved in small business enterprises as a means of supporting the church, and the church was quite dependent, of course, on donations by its members. But now, as the expansion of the church throughout the empire required the building of numerous new churches, the acquisition of art, and an increasingly elaborate system of administration, the church began to invest heavily in order to meet its expenses. The temptation of wealth and business was at least great enough that the Nicene Council produced a canon saying that any ecclesiastic found guilty of usury would be unfrocked.

A second problem for the church was that it became filled with nominal Christians. In the days of persecution, to be a Christian was not only unpopular but a threat to one's life. There was no "cheap grace" in the early church; it cost a person something to be a follower of Christ. For this reason, the doors of the church were open only to the faithful. Involvement in the church came only after an intense three-year period of catechetical teaching followed by baptism. But now the doors of the church were flung open. It was "popular" to be a Christian; the requirements, at least superficially, appeared to be little more than that the convert acquire certain virtues and niceties that were expected of those who were "well-bred."

A third problem was that the sharp distinction between the ideal of the kingdom and the ideal of humanitarianism was lost. The danger, as we have seen with Lactantius, is that of confusing Christian moral teaching with similar ideas from the pagan philosophers. This confusion of Christian and pagan ideals served to blunt the edge of Christian eschatology. The hope was no longer in the kingdom to come or in a thorough understanding of the presence of the kingdom in the world. Rather, the hope was in making the world a better place to live and in making it safe for Christianity.

Finally, the church became a powerful institution. Its members (many of them nominal) filled government and administrative posts throughout the empire, and the emperor continually favored the church. In time, the emperor, with the sanction of the church, turned against the pagan and Jewish elements of society and persecuted them. The hunted became the hunters. By 381, Theodosius I took measures against non-Christians and stated in his decree *Nulles haereticus* that "we permit no heretics to hold their unlawful assemblies in the towns. If they attempt any disturbance, we decree that their fury shall be suppressed and that they shall be expelled outside the walls of the cities."[10]

COMPARISON WITH THE EARLIER CHURCH

We may now ask how the relationship between church and world during the Constantinian era differed from that of the earlier church of the New Testament and pre-Constantinian era. In theology it continued to affirm God as Creator, sin as the perverter, Christ as the re-Creator, and the end times as the consummation of the world. But in practice certain significant shifts had taken place.

First of all, the influence of Christianity was felt more through legislation and less through evangelization. This was particularly true as a result of the far-reaching changes made by Theodosius, who revised the laws of the Roman Empire to turn it into a Christian state. For example, he instituted laws to reflect Christian principles: No criminal trials during Lent; persons imprisoned for lesser crimes were released for Easter; and death sentences were to be delayed for thirty days. He also revised existing laws regarding marriage and divorce. Further, Theodosius instituted sweeping laws against the pagans and the heretics. Paganism was outlawed, temples were nationalized and turned into museums, priests were forbidden to worship or lead in worship, the pagan calendar was abolished, and pagan festivals were made illegal. Laws were also enacted to make it much more difficult to live in the empire as a heretic. Heretics such as the Manicheans, Eunomians, Arians, Macedonians, Pneumatomachians, and Apollinarians no longer had any rights in the courts. Their properties were confiscated and they were not allowed to hold office in the government. In short, Theodosius was attempting to enforce the uniformity of Christian belief by making it exceedingly difficult to live in the empire unless one was a Christian.

Second, with the seeming Christianization of the empire, the powers of evil working through the structures of existence gave the appearance of being tamed. Consequently, the church's conflict with adverse spiritual powers working through political, economic, and social structures dropped into the background while the conflict with sin shifted more toward personal habits and choices. Many Christians failed to see that the evil powers that frequently work through political, social, and economic conditions were now turned against pagans and heretics, making their lives miserable, while making the Christian lives comfortable. Since the structures of society were favorable toward the Christian, the evil which they now inflicted upon the pagans and heretics was conveniently ignored. The Christians now concentrated on personal morality and the acquisition of habits that made them more genteel and sociable.

Third, the eschatological hope shifted from the future kingdom, which worship and the church anticipated, to the present possible formation of the kingdom on earth. It appeared that Christ's victory over sin was taking hold in the social order now, ameliorating evil conditions and humanizing the structures of existence. For example, baptism, which in the earlier Christian period was an adult repudiation of the kingdom of evil (as well as acceptance of the kingdom of Christ), now became an event in which the original sin of an infant was forgiven. Worship also underwent some significant changes. What had been a simple proclamation of Christ—emphasizing His death and resurrection as the destruction of the powers, lifting the congregation toward the parousia of the exalted Lord, and bringing the Christian community into the present realization of the kingdom—became a pious representation of Christ's life, death, and resurrection. That is, worship became historical rather than eschatological, a representation of a past event rather than the formation of God's people into the eschatological community. This historical and representational form of worship served the idea of a Christian commonwealth, for it assisted people in the assimilation of the facts of the gospel. Worship became less a prophetic announcement of the downfall of the power of evil and more a symbolic repetition of facts such as the birth, life, death, resurrection, and ascension. Worship lost its cutting edge as a proclamation against the powers as it served the purpose of increasing knowledge about Christ.[11]

Finally, the church which formerly had a pilgrim consciousness and saw itself as an alien and stranger in the world now became more and more a power to shape society. Constantine had effected a commonwealth containing two orders. Theodosius had inaugurated a relationship between the two orders that resulted in the subordination of the temporal to the spiritual. Now the two kingdoms were merged into one as the spiritual superiority of the church was recognized. Unfortunately, however, it was not civilization that was Christianized as much as Christianity that was civilized. God became identified with the maintenance of human institutions, while the distinction between the church and worldly powers was temporarily extinguished. Thus, the church shifted from an incarnational approach to the world to one that assumed the lordship of Christ over the structures of existence.

However, two events were to challenge and disturb this new relationship between church and world. The rise of the monastic movement—which denounced the church as a worldly institution and called upon people to renounce the world of power and riches—restored to a certain extent the notion of a pilgrim church, the eschatological community which renounced the power of the world, the flesh, and the Devil. The second event, the fall of Rome and its final dissolution, resulted in the temporary separation of the church from the secular government. Yet the vision of the church conquering the world remained, to appear again in the medieval period.

6

MEDIEVAL CHRISTENDOM

The concept of the church and world in the medieval period goes back to Augustine. Although Augustine's understanding of the relationship between church and world differs significantly from that of the thirteenth century, the roots of medieval thought go back to Augustine's vision expressed in *The City of God*. We will begin with a summary of the ideas contained in this classic work as a basis for understanding the later medieval doctrine of church and world.

THE ROOTS OF MEDIEVAL THOUGHT

As we have noted, Augustine's view of the relation of the Christian to culture is most clearly expressed in his work *The City of God*. In Book XI, he develops the concept of "the two cities that are confused together in this world, and distinct in the other."

The Two Cities

The two cities discussed in Augustine's book are the city of God and the city of man. The city of God is made up of all those who follow the true God, whether they be inside or outside the church. Likewise, the city of man is made up of all those who worship false gods, whether they be inside or outside the church. Augustine bases his definition of these cities upon the idea of two kinds of love: "The earthly city was created by self-love reaching the point of contempt for God, the heavenly city by the love of God carried as far as contempt of self. In fact, the earthly city glories in itself; the heavenly city glories in the Lord."[1] The two cities cannot, therefore, be identified as strict visible entities. They have a spiritual existence and find their way into opposite attitudes that come into conflict through the shape people give to culture.

One must understand the origins of these two cities if one is to understand their character. The city of God originates with the creation of light (i.e., with the angels), and the city of man begins with the sin of Satan. Sin is not something intrinsic to creation. Rather, sin is a defect of will. God's creation is therefore not evil; created beings become evil by choice. What is true in the realm of angels is also true in the realm of the created world and man. When God created the world He knew full well that the unity of society, though desirable, would not be accomplished. Human beings too would eventually form two opposing societies.

These two societies, though already present within Adam himself, emerge specifically in Cain and Abel. "Cain founded a city, whereas Abel, as a pilgrim, did not found one," says Augustine. "For the city of the saints is up above, although it produces citizens here below, and in their persons the city is on pilgrimage until the time of its Kingdom comes."[2] For this reason, the one city is rooted in "worldly possession" and the other in "heavenly hopes."

Next, Augustine traces the history of these two cities from Noah to Abraham and from Abraham to David. Abraham is promised that he will be the spiritual father of the city of God. This promise is continued in the descendants of Abraham to David. David ruled in the earthly Jerusalem. At this time the prophecies of Christ became more clear, especially in the Psalms. These prophecies were finally realized in the death and resurrection of Christ and the beginning of the church. In the meantime, the course of the city of man continued to parallel that of the city of God, and the city of man came to fruition in the Roman Empire. Nevertheless there is a mixture of the elect and the reprobate in the church as well as in the empire. The confusion between the city of God and the city of man will continue until the Judgment, when they will be severed forever and receive the reward of their works.

This brief sketch of *The City of God* provides a general background against which we will look more specifically at the relation between (1) the state and the city of man, and (2) the church and the city of God.

The State and the City of Man

Augustine does not equate the state with the city of man. As John Figgis points out, "The primary distinction is always between 'two societies,' the body of the *reprobate* and the *communis sanctorum*; not between church and state."[3] For Augustine, the state is human society organized, and as such it contains members of both the city of God and the city of man. This persuasion provides a clue to Augustine's view of church and world. If those who control the state have at the same time a final commitment to God, their influence will be felt in the social order.

Because of the interplay between the state, the city of man, and the city of God, it is impossible to pin Augustine down to a specific and manageable political view. Nevertheless, certain emphases are quite clear in his writing:

First, we may say that Augustine is not against the state as such, nor is he against the involvement of Christians in the administration of the state. He often quotes with approval the apostolic teaching on submission to the powers that be. He insists that Christians are to give to Caesar what belongs to him, and he values highly family life and social relationships.

However, Augustine does condemn the lust for power. "Is it reasonable, is it sensible," he asks, "to boast of the extent and grandeur of empire, when you cannot show that men lived in happiness, as they passed their lives amid the horrors of war . . . ?"[4]

Justice, not power, is the essence of the state. "Remove justice," he insists, "and what are kingdoms but gangs of criminals on a large scale? What are criminal gangs but petty kingdoms? A gang is a group of men under the command of a leader, bound by a compact of association, in which the plunder is divided according to an agreed convention."[5] The point is that justice cannot be had where the true God is not worshiped. Therefore, true justice exists only in the society of God, and this will be truly fulfilled only after the Judgment. Nevertheless, while no society on earth can fully express this justice, the one that is more influenced by Christians and Christian teaching will more perfectly reflect a just society. For this reason, Christians have a duty toward government.

The Church and the City of God

The relation between the church and the city of God is similar to the relation between the state and the city of man. They must not be confused. The church is not the city of God as such. The universal church contains both the wheat and the tares; it has people in it who belong to both the city of God and the city of man. The real church is the *communis sanctorum*—the body of the elect. Many of the elect are in the church, but some are not. Nevertheless, the church is the symbolic representative of the *civitas terrena* (the city of God on earth).

It is in Augustine's view of the church, particularly within the complex context in which he develops it, that the idea of the church's transforming the world becomes more clear. Augustine leaves us a legacy that is quickly developed into a model of the church over the world. This legacy includes five ideas that provided the foundation for a complex transformational model:

First, Augustine identifies the *civitas dei* as the elect. In this sense, the city of God transcends the New Testament church and includes all God's people from the beginning of history, whether they belong to the visible church or not. He is much more universal than Cyprian, who insists that "he who has not the church for his mother has not God for his Father." The real issue between Cyprian and Augustine is whether or not the church is pure, made up of believers only. Cyprian argues that it is. Augustine argues that it contains a mixture of saints and sinners—that is, redeemed and unredeemed.

Augustine nevertheless insists, and this is the second point, that the visible church is the kingdom of God on earth. "It follows," he writes, "that the church even now is the kingdom of Christ and the kingdom of heaven. And so even now his saints reign with him, though not in the same way they will then reign; and yet the tares do not reign with him, although they are growing in the church side by side with the wheat."[6]

The third idea is that the Millennium is not a *future* reign of God, but that the church is now in the Millennium. "In the meantime," he writes, "while the Devil is bound for a thousand years, the saints reign with Christ, also for a thousand years; which are without doubt to be taken in the same sense, and as denoting the same period, that is, the period beginning with Christ's first coming."[7]

The fourth point is that, given the facts that the church is the kingdom of God and that the period between Christ's first coming and second coming is the Millennium, the church is now the *regnum dei*, the rule of God. God is now ruling in His world through the church. In this respect, Augustine interprets Revelation 20:4 ("I saw thrones on which were seated those who had been given authority to judge") as "the seats of the authorities by whom the church is now governed, and those sitting on them as the authorities themselves." Consequently, he concludes that "the best interpretation of the judgment given is that referred to in the words: 'whatever you bind on earth shall be bound in heaven; and whatever you loose on earth will be loosed in heaven' " (Matt. 18:18).[8]

The fifth point is clear from the preceding four: Augustine believes that the church assumes the shape of a society. But this idea emerged not so much through theological or philosophical speculation as through practical implication. The occasion for this emergence of the view of the church as a society was the Roman church's contest with the Donatists.

The challenge that the Donatists offered the Catholics was in the area of ecclesiology. They claimed to be the true church. The issue for Augustine, at least in part, was the unity and peace of the church and the Roman Empire. To preserve unity and peace, Augustine turned to the state and developed an argument in favor of using force in religious matters. He based it on the words of Christ, "Compel them to come in" (Luke 14:23 KJV). Penalty, he argued, was useful because it helped one to reflect on error, turn away from it, and embrace the truth. It was, one might argue, persecution for the sake of good. Augustine called upon the state, then, to use force as a means of extending the kingdom of God. The state was in the service of the church.

All these ideas and the context in which they were developed tended, in the words of John Figgis,

> to develop a state of mind which will picture the *civitas dei* as a Christianized Church-State, from which unbelievers are excluded, and which would claim, directly or indirectly, the supreme power in that state for the leaders of the hierarchy. If we add to this the effects of the church's long continuance in concentration upon earthly activities, the development of vast administrative machinery, the fact that she became to the conquering barbarians the symbol and the source of all culture, we are well on our way to such a conception of church-power as was represented by Innocent III.[9]

The Implications of *De Civitate Dei* for the Medieval Era

It is generally recognized that Augustine himself did not develop his thought into an argument for Christendom.[10] Although he saw the vision of a world under God, he did not see the implications of this *on earth* in the same way that his students of the medieval era did. Several examples must suffice to illustrate the point.

A shift toward Christendom is noticeable in the thought of Pope Gelasius (492–96). He attempted to make the relation between kingly and priestly power more clear. In a letter to the Eastern emperor Anastasius, he wrote, "Two there are, august emperor, by which this world is chiefly ruled, the sacred authority of the priesthood and the royal power. Of these the responsibility of the priests is more weighty insofar as they will answer for the kings of men themselves at the divine judgment."[11] This declaration, which appears over and over again during the controversies between king and pope in the medieval period, throws the weight of governing power over the world toward the church. For our purposes, it is important to see the growing concept of a single Christian society that includes within it the arm of the state and the arm of the church.

This sense of a Christianized society was central to the thinking of Charlemagne (742–814), who aimed for a unified realm in which Christ was king and all the earth was subject to him. As a reader of Augustine, he envisioned a Christian empire, the city of God on earth. Both he and Otto I

(912–973) sought to create an empire that was holy and Roman. Theirs was a calling to create a Catholic commonwealth with two swords governing the secular and sacred life of their inhabitants.

It was their hope, as well as the hope of Innocent III (1161–1216), to organize all of human life under God. The vision was for the church and the commonwealth to become one. The kingdom of God on earth was considered to be a great church-state.

INNOCENT III

It was during the pontificate of Innocent III (1198–1216) that the medieval *synthesis* between the church and the world actually took place. The church became an international state incorporating within its jurisdiction the lands and policies of other states. It became the Roman church founded by God with universal authority exercised by the pope. The pope had the final authority over all ecclesiastical bishops and legates. He could appoint, depose, and reinstate other bishops. He could make new laws, call a council, and annul decrees made by anyone. His power also extended over emperors and kings. He could depose emperors, command subjects to disobey their rulers, and absolve subjects from their oath of allegiance to wicked rulers. All princes were to kiss his foot and no one was free to judge him or depose him. In short, these leaders believed that in the Roman church the city of God had been established on earth, as the church became a theocratic superstate governing the whole world. The great idea of a world state, overruled by an absolute monarchy through a centralized bureaucracy, had been conceived in the Roman Empire but was now the accomplishment of the papacy.

Pope Innocent III was destined to reign over this great synthesis of church and state. His own pronouncements indicate that he believed in a theocratic idea of papal monarchy. In his sermon on the occasion of his consecration to pope, he described the Roman vicar as "set between God and man, lower than God but higher than man, who judges all and is judged by no one."[12] In a letter written the same year to the archbishop of Ravenna, Innocent III declared, "Ecclesiastical liberty is nowhere better cared for than where the Roman church has full power in both temporal and spiritual affairs."[13] Again, the same year in a letter to the prefect of Acerbus and the nobles of Tuscany, he reminded the secular rulers that "just as the moon derives its light from the sun and is indeed lower than it in quantity and quality, in position and in power, so too the royal power derives the splendor of its dignity from the pontifical authority."[14] No wonder he wrote to the patriarch of Constantinople a year later that "James, the brother of the Lord who 'seemed to be a pillar' (Gal. 2:1 KJV), content with Jerusalem alone . . . left to Peter not only the universal church but the whole world to govern."[15]

Innocent III took his right to govern the empire with seriousness. In 1199, Innocent III imposed a truce upon Philip Augustus of France and Richard I of England. In 1201, he decided the dispute over succession in Germany in favor of Otto IV of Brunswick. In England, over a dispute regarding the appointment of the Archbishop of Canterbury, he succeeded not only in making the appointment but in making both England and Ireland fiefs of the papacy. Yet the judgment of many historians is that he always maintained "the need for two orders of government in Christian society, a priestly one and a royal one, and he never claimed that either order could be abolished or wholly absorbed by the other."[16] What was unique about his governance was the conviction that the pope was head over both the so-called secular and sacred realms.

As spiritual leader of both church and society, Innocent III was supposed to be in possession of *plenitudo potestatis,* that is, fullness of power. Through his administrative authority all ecclesiastical officials became the agents of the pope. He governed the finances, the appointments, the councils, and the courts. There was nothing that was not finally and ultimately under his power.

Nevertheless, this papal power—both temporal and spiritual—was not destined to last beyond the thirteenth century. In the fourteenth and fifteenth centuries, the breakdown of papal morality, the rise of nationalism, the emergence of a new economics, the reaction against the church by reforming groups, and the rise of the Renaissance paved the way for new religious, political, economic, and social ideas which were to drastically change the face of Christianized Europe and make havoc of a unified church.

EVALUATION AND COMPARISON

What are we to make of this medieval synthesis of church and world? How does it compare to the New Testament church, to the early church, to the church of the Constantinian era?

Obviously, medieval thought about church and world affirmed the doctrine of creation and sought to bring the whole world under the reign of Christ through the church. For medieval thinkers, the so-called secular powers were far from being an antithesis to the church. Indeed, in the medieval period all aspects of creation were integrated with a Christian world view. Redemption supposedly extended to art, literature, music, philosophy, law, science, medicine, and city planning. The world seemed to have been wrestled from the lap of the wicked one and brought into submission to the lordship of Christ who exercised his rule through the pope, His vicar on earth.

The ancient idea that the Fall resulted in the release of adverse spiritual forces who worked through the structures of existence faded into the background in favor of a more individualistic concept of sin. The Fall of our first parents was thought to have introduced original sin, which was passed down from generation to generation through procreation. Baptism not only remitted sin but brought one into the church, the institution through which salvation was guaranteed through the continual sacrifice of Christ, the benefit of which was communicated through the Eucharist. For sins of concupiscence, the system of penance had been established to maintain continual forgiveness.

Further, the ancient notion of Christ's death and resurrection as a victory over sin, the Devil, and the kingdom of evil was replaced by the Anselmic notion of satisfaction. This legal approach to Christ's death was more in keeping with the Catholic concept of jurisprudence and of the church as an institution which dispensed salvation through the sacraments. The central idea was that God in Christ's death had offered a satisfaction for sin which was not only acceptable to the Father, but which vindicated His holiness and set Him free to be just while justifying the unjust. Christ's death was less a victory over the Devil and more a satisfactory legal arrangement between Father and Son, through which the Son received punishment for sin as a substitute for the sinner.

The medieval concept of the church reflected the Catholic view of the world, of sin, and of Christ's death. The church was not a pilgrim people connected by the Christ event and the eschaton. Rather than anticipating the future, the church became an institution bent on establishing Christ's reign on earth. This institutional nature of the church was buttressed by its sacramental system. The Eucharist, for example, was viewed less as a proclamation of Christ's death through which the church became the eschatological community, more as the historical repetition of the sacrifice of Christ for sin. Instead of looking forward to the eschaton, this sacrament looked backward to the Cross. It became a mechanical means through which salvation was made available in the institution. It no longer defined the people of God as those who were anticipating and moving toward the kingdom. It no longer had anything to do with the individual's role in the world. It became a personal sacrifice for the sins of the individual.

Rather than defining the nature and mission of the church, eschatology became a theological discipline for considering the end times. The church was less interested in the coming of the kingdom and the overthrow of evil because the adverse powers of evil had been conquered and tamed by the church. The kingdom was a present reality, not a future hope. It had been established on earth now. The church's actual authority over the world was a hierarchical reflection of the heavenly reality. Thus, as petitioned in the Lord's Prayer, the kingdom had come, his will had been done.

The medieval church was a long way from the simple church of the New Testament. It appeared as though the powers of evil were not only tamed, but harnessed. The lordship of Christ over the powers of evil was now exercised through the church by the pope, who was Christ's vicar on earth. But this view of Christendom did not last long; it was a short turn in the long history of the church. The process of secularization soon forced the church to grant autonomy to the various structures of existence. However, before turning to the story of secularization, we must examine the viewpoint of the Reformers who were caught in the middle of this changing world. Caught between the death throes of medieval Christendom and the emergence of a new order, in which the structures of existence were given an autonomy from the church, the Reformers were forced to face the relationship between church and world in fresh ways. In their struggle to relate the Christian faith to the various orders of existence, the Reformers expressed three models which Richard Niebuhr identified as *church and world in antithesis, church and world in paradox,* and *church transforming the world.* Since Christians still wrestle with these models today, a brief modern update of each model will be provided with a summary of its classical articulation.

B. Classic Reformation Models of Church and World

7

CHURCH AND WORLD IN ANTITHESIS

In the history of Christian thought there are three distinct theological models of the relation between church and world. We have already met these models in their historical setting in the preceding section. First, there is the witness of the church *against* the world, such as that of the early church; second, the model of the church and the world in *paradox*, which has antecedents in early Constantinianism; and third, the model of the church *transforming* culture, which is rooted in Augustine and elaborated in the medieval period. However, the classic expressions of these three theological models are found among the Reformers. Our attention will focus first on the sixteenth-century alignment of church and world delineated by the Anabaptists (church and world in antithesis); second, on Martin Luther (church and world in paradox); and finally, on John Calvin (church transforming the world).

Only recently has the Anabaptist contribution to the church begun to be appreciated by mainline Protestants and Catholics. In the sixteenth century, the Anabaptists were regarded as left-wing radicals and this onus stayed with them for a long time. The negative attitude toward the Anabaptists originated with the Reformers and other defenders of the state-church Protestantism whom the Anabaptists opposed, and historical information about the Anabaptists has been drawn mainly from these hostile sources. However, twentieth-century historical scholarship has moved behind the myth, and a more accurate view has emerged.

The word *Anabaptist* itself does not give us a clear picture of these so-called left-wing radicals. It is a Latin derivative of the Greek *anabaptismos*, meaning "rebaptism," and in its historical context it literally meant "one who rebaptizes." The word was originally used by Luther and Zwingli to describe those Protestants who separated themselves from the state church. Baptism was a distinguishing mark between two approaches to the church organization. Infant baptism was the mark of the state churches; it was a civil law that all infants were to be baptized into the church. Adult baptism (or rebaptism in the case of those converts originally baptized as infants) was a mark of a church that refused to be controlled by the state. The Anabaptists advocated this "free church" position. They would not submit to state control. So their form of baptism constituted an act of civil disobedience. The word *Anabaptist* is inadequate to describe them because it points only to the act of baptism itself; whereas the deeper cause of anger and frustration, on the part of Luther and Zwingli and others who opposed the Anabaptists, was really the issue of whether the church should be independent of the state.

Franklin Littell in *The Anabaptist View of the Church* puts his finger on the real meaning of the term *Anabaptist*: "The Anabaptists proper were those in the radical reformation who gathered and disciplined a 'true church' (*Rechte Kirche*) upon the apostolic pattern as they understood it."[1] While the word was used rather broadly, the groups I have in mind in this discussion include only those at the center, the more moderate Anabaptists such as the Swiss Brethren, the Hutterite Brethren, and the Mennonites.[2]

A concern for the restitution of the church was central to these "mainline Anabaptists." It is the key, not only to the heart of the Anabaptist movement, but also to the Anabaptist view of culture. And so we must look first to the Anabaptists' view of biblical teaching on church and world, then their view of church history, and their concern to restore the true church.

BIBLICAL BASIS

As we have seen, the problem of the Christian in the world is rooted in the tension created by living in two worlds simultaneously. The Christian lives both in the world and in the kingdom of Christ.

The antithesis model of the Christian in the world emphasizes both the necessity that the Christian live by the standards of the kingdom of God, quite apart from an involvement in the world, and that every Christian is able to do so. The *necessity* of living by the principles of the kingdom of God is grounded in the antithesis that exists between the kingdom of God and the kingdom of evil. They are two wholly distinct spheres of life. The *ability* of the Christians to live in one sphere and not the other resides in the individual's power of choice. "Choose you this day whom ye will serve" (Josh. 24:15 KJV), "Come out from among them, and be ye separate" (2 Cor. 6:17 KJV)—Anabaptists believed these are not to be regarded as mere word games. They describe actual choices that the Christian must make. The separation from the kingdom of evil is ultimately a matter of Christian obedience.

Those who follow the antithesis model believe that the Bible abounds in examples of this kind of radical obedience. For example, Noah was chosen to build an ark for eight people in the midst of a culture so wicked "every inclination of the thoughts of [man's] heart was only evil all the time" (Gen. 6:5). Abraham was called *out* of his country to establish a new people: "Leave your country, your people and your father's household and go to the land I will show you" (Gen. 12:1). Abraham had no attachment to the city of man, for "he made his home in the promised land like a stranger in a foreign country; . . . For he was looking forward to the city with foundations, whose architect and builder is God" (Heb. 11:9–10). Likewise Moses refused to be identified with the Egyptians who reared him. "He chose to be mistreated along with the people of God rather than to enjoy the pleasures of sin for a short time" (Heb. 11:25). The same is true of the prophets: "They were stoned; they were sawed in two; they were put to death by the sword. They went about in sheepskins and goatskins, destitute, persecuted and mistreated—the world was not worthy of them. They wandered in deserts and mountains, and in caves and holes in the ground" (Heb. 11:37–38). What all these people have in common is that they separated themselves from the culture of the world.

Anabaptists regarded this theme, that Christians are to be separate from the world, as the explicit teaching of Jesus and the disciples. They believed that Jesus' teaching in the Sermon on the Mount supports the idea of an antithesis between the followers of Christ and the world. Jesus stated that "no one can serve two masters. Either he will hate the one and love the other, or he will be devoted to the one and despise the other. You cannot serve both God and Money" (Matt. 6:24). Furthermore, Peter described the Christian community as "aliens and strangers" (1 Peter 2:11) and John supported the antithesis by admonishing Christians not to "love the world or anything in the world. If anyone loves the world, the love of the Father is not in him. For everything in the world—the cravings of sinful man, the lust of his eyes and the boasting of what he has and does—comes not from the Father but from the world" (1 John 2:15–16). This attitude, as directed against the state, is particularly evident in the Book of Revelation, where John sees Rome as "the beast" (Rev. 13:1ff.).

Finally, separation from the world, according to the Anabaptist view, is grounded in a proper understanding of the two kingdoms. The separatist maintains that the two are so radically different that one can live in one or the other, but not both at the same time. This is the doctrine of the "radical antithesis." It assumes that sin has permeated every area of the world to such an extent that the true Christian cannot traffic with the world without compromising with sin and becoming contaminated by it. The church is therefore a counterculture, a culture within the culture, which lives by kingdom principles and values. The church is a pilgrim-people, sojourners whose citizenship is above. Any attachment to this world—to its goals, its pleasures, its wealth—must be denied for the sake of the kingdom of God.

ANABAPTIST UNDERSTANDING OF CHURCH HISTORY

The heart of the Anabaptists' view of the church is their desire to follow the New Testament pattern of the church, which is expressed in a kind of voluntarism. Littell calls this a "primitivism."[3] Their objective was to restore something old, to return to the pure, primitive, unspoiled church of a bygone age.

Actually, a kind of primitivism was already in the air in the sixteenth century. Many felt that the turmoil and revolution of the times was symptomatic of a fall that had occurred in national affairs, in the church, and in the age. Consequently, there was a longing for the past, for the restoration of a purer era. For the church, the past model was the New Testament era and the pre-Constantinian church. Erasmus, for example, pointed to gospel simplicity as a way to rejuvenate the faith and the church. But Erasmus never broke with the Catholic church. Zwingli, another student of the Bible and the early Fathers, called for a return to the New Testament and to Christ. But Zwingli never repudiated the church-state connections of the Swiss city-state. Unlike Erasmus or Zwingli, the early Anabaptist leaders were willing to carry out the logic of their convictions. They were willing to turn their back on the present—on the Catholic church and on the state-church establishment—to restore the past.

This interest inevitably led them to conclude that the present church had fallen. In general, their consensus was that the church had fallen during the time of Constantine, when Christianity was declared to be the state religion (A.D. 324). This event marked a turning point for the church; no longer independent, it began to turn to the state for support. The church had therefore been in a fallen condition ever since Constantine.

This attitude of the Anabaptists inevitably led them to find certain "marks" of the fallen church.[4] The most obvious mark was the union of church and state. Through this compromise, the church ceased to be a voluntary association of believers; the state was able to use power and coercion as a means of bringing people into the church. It made the church little more than another human institution. A second mark of the fallen church was seen in the wars conducted in the name of Christianity. Violence of any kind and under any condition was rejected as alien to the spirit of New Testament Christianity and that of the early church. That the church could carry the sword, take an oath of allegiance, and enforce political, economic, and religious control through the use of power was obviously wrong. Another mark of the fallenness of the church, in the eyes of the Anabaptists, was the dead formalism that characterized its life and worship. The Anabaptists argued that spiritual strength was found in the inward man, in the heart, and not in the pomp of the Mass. This concern for external appearances fostered another mark of the fallen church—the lust for ecclesiastical position and the power that went with it. This unseemly desire for achievement stood behind the rise of the church hierarchy. And through the hierarchy, power was abused.

The Anabaptists' rejection of the present state of the church caused them to focus on the early church, where none of these marks were present. The early church was characterized instead by the separation of church and state, by a true inward spirituality, by a spirit of community and brotherhood, and by equality among Christians. The Anabaptists' desire to restore the early church led them into a view of eschatology that looked for the dissolution of the established church in the near future, the emergence of the inner church from it, and then an age of the persecution of the true church by the established church (the Antichrist). After this would come the return of Christ.

Underlying all these convictions is a basic theological conviction, the ardent belief in the two kingdoms.

The Doctrine of Antithesis

Even though the Anabaptists glorified the pre-Constantinian church, they were unlike the early Christians in one major respect: they had a well-developed theology of the kingdom.[5] This theology was rooted in a fundamental dualism that they found in the New Testament. It was, they believed, the major concern of Jesus to proclaim the presence of the kingdom. Entrance into the kingdom of Jesus was through the new birth, a radical reorientation in one's view of life and style of life in which one turned away from the sin of the world (the kingdom of evil) toward the values, virtues, and lifestyle of Jesus. They took seriously the admonition of Paul that "our struggle is not against flesh and blood, but against the rulers, against the authorities, against the powers of this dark world and against the spiritual forces of evil in the heavenly realms" (Eph. 6:12). They were unwilling to compromise with the world, to flirt with its passing fancies, or to be related to it in any way.

This concern to be separate from the world dominated the Schleitheim Confession of Faith,[6] a major Anabaptist statement written in 1527 by the Swiss Anabaptists. In the third article the authors state that "all those who have fellowship with the dead works of darkness have no part in the light" and that "all who follow the devil and the world have no part with those who are called unto God out of the world." The fourth article states that "all creatures are in but two classes, good and bad, believing and unbelieving, darkness and light, the world and those who (have come) out of the world, God's temple and idols, Christ and Belial; and none can have part with the other."

A more elaborate statement of the same idea is found in the anonymous *Great Article Book* of the Hutterites. This is generally regarded as having been written by Bishop Peter Walpt around 1577.[7]

> Between the Christian and the world there exists a vast difference like that between heaven and earth. The world is the world, always remains the world, behaves like the world and all the world is nothing but world. The Christian, on the other hand, has been called away from the world. He has been called never to conform to the world, never to be a consort, never to run along with the crowd of the world and never to pull its yoke. The world lives according to the flesh and is dominated by the flesh. Those in the world think that no one sees what they are doing; hence the world needs the sword [of the authorities]. The Christians live according to the Spirit and are governed by the Spirit. They think that the Spirit sees what they are doing and that the Lord watches them. Hence they do not need and do not use the sword among themselves. The victory of the Christians is the faith that overcometh the world (1 John 5:4), while the victory of the world is the sword by which they overcome [whatever is in their way]. To Christians an inner joy is given; it is the joy in their hearts that maintains the unity of the Spirit in the bond of peace (Eph. 4:3). The world knows no true peace; therefore it has to maintain peace by the sword and force alone. The Christian is patient, as the apostle writes (1 Peter 4:1): "As Christ hath suffered . . . arm yourself likewise with the same mind." The world arms itself for the sake of vengeance and (accordingly) strikes out with the sword. Among Christians he is the most genuine who is willing to suffer for the sake of God. The world, on the contrary, thinks him the most honorable who knows how to defend himself with the sword.

To sum up: friendship with the world is enmity with God. Whosoever, therefore, wishes to be a friend of the world makes himself an enemy of God (James 4:4). If to be a Christian would reside alone in words and an empty name, and if Christianity could be arranged as it pleases the world; if, furthermore, Christ would permit what is agreeable to the world, and the cross would have to be carried by a sword only . . . then both authorities and subjects—in fact, all the world—would be Christians. Inasmuch, however, as a man must be born anew (John 3:7), must die in baptism to his old life, and must rise again with Christ unto a new life and Christian conduct, such a thing cannot and shall not be: "It is easier," says Christ, "for a camel to go through the eye of a needle than for a rich man (by whom is meant here the authorities in particular) to enter the Kingdom of God or true Christianity" (Matt. 19:24).[8]

The striking feature of the Anabaptist theology of the kingdom is the absolute antithesis it sees between the kingdom of Christ and the kingdom of this world. As the *Great Article Book* points out, the kingdom of this world is "according to the flesh," "needs the sword," and "knows no true peace." On the other hand, the kingdom of Christ is "according to the Spirit" and "governed by the Spirit," and to it "an inner joy is given." The conclusion is reached that "whosoever, therefore, wishes to be a friend of the world makes himself an enemy of God."

This theology of the kingdoms and the view of the absolute antithesis between them lies at the heart of the Anabaptists' view both of the church and of the state. We cannot understand their view of Christians in the world without understanding this. We turn, then, to the implications of the antithesis between the two kingdoms and the Anabaptist view of the church and of the state.

The Anabaptist View of the Church

To begin with, it must be recognized that the Anabaptists would have nothing to do with the state-church concept prevalent in the sixteenth century. This was the main point of their separation from the Lutherans, the Zwinglians, and the Calvinists. The Anabaptists were all united in their conviction that the state church was a kind of culture religion that had to be rejected before the true church (which was to have no connection with the culture of the world) could emerge.

This view forms the background for three Anabaptist convictions about the church. They believed that the church was a free association of believers, that it was a brotherhood of believers, and that the believers were characterized by radical obedience.

First and foremost, the Anabaptists regarded the church as a free association of believers. The institutional idea of the church to which people were admitted through baptism was, to them, a perversion of the New Testament ideal. They wished to restore the early church as it was at Jerusalem, a community of Christians who had in common their new birth by the Holy Spirit and the desire to worship God in purity of spirit and simplicity. This concern, to have a free church, must not be confused with the modern notion of individualism wherein each person has a private experience of conversion and growth in Christ somewhat unrelated to that of the rest of the Christian community.

This brings us to their second conviction about the church, that it is a brotherhood of believers. The concept of brotherhood attempts to take seriously the idea of a visible community of believers into which the Christian enters and to which he is responsible. Likewise the community is responsible for each person. As Robert Friedmann describes it, "One cannot find salvation without caring for each other, as it was commanded to the disciples of Christ as the way to God's Kingdom."[9] This concern for brotherhood is illustrated by the Anabaptist use of the "ban." Whenever a brother fell out of line with the Christian practice expected of him, he was banned from taking part in "the breaking of bread" as a method of punishment and correction.

The third conviction about the church was that it must be characterized by radical obedience. Once a believer has come to know God's will—through the Bible and in the community—there is nothing left for him to do except to obey. The Anabaptists looked on the commands of God as something to be taken literally and not spiritualized as Luther or Calvin would do. For example, the command to "forsake all" meant actually to forsake all and not merely to be *willing* to forsake all.

These three points illustrate the vast distance between

the Anabaptists and the accepted state-church view of their time. It was the reason for which they suffered and the basis for their view of the state.

The Anabaptist View of the State

As mentioned previously, the Anabaptists believed that the state belonged to the kingdom of this world. Therefore, because of the antithesis between the two kingdoms, the Anabaptists "acknowledged the primacy of the claims of God over the claims of government."[10]

This does not mean, however, that they did not recognize the state as a valid institution. Indeed, as the Schleitheim Confession states, "The sword is ordained of God outside the perfection of Christ. It punishes and puts to death the wicked, and guards and protects the good. In the law the sword was ordained for the punishment of the wicked and for their death, and the same [sword] is [now] ordained to be used by the worldly magistrates."[11] In this respect Romans 13 was used as the basis for all discussion about civil authority.

Consequently, the Anabaptists insisted that Christians owed an obedience to the civil authorities as long as this obedience did not stand in the way of their primary commitment to God. They paid their taxes and followed the general customs required by the magistracy. In the beginning of the movement, when the government began to suppress it, the Anabaptists begged the government not to do so, sought official permission to publish their writings, asked for public hearing, petitioned for safe-conduct papers, and generally attempted to be obedient to Christ in a way that would be acceptable to the civil authorities. However, as they continued to be suppressed, they gradually had to move into civil disobedience on certain levels in order to remain obedient to their higher calling. They continued to meet and to preach despite the regulations against them. They refused to divulge the names of their brethren. They hid in the forests and mountains in an attempt to escape their persecutors, and they sometimes refused to surrender themselves to the court.[12]

Within this context it is easy to see that the Anabaptists would not support involvement in the state on any level. The Schleitheim Confession addresses three points in particular:

First, "whether a Christian may or should employ the sword against the wicked for the defense and protection of the good." Second, "whether a Christian shall pass sentence in worldly disputes and strife such as unbelievers have with one another." And third, "Shall one be a magistrate if one should be chosen as such?" The argument in each case, against involvement in the state, is that "Christ did not . . . ; therefore we should do likewise." The government operates according to the flesh, but the Christian operates according to the Spirit. The Christian may be in this world, but his Christian citizenship is in heaven, and therefore Christian allegiance belongs to Christ alone.[13]

This radical doctrine that underlies the Anabaptists' view of the church and state also determines their view of life in the world.

The Anabaptist Lifestyle

In the first place, the Anabaptists had a strong sense of Christian discipleship. They insisted that there was a difference between reflection upon Christ and obedience to Christ. A major problem in the church, they thought, was that Christians spent too much time reflecting on Christ and not enough time imitating Christ. For them, the apostolic norm—to which all Christians were called—was an active, energetic attempt to be like Christ, to live as He did, to follow Him. The Sermon on the Mount was viewed as an expression of principles that were to be carried out in this world, in the here and now. It did not contain commands for a select few (monastics, for example), or teaching for a future age, or principles that were only for the inner man. As a consequence of this view, Anabaptists rejected the traditional concept of monasticism and emerged with the view that all Christians were called into a kind of monastic life. The radical claims of Christianity were no longer for the few but for all. Such a radical view of discipleship had the effect of changing social structures for the Anabaptist community and, if accepted by all, had the potential of totally revolutionizing the structures of human society.[14]

This radical view of Christian discipleship caused the Anabaptists to be active in social service; they believed they were forerunners of the time when God would establish His kingdom on earth. This eschatological element of their thinking was, therefore, a strong motivating factor in their witness to the world. They did not hope to save the present world so much as they lived in anticipation of the new order that God Himself would establish. Klassen, in his thorough treatment of this subject, writes:

> The practice of mutual aid was considered a necessary and natural concomitant of spiritual fellowship. At secret meetings in cellars, fields, gardens, or forests, the persecuted groups would gather money, food, and clothing for those in need. Members were encouraged to place their gifts in the boxes and sacks provided for that purpose. . . . If the destitute were ill and unable to attend the meetings, their unfortunate circumstances were not forgotten.[15]

Another aspect of the Anabaptist life in the world was their insistence on nonresistance. "The Brethren understood this to mean complete abandonment of all warfare, strife, and violence, and of the taking of human life," comments Harold Bender.[16] It should be remembered that this lifestyle was adopted at a time when the sword was being used in the name of religion. In this sense, the Anabaptists were forerunners of those who hold to the modern concept of pacifism.[17]

A natural outcome of the doctrine of nonresistance was the Anabaptists' insistence on religious liberty. This arose, says Bender, "not from any merely prudential, rationalistic, or ethical considerations, but from its central understanding of the nature of Christianity."[18] The Anabaptists believed that a person's conviction of the truth of Christianity came by the Holy Spirit and not by force. Therefore a person's conscience was not to be bound to the state but was to be free under God.

EVALUATION

This brief analysis leads us to the firm conclusion that the Anabaptists belong to the separatist model of Christians in culture. They believed Christians were to create a culture within the culture, called to witness and to suffer in this world. Anabaptists believed the kingdom of God had come and was taking shape in a hostile world. The Christian society was therefore to be built through the church, for this was where Christ reigned in the world. But how are we to view the Anabaptists of the sixteenth century in light of the powers of evil, their destruction by Christ, and the church's continued witness to them? A brief critical evaluation of their teaching, pointing to both strengths and weaknesses in their thought, is in order.

First, mention may be made of several strengths of Anabaptist teaching. Their sensitivity to evil agencies at work in the world should be considered from a New Testament perspective. Like Paul, the Anabaptists seem to be keenly aware of the presence and power of satanic forces. Menno Simons, the evangelical leader of the movement, described Satan as "a shrewd, cunning deceiver, shameless, scheming liar, and proud and haughty murderer, what a hateful envier of the honor and truth of God; a falsifier of his Holy Word, and a deadly enemy of pious souls." He further described the work of Satan as "seditious, factious, unruly, schismatic, envious, perverse, and devoid of love; one who can only bring forth hatred, slander, falsehood, deception, suspicion, impure hearts, shame and disgrace."[19] Further, Simons claims Satan has risen "to full dominion and has gained the mastery of the whole earth by his seductive doctrine, explanations, glosses, statutes, commandments, idolatry, tyranny, and violence."[20] While Simons does not deal explicitly with the idea of demonic powers that work through the structures of existence, he gives implicit support to this doctrine of Paul through his view of the state,[21] papal religion,[22] and the ban.[23] According to the Anabaptists, evil powers became present to the world through the state and the Roman church. That is why the Christian must separate from them. Further, the ban was a way of calling church members who have fallen into the snare of Satan back to the church and Christian fellowship. To be banned from the church was to be consigned to Satan.[24]

The Anabaptists also exhibit a profound sense of the church as a community of God's people in the world. Like the New Testament writers, they root the origin of the church in the Christ event, and look upon themselves as the people of that event. The church is not an institution or political power. Rather, it is dressed in the garb of simplicity, and functions under the exalted Christ by the power of the Spirit as a pilgrim community on earth. Heaven is its home; but here on earth the church suffers and endures till the end.

Hence, while the church is a society of people in this world, it tastes nothing of the dregs of the world nor of its allurement.[25]

In spite of these strengths, there is a fundamental weakness in the Anabaptists' doctrines of redemption, creation, ecclesiology, and eschatology. The root problem lies in the Anabaptist concept of redemption, which in turn affects the Anabaptist view of creation, ecclesiology, and eschatology.

For example, Menno Simons sets forth a stark contrast between the unbeliever and the believer which may be described as "radical regeneration." In his work *The New Birth* he describes the Christian as follows: "Once they were earthly minded, now heavenly; once they were carnal, now spiritual; once they were unrighteous, now righteous; once they were evil, now good, and they live no longer after the old corrupted nature of the first earthly Adam, but after the new upright nature of the new and heavenly Adam, Christ Jesus."[26] This statement, typical of the Anabaptists' central commitment to the antithesis of the Christian with the world, does not allow adequate room for the presence of the good among the unregenerate and the presence of evil among the regenerate.

Furthermore, this literalistic interpretation of the absolute antithesis between the regenerate and unregenerate lends itself to an inadequate view of the natural world (creation). While the world which the Anabaptist is against is the world of adverse power of evil, the world they appear to be against is the natural creation and the structures of existence. Creation appears to be intrinsically evil, and any vocation in the world as a joyful exercise of faith is negated.

This total rejection of the world leads to an ecclesiology of separationism that reflects the absolute antithesis. Since the Anabaptist church is the church of the regenerate, all other false and unregenerate churches can be easily and quickly identified. Consequently, Simons can write:

> Here is faith, there unbelief; here truth, there falsehood; here obedience, there disobedience; here believers' baptism according to God's Word, there infant baptism without scriptural warrant; here brotherly love, there hatred, envy, tyranny, cruelty, and plentiful bloodshed; here a delightful service of others, there a much wrangling, legal action, gossip, cheating, and in some cases,

also theft, robbery and murder. Here we see instruction, admonition, consolation, reproof in righteousness; there we hear only hurt, accusations of heresies, vituperation, and slander; here is blessing, praise, thanksgiving; there cursing and swearing by the passion and wounds of Christ, by the sacraments, flesh and blood, and judgment; here is patience, there anger; here humility, there haughtiness; here pity, there abuse; here true service of God, there idolatry; here spirit, there flesh; here spiritual wisdom, there folly. Here men pray in the spirit and in truth, there they mock in a flood of empty words; here men pray for God's truth, there they persecute God's righteousness; here is trust in Christ, there is idolatrous rites. In fine, here is Christ and God, and there is antichrist and the devil. Yes, dearly beloved brethren, the pure, chaste, and spotless bride of our Lord Jesus Christ (judge for yourselves) is quite different from this carnal, unclean, adulterous, and shameful affair.[27]

This view which locates the true church in the Anabaptist community contains eschatological implications that are not in keeping with the biblical and historical experience of the church. Traditionally, the church has not viewed itself as the realized eschatological community. Rather, it has seen its holiness as an eschatological goal. Consequently, the experience of the church has been one of eschatological tension; knowing that its call is to holiness, yet experiencing the presence of sin and imperfection in its own body, the church has been characterized by an eschatological longing for its fulfillment. However, among the sixteenth-century Anabaptists, the radical concept of regeneration suggests that the one holy, catholic, and apostolic church finds expression in the perfection attained through Anabaptist discipleship. This sense of a near perfection on the part of the church reduces the intensity of the eschatological. For why should one hope for what has been achieved?

Finally, the Anabaptists seem to have interpreted the New Testament's christological approach toward church and world primarily in terms of the ecclesiological community. But the incarnational presence of Christ within the church calls for servanthood in the world. Further, the lordship of Christ over the powers of evil are to be realized within the Christian community as well as within the world. But the Anabaptists' convictions would tend to lessen the impact which the church makes on the world, turning the church into a distinct society in which Christ's presence and lordship are experienced, while the rest of the world remains apart from Christ's presence and lordship, enslaved under the dominion of Satan.

A CONTEMPORARY INTERPRETATION

Anabaptist history and theology have been greatly neglected during the modern era of Christianity. The dominant Protestant viewpoints on church and world have been those of Calvin and Luther, while the Anabaptist view of the church and the world has been scorned as irrelevant and out of touch with modern thought. However, in the last three decades modern Anabaptists have reasserted themselves and gained a significant hearing. In part, the restoration of Anabaptist thought has been accelerated by the rise of a secularistic society, making the idea of antithesis to the world more reasonable. Further, a resurgence of interest in the Anabaptist vision of life by scholarly members of its own community has placed it in the mainstream of discussion once again. It is no longer an isolated viewpoint held by few, but an option that competes with the models set forth by Luther and Calvin. More importantly, significant alterations of the classical Anabaptist position have been made to fit the changing cultural situation in which the Anabaptist lives and works. Nevertheless, these changes stand in continuity with the original Anabaptist vision and do not represent a radical departure from the classical teaching on antithesis. The most articulate contemporary Anabaptist perspective is set forth by John Howard Yoder, a Mennonite and professor of Christian ethics at Notre Dame University.[28] A brief summary of his viewpoint will serve as an example of the contemporary Anabaptist church and world concern.

Yoder's writing on church and world is done within the context of the current discussion of the powers. He asserts that "Paul has made three fundamental declarations in the language of his time, concerning the structures of creaturely existence: (a) these structures were created by God . . . (b) these powers have rebelled and are fallen . . . (c) despite their fallen condition the powers cannot fully escape the providential sovereignty of God. He is still able to use them for good."[29] In these assertions Yoder makes a clearer affirmation of creation than his predecessors. Clearly, God is the Creator of all things, creation is good, and the structures of existence may function in ways that are beneficial for human kind. Furthermore, Yoder acknowledges that Christ has broken the sovereignty of the powers. "If then God is going to save man *in his humanity*," Yoder states, "the powers cannot simply be destroyed or set aside or ignored. Their sovereignty must be broken. This is what Jesus did concretely and historically."[30] Next Yoder recognizes that the church which is the unique response to the Christ event, the event through which the powers have been overcome, is called to witness in the world to the triumph of Christ over the powers. "It is," he writes, "a fundamental error to conceive of the position of the church in the New Testament in the face of social issues as a 'withdrawal.' . . . It consists in her being a herald of liberation."[31] At first, these words may appear to set the function of the church into an aggressive role more clearly associated with Calvinism. However, further reading contradicts this superficial conclusion. Yoder believes that the church fulfills its "herald" role *not through its action but through its existence*. "The very existence of the church is her primary task," he insists. "It is in itself a proclamation of the Lordship of Christ to the powers from whose dominion the church has begun to be liberated. The church does not attack the powers; this Christ has done. The church concentrates upon not being seduced by them. By her existence she demonstrates that their rebellion has been vanquished."[32] The question, then, of the relationship between the church and the world is not "What must the church do?" Rather, it is, "What must the church be?" This concern for the existence of the church lies in fundamental continuity with the Anabaptist vision of the sixteenth century. Consequently, an examination of the role Yoder assigns to the church in the modern world will provide us with an insight into a contemporary Anabaptist view of church and world. The role of the church in the world may be captured by three phrases: revolutionary subordination, the refusal to "manage history," and accepting power-lessness. Yoder develops these themes in his classic work, *The Politics of Jesus*.[33]

Yoder roots the concept of revolutionary subordination-ism in the life, teachings, and ministry of Jesus. Jesus subordinated Himself to the powers of evil that put Him to death, but by doing so He destroyed the power they had over him. This revolutionary action has practical implications for the role of the Christian and the church in the world. For example, in the primitive church the ethical instruction given to the Christians (Col. 3:18–4:1; Eph. 5:21–6:9; 1 Peter 2:13–3:7) calls upon the Christian to enter into a "willing subordination to one's fellow man."[34] When the woman is told to be subject to her husband, when the children are to obey their parents, when slaves are instructed to be obedient to their masters, they are called into subordination. According to Yoder, this "subordination means the acceptance of an *order*, as it exists, but with the new meaning given to it by the fact that one's acceptance of it is willing and meaningfully motivated."[35] But another revolutionary factor here must not be ignored. It is that the person in the dominant order is also to be in subordination; and in each of these cases, subordination is to the lesser status. Thus, "parents are asked not to irritate their children, husbands are called upon to love (*agapan*) their wives. Philemon is invited to receive Onesimus."[36] What is revolutionary about this is the reciprocal relationship of mutual submission. But the reason is not practical or prudent, but theological: They are both subordinate to a higher master. This is an ethic, claims Yoder, that "is derived in its shape and in its meaning, and even in its language, from the novelty of the teaching and the work and the triumph of Jesus."[37]

It is an ethic that will have a missionary impact on the world, for it is a new way of living. It shuns the quest for dominance and control. Like Jesus, it assumes the role of servanthood, and thus shows that the powers of this world are not normative, but the Christian is attached to a power of a higher order.[38]

Consequently, the Christian is unwilling to "manage history." The nonbeliever attempts to control and manage the destiny of history; but from the Christian point of view the management of history belongs to God. It is the "Lamb who was slain" that has the power to determine the course of human events, to manage nations, and people, and cultures—the Lamb who is "worthy to receive power," and is the one who was executed under the superscription, "King of the Jews."[39] He who became subordinate to the powers of death now rules the destiny of all. This is the meaning of the Christ hymn in Philippians 2:1–11. "His emptying of himself, his accepting the form of servanthood and obedience unto death is precisely this renunciation of lordship, his apparent abandonment of any obligation to be effective in making history move down the right track. But the judgment of God upon this renunciation and acceptance of defeat is the declaration that this is victory."[40] Consequently, the philosophy of history that is affirmed by the example of Jesus is one "in which renunciation and suffering are meaningful."[41] What Jesus renounced in His earthly ministry was the compulsive desire to rule others that would lead to the violation of the dignity of others. But by refusing this power through weakness, He actually attained it. For us "the point is . . . that our readiness to renounce our legitimate ends whenever they cannot be attained by legitimate means itself constituted our participation in the triumphant suffering of the Lamb."[42]

Since it is not for the Christian to manage society, the best stance toward the world—that which Jesus Himself took—is one of accepting powerlessness. Jesus was not willing to accept complicity with the powers of evil. Rather than play the power game and defeat them on their own terms, He chose to be powerless. He chose to overcome evil through the good, not through violence or power. For us, then, the call of discipleship is a simple obedience that reflects "the character of the love of God."[43] The greatest good can only come by accepting our own powerlessness; through that means, we participate in "the war of the Lamb" and the ultimate defeat of all evil.

Yoder, like the Anabaptists before him, points to the example of Christ as the crucial factor in church and world relations. Like his Anabaptist predecessors, he eschews a Christian political action that attempts to enthrone justice or righteousness directly. Christians are not called to political power, to political domination, or manipulation. They are called to an obedience to Jesus Christ which emulates His character and example. Even as Jesus sought no power in His world and allowed Himself to suffer at the hands of the power that ruled His world, so the church today and every day is called into the Cross, into the death and suffering of Christ, into His stance of subordination, into His refusal to manage society, and into His powerlessness. In and through the acceptance of the Cross, we are free to participate in the triumph of the Cross over all power of evil. For in our submission to the powers that rule our world (political, social, economic), we do not acknowledge them as lord, but acknowledge rather that they have been defeated by the Cross and that our allegiance and commitment are given to the one who has already defeated the powers.

Yoder, unlike his Anabaptist predecessors, is deeply concerned to apply a christological view of the church beyond the borders of the church to the world. Yoder advocates the role of the church as servant to the world. But this servanthood, which derives from the Incarnation, is related to the lordship of Christ as an expectation and not as an actualization that would attempt to Christianize the structures of existence. The actualization of the lordship of Christ occurs in the church, in the community of believers who now witness by their corporate lifestyle that the power of evil has been conquered in their midst. Thus the church is the sign of the future in the present world order.

8

CHURCH AND WORLD IN PARADOX

We have seen that the central reformational point about the Christian's life in the world is that one must live in relationship to two rules simultaneously. The problem for each person and for the church is finding out how to do this.

The separatist's answer is to live in one world and not the other; a sharp distinction is drawn between the two. Others however feel uncomfortable with this antithesis and seek to resolve the problem through *paradox*. The paradoxical approach sees both sides of an issue and resolves it by affirming that both sides are true. The Christian is to live both in the kingdom of Christ and in the world. Exactly how this is accomplished is not necessarily agreed upon by all those who believe that the Christian life in the world is a paradox. Since Martin Luther, the sixteenth-century reformer, succeeded in articulating the church and world in paradox, we will concentrate on his thought and that of contemporary Lutherans today. But first, a brief account of Scripture passages that illustrate the paradox of living in both worlds simultaneously is in order.

BIBLICAL BASIS

The Bible abounds in examples of believers who played a leading role in culture. For example, Joseph rose to the position of second in command to Pharaoh in Egypt. He was set "over all the land of Egypt" and was arrayed in garments of fine linen. A gold chain was put around his neck, and as he rode in the chariot people called out, "Bow the knee!" (Gen. 41:43 KJV). Likewise, Daniel was given a position of authority in Babylon. He was one of three presidents over the 120 satraps under whom the entire government was organized. Daniel became the most distinguished of these presidents, so that "the king planned to set him over the whole kingdom" (Dan. 6:3).

Jesus Himself was identified with the world: the Son of Man "came eating and drinking, and they say, 'Here is a glutton and a drunkard, a friend of tax collectors and 'sinners!' " (Matt. 11:19). Jesus also had friends in government, such as Nicodemus, and insisted that His followers "give to Caesar what is Caesar's" (Matt. 22:21).

Furthermore, the accounts of the early church in Acts indicate that Christians were drawn from all areas of life and that the gospel did not demand that they turn away from their occupations. This is true with the Ethiopian eunuch in Acts 8; Cornelius the centurion in Acts 10; Manaen, a member of the court of Herod the tetrarch, in Acts 13; and the Philippian jailer in Acts 16. The same kind of evidence is found in the Epistles. In Paul's letter to the Philippians, written from jail in Rome, he said, "All the saints send you greetings, especially those who belong to Caesar's household" (4:22).

Even more important is the direct teaching of the Epistles concerning the Christian's duty toward the government. Paul in Romans 13 clearly sets forth the rule of government as an arena in which God is at work. In admonishing Christians to be subject to the governing authorities, Paul insists that "there is no authority except that which God has established" (v. 1). He calls a ruler of the world "the servant of God" and insists that we are to treat him as such, thus suggesting that work in the government is a high and perhaps even a holy calling.

These biblical examples are further substantiated by the theological undergirding of the doctrines of creation, incarnation, and redemption and by the understanding that the Christian is *simul justus et peccator*, both just and a sinner at the same time. The doctrine of creation teaches that this is God's good world, that all of it belongs to Him. The doctrine of the Incarnation teaches that Christ assumed the created order and participated in it. The doctrine of redemption insists that because God is the Creator and because the Creator assumed the creation, the whole creation therefore, through the life and death of Jesus Christ, has been redeemed (potentially). The Christian is thus *simul justus et peccator*. Before God, the believer is saved; but in the world, the believer is still a sinner. This same paradoxical principle is true of creation. Because of Christ, the creation has been released from its bondage to decay. But it will still be under decay and in bondage until the Second Coming, when God's redemptive work will be consummated. Consequently, the justified sinner and the entire created order are caught in the tension between what is and what will be. In the context of this tension, "all things are lawful" (1 Cor. 6:12 KJV). The Christian is free to affirm all of creation, to enter all callings, and to work and live before God in every aspect of life.

LUTHER'S TEACHING

Luther's view of the Christian in culture is rooted in a basic dualism that he found at the very heart of the Christian understanding of life. Gerhard Ebeling observes:

> Luther's thought always contains an antithesis, tension between strongly opposed but related polarities: theology and philosophy, the letter and the spirit, the law and the gospel, the double use of the law, person and works, faith and love, the Kingdom of Christ and the Kingdom of the world, man as a Christian and man in the world, freedom and bondage, God hidden and God revealed.[1]

Luther's approach to the question of the Christian in culture builds on this dualism: There are two realms of existence, one for the non-Christian and the other for the Christian, although the Christian lives in both realms simultaneously.

According to Luther, the teaching that human existence is to be understood in two realms is rooted in Scripture. Certain passages dealing with the authority of the state (Rom. 13; 1 Peter 2:13–14; also note Old Testament statements such as Gen. 9:6 and Exod. 21:14, 22ff., which sanction the use of the sword) are binding upon everybody. All God's creatures are under the authority of the state and are to abide by the divine laws of creation. But other passages, such as the Sermon on the Mount and the apostle's statement about the "law of of the Spirit of life" (Rom. 8:2), refer only to Christians, who are to live by love and not by force.[2] These biblical references point to the two realms of human existence: the first, rooted in creation and the Fall, in which all people participate equally; the second, rooted in Jesus Christ and the church, in which only believers participate. This insistence that there is a Christian existence in Christ and a Christian existence in the world is the key to Luther's understanding of the relation between Christianity and culture.

While on the surface Luther's explanation of the two kingdoms appears complicated, it is basically simple. In sum, the kingdom of this world rightfully belongs to God by creation. All human beings live in this world. But the kingdom of Christ, which is made up of true believers only, is part of this world. Because Christians belong to this world and to Christ, they wholly belong to two worlds. Satan does not have a kingdom as such. He does not own creation; it is God's. Instead, Satan's influence extends throughout God's creation, beginning in the hearts of fallen men and extending through their exercise of authority over creation.

The Christian must therefore learn how to live life before God in two existences at once. The believer is a saint because of a heavenly standing, and is a sinner/saint because of an earthly existence. Exactly how the Christian is a citizen of two worlds simultaneously, and what this means to one's way of life on earth, is a problem Luther continued to wrestle with throughout his life.[3]

In order to understand Luther's position more thoroughly, let us look first at the nature of the two realms, then at the rule of God in these realms, and finally at the application of all this to the life of the Christian in the world.

The Two Realms of Human Existence Are the Two Kingdoms of This World.

In a treatise entitled "Temporal Authority," Luther speaks of the two realms of existence as two kingdoms[4]: "We must divide the children of Adam and all mankind in two classes, the first belonging to the Kingdom of God, the second to the Kingdom of the world. Those who belong to the Kingdom of God are all the true believers."[5]

The kingdom of this world originated in God's act of creation.[6] God not only brought the natural order into existence, but also established the institutions of the world such as marriage and the family, business, and secular government. Consequently, everything earthly, temporal, and physical belongs to God, not to the Devil, and is under his sovereign control. And so every human being, Christian or not, lives in this world under God. Human rule over the earth is under God for the purpose of preserving earthly life.

On the other hand, the origin of the kingdom of God is rooted in redemption. God established a heavenly people for Himself through His act of redemption in Jesus Christ. Redeemed people belong to a spiritual kingdom that is at once in heaven and on earth.

God is at work in both realms of existence. His goodness, love, and mercy are present through Jesus Christ, the Word, and the sacraments in the kingdom of God and through natural law, providence, and divine law in the kingdom of the world.

But there are differences between the two kingdoms and in the way God works in them. First, the kingdom of God outlasts the kingdom of the world. Secular government serves only the world, which passes away, but the spiritual government of God serves eternal life and God's ultimate purpose. Second, there is an equality in the kingdom of God that does not exist in the kingdom of the world. In the priesthood of believers, all Christians stand on an equal plane before God; but in the kingdom of this world there are differences between people in the variety of functions necessary to govern the world. Some have positions of authority and others of dependence. Third, God rules by love, justice, forgiveness, and the Holy Spirit in the kingdom of God, but by justice, retribution, punishment, and reason in the kingdom of the world.

Nevertheless, the two kingdoms are dependent on each other. The kingdom of this world should provide an atmosphere of peace in which the kingdom of Christ is able to carry out its function. The gospel could never provide this climate of peace because it cannot force disorderly people to change their ways. On the other hand, the preaching of the gospel results in good works, and this helps to stabilize society and reduce evil in the world.

In the kingdom of God the Christian is a saint, but in the

kingdom of the world a sinner/saint.[7] Herein lies a further
dualism that complicates our understanding of Luther. He
holds that in the world the believer is both sinner and saint
at the same time—not partially the one and partially the
other, but wholly both. That is, before God the Christian is a
saint, but in the world a sinner/saint, working out in time,
space, and history the reality of membership in the invisible
community of believers. This is Luther's doctrine of gradual
sanctification, a doctrine that accounts for the believer's lack
of perfection in the world.

This dualism that characterizes the believer's personal
life is also expressed on a more corporate level in his function
in church and society. In the church the believer functions
under the rule of Christ, both immediately, in personal
submission to Christ, and mediately, in submission to God's
appointed ministers of his Word. In society the believer
functions under the rule of God immediately, by obeying the
laws of creation, and mediately, by living in submission to
God's appointed rulers in the land. The unbeliever may also
function in the church without being a part of God's invisible
kingdom. The wheat and the tares grow together also in the
church, a fact that points once again to Luther's basic theme
of the dualism that permeates every aspect of human
existence.

Although There Are Two Kingdoms
In This World, God Rules in Each.

Implicit in Luther's presentation of the two kingdoms is
the notion that God's government over this world can be
understood only through a double expression. His rule is
one thing in the kingdom of the world and another in the
kingdom of God. Yet there are not two distinct rules, as
though the unbeliever were under one set of laws and the
believer another. Instead, both rules affect everyone in two
different areas of the same life.

This approach is consistent with the dualistic motif of
the rest of Luther's thought. But Luther would not want us
to divide life into two distinct parts, the secular and the
sacred. Instead, he is asking us to stand in God's place, as it
were, and see our world and ourselves as He sees it. God
sees His creation divided between the believer and the
unbeliever, the church and society. But He sees His rule in

the believer having an effect on the unbeliever, who cannot escape the presence of the kingdom of God in its earthly manifestation. And since God also rules in the kingdom of the world, His rule affects each person in both his earthly and spiritual existence. God rules over the whole person. These thoughts are most clearly presented in "Temporal Authority," where Luther wrote,

> God has ordained two governments: the spiritual, by which the Holy Spirit produces Christians and righteous people under Christ; and the temporal, which restrains the un-Christian and wicked so that—no thanks to them—they are obliged to keep still and to maintain an outward peace.[8]

A closer examination of God's rule in each of these two kingdoms will help to clarify this distinction. We will look first at the rule of God in the kingdom of the world.

Luther frequently refers to the two uses of the law, the spiritual and the civil.[9] The spiritual use of the law is to bring conviction of sin and drive a person to Christ. The civil use of the law is to function as a restraining and ordering influence in society.

Civil law, by which God governs the kingdom of the world, is, no less than spiritual law, in the world by "God's will and ordinance." It is divinely instituted and as old as creation itself. This rule, which Luther sometimes calls the "law of the temporal sword," is set forth in Romans 13 and 1 Peter 2:13–14. It also finds expression throughout the Old Testament, beginning with God's dealing with Cain. Luther believed it was confirmed after the Flood, again in the law of Moses, and finally in the teaching of Jesus (Matt. 26:52).

This rule of God in the temporal human affairs is always expressed through the secular government, whose God-given responsibility is to rule in society. Here Luther's view of sin comes into view. Because humans are "altogether sinful and wicked," God puts them under the law to restrain their wicked deeds. The law holds back the sinfulness of people. It keeps the world from destroying itself through its own wickedness.

The law has a positive use also: it promotes goodness. Through political authorities and the laws of the land, people are protected from evil men. For this reason, Luther can refer to the authorities as "saviors" and give them the same recognition attributed to fathers and mothers and doctors and lawyers whose help people cannot do without.

Justice, therefore, serves both a negative and a positive function: It punishes the wrongdoer and it encourages peace. For this reason, the government is to be obeyed and honored by all people.

The second area of the rule of God is in the kingdom of God. In the spiritual kingdom all true believers are under Christ, who is King in God's kingdom. Christ came into the world to establish God's kingdom in the world, a kingdom that is not "of the world." In this kingdom there is no need of the temporal law of the sword, for Christians are ruled by the Holy Spirit, who teaches them "to do injustice to no one, to love everyone, and to suffer injustice and even death willingly and cheerfully at the hands of anyone."[10]

How are these two rules of God related? Since temporal existence and spiritual existence are both under God, Luther argues that "neither one is sufficient in the world without the other." We must recognize the need for both, "the one to produce righteousness, the other to bring about external peace and prevent evil deeds."[11]

However, the one must not invade the territory of the other and presume to rule where it has no right. The temporal government, for example, has laws that extend no further than to matters of life and property and external affairs on earth, for God will not permit anyone but Himself to rule over the soul. For the state to attempt in any way to coerce people into belief would be a violation of its function, an invasion of a realm not under its jurisdiction. Only God Himself, through the Spirit, creates belief; the heart cannot be compelled against its will.

On the other hand, the rule and authority of the priests and bishops has—contrary to the example of the medieval period—nothing to do with man's temporal existence. Their government, Luther insists (on the basis of the priesthood of all believers), is "not a matter of authority or power, but a service." In their Christian existence believers are ruled only by God's Word, which instructs them in all matters pertaining to their spiritual existence.

The Christian lives under both rules. While Luther separates the two and speaks of human existence under God's secular authority and the Christian's existence under Christ or biblical authority, he does not mean to separate them as though the believer lived *only* under the authority of Christ, nor does he bring the two together in such a way to make the believer appear schizophrenic. He is viewing two aspects of the same existence.

Christian persons live under the Word of God in their spiritual existence and the secular authority in their temporal existence. They owe obedience to both under God. For this reason, says Luther, the Christian "submits most willingly to the rule of the sword, pays his taxes, honors those in authority, serves, helps, and does all he can to assist the governing authority, that it may continue to function and be held in honor and fear."[12]

Not only does the Christian submit to the law of the sword, but the believer is also encouraged by Luther to "serve and assist the sword" because it is "beneficial and essential for the whole world and for your neighbor." However, while Luther encourages the believer to participate in every aspect of society, he insists that the Christian should never use secular authority for self or personal reasons. Rather, Christians should "wield it [the sword] and invoke it to restrain wickedness and to defend godliness" on behalf of their neighbor. The Christian can serve in this area because it is a "divine service."

Here again we are confronted by the tension of living in two worlds. Christians are to serve the secular authority in temporal matters, living according to a law that appears contradictory to Christian persuasion. This is the problem of Christian existence in the world.

How Are Christians to Live In Two Worlds Simultaneously?

Luther's position on the Christian in the world cannot be understood apart from his interpretation of the Sermon on the Mount.[13] In interpreting the Sermon, Luther had to oppose the convictions, held by two different groups of Christians, that Jesus' teachings in this passage could be practiced only by those who completely withdrew from the world. One group, the Roman Catholics, held that the ethical teachings contained in the Sermon were intended not as unconditional *commandments* for everyone but only as *counsels* for those who wished to achieve perfection. This position fit the Roman Catholic view that there are two stages of discipleship for Christians. In the second stage, the ascetic ideal, one attempts to fulfill the requirements of Jesus in the strictest sense by withdrawing from the world into a monastic community.

On the other hand, Luther had to defend himself over against the Anabaptists, who also insisted that radical obedience could be achieved only through a complete forsaking of the world and its ways. They believed that discipleship meant refusing to participate in the institutions of the world, in its occupations, and in its power. True discipleship could be expressed only in Christian communities cut off from the outside world, where Christians were free to create a whole new way of life, a culture in conformity with the teachings of Christ. While the majority of Anabaptists withdrew to form their own culture, a small minority of Anabaptist millennarians were convinced that it was their responsibility to revolutionize the world, reshaping it to live by the standards of the kingdom, and thus bringing about the kingdom of God on earth. These active enthusiasts were the ones Luther confronted in the Peasant's War.

Luther's interpretation of the Sermon on the Mount is consistent with the dualism that runs through his entire approach to the Christian faith. His perception is rooted in his view of freedom and love. The freedom to which Christ calls us must govern our attitude toward the material good of the world; Luther warns us against raising material goods to the status of idols in our lives. He believes that freedom is an inner quality, an attitude of the heart toward possession. Owning property and enjoying this earth's goods are not inherently wrong, since this is God's world and His ownership extends over all things. But we are to be free from the service of this world's goods. We are not to set "our confidence, comfort, and trust on temporal good." Poverty is also an inner thing, a matter of the heart. We are not to be attached to earthly goods in any way. This is the inner freedom that Paul describes in 2 Corinthians 6:10 as "having nothing, and yet possessing everything." Sometimes God may call a person to abandon earthly possessions, literally, but this would be the exception. Nevertheless, the believer must be ready at all times to drop everything if God should so demand. For Luther, this position is never an excuse to accumulate riches. He himself lived a frugal life. He insisted that the believer should not own more than he really needed, giving the rest to his neighbors and to the poor.

Although Christians live by freedom in the realm of material goods, they live by love in human relationships. For Luther, the standard of love extends not only toward other believers in the kingdom of God, but also toward the unbelievers in the kingdom of this world. Although man is free economically, to own property and to trade, and free politically, to support the state or serve as a judge or statesman or soldier, he must always do so by the ethic of love. Love forgives, suffers injustice without demand for retribution, and places the interest of others above its own. Love creates a style of life in utter antithesis to the selfishness and greed of the normal sinful approach to life.

Through freedom and love, Luther believed, the Christian is able to live in the would in a manner consistent with the teaching of Jesus in the Sermon on the Mount. From this arose Luther's view of Christian calling.

Like everything else, Luther's view of calling is rooted in the dualistic understanding of Christian existence in two realms[14]: There is the invisible and spiritual calling, by virtue of the believer's being totally just in Christ; and there is a calling in daily life, in which the believer actively lives out his sanctification.

Luther's view of the sacredness of all callings in life was forged against the common notion that certain aspects of life were spiritual and others secular. Unlike Roman Catholics—who confined spiritual callings to the priesthood, monastic life, or other service within the church—Luther insisted that all believers are equally justified before God and therefore they are called to live as believers, demonstrating their justification and working out their sanctification in every function of life. The believer's life in this world is where he is called to live out, in freedom and love, a heavenly or spiritual standing. Consequently, Luther can refer to every "estate" (a word he used to mean a person's specific function) as a calling in life that is ultimately spiritual in nature. A priestly estate is no more sacred than that of a teacher, carpenter, or prince.

However, this view of the equality of all callings did not keep Luther from making distinctions among the estates. This is clearly seen in his so-called three hierarchies: the priestly office, the married estate, and the world magistracy. These are special callings in which persons are more able to fight the Devil. But they are no more spiritual than any other calling, and they are not means by which one is able to do good to obtain salvation.

For Luther, marriage belongs in the kingdom of this world.[15] Love, marriage, sexual desire, and parenthood are parts of God's natural order, ordained in the creative act of God. God told Adam to "be fruitful and multiply," and he sanctified marriage and sexual love, not only for procreation, but also for enjoyment and pleasure.

But because of sin, love is no longer pure. Persons seek to satisfy themselves rather than their partners. Consequently, the physical joy of marriage has become lustful; conception has lost its purity, as the psalmist indicated: "Surely I was sinful at birth, sinful from the time my mother conceived me" (Ps. 51:5). Because of sin, marriage has an added dimension: It restrains and controls sexuality which, because it has been distorted by sin, now needs limits. Even in marriage the impurity of lustful desires cannot be avoided, so people in this order of creation, as in others, are not able to escape sinning. But Luther says that God forgives married people of this sin because marriage is his work; he instituted it and continues to will it.

Because marriage is for everyone and belongs to the order of creation rather than the order of redemption, Luther does not view marriage as a sacrament, and speaks of it as a secular affair. It is under the jurisdiction of the state, not the church; subject to civil law, not ecclesiastical law.[16] This does not mean, though, that there is no difference between a Christian and a non-Christian marriage. Christians have the power of the Holy Spirit and the love of Christ (depicted as a marriage relationship between Him and the church) to enable them to fulfill the ideal of marriage better than non-Christians do.

Work is also related to God's natural law and belongs to the kingdom of this world.[17] God ordained work before the Fall; Adam was given responsibility to till and to keep the Garden of Eden. Therefore, work is an honorable thing and a sphere in which we can expect to find God's blessing.

Because of sin, work is also a tiresome and burdensome responsibility. It involves toil, discouragement, and difficulty. Humans must often fight against the elements to make their living by the "sweat of their brow." And people who see things through the eyes of the flesh see work mainly in this way. But for the Christian there is a difference, because believers see work through the eyes of the Holy Spirit. The believer knows that work is a form of obedience to God and is therefore approved by Him. So although human labors are under a curse, they are also under a blessing; work is meaningful and ultimately of great personal value.

The ownership of property also belongs to the kingdom of this world.[18] Luther could not find any specific statements in the Bible affirming the right of private ownership. Therefore he comes at the question in a rather roundabout way. He argues for example that Jesus' statement, "see what you have," presupposes private property, as does the biblical injunction to give to one's neighbor. If we do not have anything, we are not able to give; therefore, private ownership must be ordained of God.

Although Luther rejects the communism of radical Anabaptists, he does insist that the Christian is called upon to make his property available to those who are in need. Of course, he is to meet the needs of his own family first. But what is left over belongs to his neighbor. For the most part, Luther viewed business and the money economy of his time as corrupt; he believed that business is motivated mostly by the selfish desire for profit. Consequently, he argued against usury and insisted that people look for a reasonable way to arrive at prices through an analysis of cost.

Luther felt that the state is also a part of the kingdom of this world.[19] The state is an order created by God, and like everything else He has created, it is good.

But the *function* of government in the work is shaped by the Fall. Because of sin, human beings have become wicked and perverse in their ways and need control lest they destroy themselves. The purpose of government in this fallen world, then, is to protect the people under its care against the cruelty and exploitation of their fellow-men. It preserves peace and order. But it performs its duty as a parent, as one who cares for those whom it controls. In this sense, the government stands before the people as God. It rewards the good and punishes the evil so that God's goodness and His wrath are known through the administration of government. Therefore, the government has power over life and death, the power to impose the death penalty or to wage war.

Now the Christian, who lives both in the kingdom of God and in the kingdom of the world, is to act responsibly toward God in both realms. Because the state is God's work and because God rules through the state, the Christian's existence in the world is under God through the state. He is to be obedient to the state and to serve and assist the state. Even if the state acts unjustly, he is still to obey its dictates. Only if the state forces the Christian to act contrary to God's Word does its authority over the Christian end.[20]

Luther's view of the church in the world follows the same pattern as his view of the Christian in the world. The church is to be found in two realms of existence. In the heavenly realm it is totally just before God; but in its earthly and visible manifestation it expresses itself simultaneously in the kingdom of God and the kingdom of the world. Consequently, its existence in Christ is a spiritual and internal communion while its existence in the world is an external communion.[21]

The problem here is to understand the relation of the outward, visible communion to both the kingdom of God and the kingdom of the world. Luther rejects outright the notion of a pure church without sin. For one thing, he recognizes that the church is "mixed," containing sinners who are not part of the internal communion. Furthermore, even the Christians in the church are sinners. So the church, at its best, is both just and sinful.

Luther regarded the church, in its outward form, as a kind of mask. The mask is its costume or shell in which it is heard, seen, and grasped. A mask may be the kind of building used, the time of service, the organization of the church, and even the authority of any person in the organization such as a pastor or a bishop. In these *masks*, God is hidden. But there are also *signs* through which God reveals Himself, and these are the preaching of the Word and the sacraments. Masks belong to the kingdom of this world and signs to the kingdom of God. So the Christian in the church, as in other aspects of society, finds himself wholly in both realms of existence.

As we have seen, Luther's primary point of emphasis is the dualism between the two realms of human existence for the Christian. This concept of dualism is rooted in the beliefs that creation is good, that the Fall introduced an element of disorder into God's good order, and that redemption in Christ is the only means for human reconciliation. Luther's dualism makes a very positive contribution to a realistic assessment of the believer's role in society. The believer is involved in the sins of the world. One cannot escape participation in the rebellion against God from which one has been redeemed. As Paul described it in Romans 7, the believer is tossed between what is and what ought to be. One can never fulfill one's heavenly existence on earth, simply because one is in an earthly existence. One is still a creature of the world, a prisoner of the sinful nature.

But the believer is not thereby free to do whatever is desired, to be licentious or reckless. As we have seen, Luther stresses the need to be a responsible Christian, living in the world according to the transcendent principles of the Sermon on the Mount, which can indeed be lived out in the world and need not be relegated to some ascetic or other separate existence. In this way the Christian will function as a creative and dynamic force within society, bringing the gospel of the kingdom of God to bear on the structures of the kingdom of this world.

How are we to view Luther and his perspective in light of the powers of evil, their destruction by Christ, and the church's continued witness to them? A brief critical evaluation of the teaching of Luther, pointing to both strengths and weaknesses in his thought, are in order.

EVALUATION

Within Luther's writings there seems to be a vivid sense of the extensive power of evil. Readers of Luther are well acquainted with his frequent references to the Devil. The Devil, he claims, may have power over our personal lives. For example, in the *Bondage of the Will* he refers to the human will as a beast between the two worlds: "If God sits thereon, it wills and goes where God will . . . If Satan sits thereon, it wills and goes as Satan will. Nor is it in the power of its own will to choose, to which rider it will run, nor which it will seek, but the riders themselves contend which shall have hold of it."[22] The power of the rider implied in this quote appears to extend beyond the personal. For example, Luther often refers to the Devil's power in biblical language such as "the God of this world."[23] Sometimes he refers to the Devil and his work in the world in such a way that the structures of existence may be in mind. Thus, he speaks of the Turk as "the servant of the raging devil."[24]

Central to Luther's view of church and world is the

destruction of evil powers by the work of Christ. Christ has come to "deliver us from the devil's power and to bring us to Himself and reign over us a king of righteousness, of life and salvation, defending us from sin, death and an evil conscience."[25] Consequently, the church is now called to fight the Devil and the powers of evil. "For the church ought not strive or fight with the sword; it has other enemies than flesh and blood; their name is the wicked devils in the air; therefore it has weapons and swords and other wars, so that it has enough to do, and cannot mix in the wars of the emperor."[26]

Gustaf Aulen has shown in his work, *Christus Victor*, that Luther's view of the atonement stands in continuity with that of the early Fathers.[27] Since the victory of Christ over the powers of evil may be understood in the broader sense of victory over those powers that work through the structures of existence, it is a temptation to argue that Luther's references to evil may be read as adverse spiritual powers working through the structures of existence. However, further work in Luther would have to be done to argue the case more effectively. Nevertheless, the outline of the more modern understanding of the powers is in Luther, however faint.

Second, Luther's view of the two realms of human existence in the world resulted in several positive insights. For one, it managed to break through the theocratic ideal of the medieval period in which the church ruled over temporal authority. By establishing the concept of two distinct kingdoms or governments in this world (church and state), and by affirming that God rules in each simultaneously, Luther managed to provide a base for asserting the authority of the government which was free of interference by the church. The prince is to rule, not by the gospel, but by reason and common sense. And the preacher is not to tell the prince how to rule, although he may instruct the prince in the Christian faith and values, and through that means influence secular decision making.

By affirming that the secular order is under God, Luther escaped the Anabaptist problem of dividing the two realms—putting one under God and another under Satan. Further, Luther's recognition that God is Lord over the entire creation paved the way for Christians to function in the secular order. Since he could affirm that God is present to

His world through creation, and that God's rule over the world is exercised through the government, Luther established a view of vocation which affirmed that all legitimate vocations in the world are under God and therefore works of religious service. It was no longer necessary to become a monk or priest to do God's work. According to Luther's viewpoint, one could work for God in all spheres including the political and economic.

A third strength of Luther is that he managed to break through the institutionalization of the church. This motif of the church is best expressed in Luther's image of "the hidden church." By this term he did not suggest the usual contrast between *visible* and *invisible*; rather, he meant that the church as the true body of Christ is only visible to the eye of the faith. The church, he said, "is a high, deep, hidden thing which nobody can perceive or see, but only grasp and believe in baptism, sacrament and word."[28] The institutional church in its visible setting, as a power in the world, was replaced in Luther's thinking by the hidden church of faith which cannot be seen by the world. The shift epitomizes Luther's understanding of the church in the world. Whereas for the medievalists it was a church over the world, now for Luther it is the church within the world. The role of the church in the world had shifted in Lutheran thinking from an institutional power to a redemptive presence.

Finally, Luther is characterized by a strong eschatological sense of history. It is well known that Luther interpreted the events of his day as signs of the imminent return of Christ. He believed the judgment would come suddenly and soon. Preparations were being made for the final battle which could take place at any moment. Consequently, Luther had no hope for a changed and transformed world. The work of the church was to witness to the end when Christ would establish the new heavens and the new earth.

It is not uncommon to find the weaknesses of a position in the center of its strengths. This is the case with Luther's concept of the two realms; several weaknesses are found. Most obvious, and the one most frequently cited, is that Luther seems to put the Christian in the position of living by two ethics, one for the church and another for the state. The church is ruled by the Spirit, whereas the state is ruled by the sword. Living in both worlds, the Christian must frequently shift his allegiance from one authority to the other. The

Christian must at times compromise his Christian ethics to function in the secular order on its terms. But Luther wants to avoid the dilemma of separationism, on the one hand, and a church-controlled society on the other hand. So he encourages Christians to "mingle with other mortals, eat and drink, make homes, till the soil, fill civil offices, and show good will."[29]

This strong emphasis on the Christian's obedience to the state may lead to the toleration of practices that are evil. The most dramatic example of this is the failure on the part of the Lutheran church to take a stand against Hitler and the extermination of the Jews in this century. Luther wrote, "For even if the government does injustice, as the King of Babylon did to the people of Israel, yet God would have it obeyed, without treachery and deception."[30] He also warned against insurrection, arguing that "insurrection is an unprofitable method of procedure, and never results in the desired reformation."[31] But Luther also claimed that Christian people were not bound to follow their prince in doing wrong, for he wrote, "We ought to obey God who desirest the right, rather than men."[32] In spite of Luther's advice not to follow the prince into evil, Lutherans have been characterized by what Richard Neibuhr calls "cultural conservatism."[33]

In sum, it may be argued that Luther's view of the church in the world is incarnational. In and through the church, Christ is present to the world. However, the lordship of Christ over the world—over the evil powers that work through the structures of existence—is exercised not through the church, but through God's governance through the law and through the princes and rulers who are called to submit to God's law in the various spheres of human existence.

The tendency toward cultural conservatism may be related to Luther's eschatology. Since Luther expected the return of Christ in his own time, he did not sense an urgency to change the world, to alter its oppressive political and economic forces. Why should one change what God will change in the consummation, which is about to take place?

A CONTEMPORARY INTERPRETATION

One of the most significant spokespersons for a contemporary understanding and application of Luther's thought today is Ulrich Duchrow.[34] It is Duchrow's contention that Luther never really formulated the two kingdom theory of church and state in any systematic fashion. Rather, Luther's writings that reflect God's twofold governance in this world arise out of situations where Luther speaks against false constructs of church and world. Duchrow believes that Luther's comments on church and world occur in reaction to four groups of people in particular: church clericalism, totalitarianism, monasticism, and the enthusiasts.[35] In each of these cases, Luther argues for the rule of God in both church and world. History, Luther believes, is "the great struggle of God against the evil of sin and destruction." The main goal of this process is the establishment of the kingdom of God in its fullness, starting already among Christian people as the Holy Spirit shapes their personal lives and ecclesiastical communities according to the mold of the Sermon on the Mount. On the other hand, insofar as the Devil is still at work, the weak must be protected through public order (Rom. 13:1–7),[36] for which God graciously provides through His "worldly governance."

A second contention of Duchrow is that Luther's original vision of God's twofold governance was corrupted by the followers of Luther (neo-Lutherans). Through the process of secularization, Luther's followers divorced God's rule from the kingdom of the world, allowing the structures of existence to become autonomous. They supported the dichotomy between private life and public life. They came to view Christ as the Savior of souls, with no authority in the "worldly realm." They "split worldly affairs from God's just and saving will for all human beings."[37] Consequently, Luther's original criteria of love and justice in the economic, cultural, political, and scientific realms of life were lost.[38]

According to Duchrow, contemporary Lutheran thought is now challenging the neo-Lutherans' corruption of Luther's two-kingdom theory and calling for a return to Luther's insistence that God rules not only in the church but also in the world. The most significant contemporary event that has led to the rediscovery of God's rule in the spheres of life is the reaction of the confessing church to the Third Reich, as stated in the historic "Barmen Theological Declaration,"[39] inspired by the leadership of Karl Barth. Since then the cutting edge of Lutheran thought has been seeking to fulfill three concerns: first, to recognize structural evil; second, to rediscover the neglected elements of Luther's teaching on the two kingdoms; and third, to ask, How do we get from the "universally dominant operator" approach to the "co-operator" approach? A comment on each of these issues is in order.

First, contemporary Lutheran thinkers recognize the reality of structural evil. Duchrow acknowledges that evil is something more than bad deeds; it is a power that permeates all the institutions of society, a power that is exercised through the spheres of life to destroy God's good creation and humankind. He speaks of the "modern potentialities of power," such as the "methodical disregard for the common good . . . the growth of the means for exercising bureaucratic and military power, the exploitation of nature, the widening gap between the centers of power and the periphery (due to the division of labor), the tightly closed circle of production and consumption as a means of manipulating people's entire lives, the mass medical industry which is programmed to intrude into the remotest sanctuary of the human mind to exercise control over it."[40]

But Duchrow does not set the church in antithesis to these powers of evil, as though there is a pure church immune to evil on the one hand and an evil world immune to good on the other hand. Instead he recognizes the power of evil within the structure of the church itself. He asks, "How can the church participate in God's multifaceted struggle against the powers of evil and their impact on the world unless it realizes, first of all, how much it is itself subject to the powers of evil in a distinctive situation?"[41] Now the question is, Does Luther offer a way to deal with these structures of evil? Duchrow's answer—which is yes—brings us to the second concern, namely to rediscover the neglected elements of Luther's teaching on the two kingdoms.

Luther, Duchrow claims, "did not urge Christians to obey blindly the powers that be; rather, he inquired into the criteria and the limitations of public institutions, as in his writing, 'Temporal Authority: To What Extent It Should Be Obeyed.'[42] Luther's analysis was based on a long-standing search on the part of the church to understand the elements which are connected essentially with the eschatological struggle of God's power against the forces of evil (i.e., the Devil), which seek to destroy His creation."[43] The biblical and historical sources for the church's evolving con- sciousness include Jewish apocalypticism,. the teachings of Jesus and Paul, and the struggle of Augustine, to name a few.[44]

Throughout history, the church has alternated between three stances toward the world:

(1) "An undifferentiated adaptation to existing power structures, without any critical examination of them." This type is expressed in the Caesaro-papism of the Eastern church or in the theocracy of Western Catholi- cism. In modern times it existed in the national church of the German Reich;

(2) "A dualistic differentiated adaptation to existing power structures without any evaluation of them." This type accepts the autonomy of the spheres of life from God's rule and seeks little or no influence in the world. It is characteristic of certain types of mystical monasticism, the Anabaptists, and the early fundamentalism of this century;

(3) "A differentiated but integrated participation in God's struggle to adapt the powers to universally applicable (language) interests of human beings in all relationships affecting their life and freedom."[45] This type of church accepts the paradox that God rules both in the church and in the world. This was also Luther's perspective.

Luther recognized the "eschatological struggle between the power of God and the powers of evil."[46] Therefore, in the comparison Luther draws between God's spiritual and temporal rule, he acknowledges a distinction between "two different forms of action on God's part."[47] In addition, those who believe in Christ and in His power over evil are liberated from "false allegiances and totalitarian tendencies." Conse- quently, they can play "a constructive role in their relation- ship with the world." In this dialectic, Christians experience both a differentiation from the powers of evil and an integration with the world for its common good. This is precisely what Luther espoused when he affirmed both "the freedom of a Christian" and "the bondage of the will." The

Christian is free from the power of evil, yet bound in conscience to serve neighbor and the world through justice and love.[48]

Third, Duchrow asks, "How do we get from the universally dominant operator approach to the co-operator approach?" Some definitions are in order. The "dominant operator" approach to the world assumes that certain powers must dominate the world with absoluteness. The co-operator approach suggests cooperation and integration of the authorities that rule life. For example, multinational corporations may be seen as "dominant operator" institutions. "They control all resources and commodities, and they handle them as they want."[49] According to Duchrow, a modern translation of Luther's treatise *On Usury* would read as follows: "Nobody may even ask the question of how to participate in the business of the corporation with good conscience. There is no other advice than to boycott them. They will not change. If the corporations remain, justice and righteousness will be destroyed." In response to this situation, Duchrow says: "I suggest we selectively try out 'economic disobedience.' This might take different forms as e.g., boycotts, public exposure of economic injustices, experiments in non-consumerists' lifestyle, etc."[50]

A second example of the dominant operator may be drawn from the current situation of apartheid in South Africa. With regard to apartheid, Duchrow insists "You only can say 'no,' and act accordingly."[51] He further acknowledges that in this situation the church is taking a "Christ against culture" model because its stance is not one of support, nor of indifference, but of resistance. Luther himself, he reminds us, "practiced critical and constructive and sometimes resisting involvement of Christians and the church in public and economic affairs."[52]

Therefore, hope for the future does not lie in perpetuating the neo-Lutheran misunderstanding of Luther's two governances. Rather, there is a need to "rediscover the doctrine of creation and relate it to our belief in Christ the redeemer . . . [and] . . . to rediscover the doctrine of the Spirit interrelating cosmology and ecclesiology."[53] Consequently, the most "visible signs of hope" are the ecumenical communities rising up around the world today. They express both a differentiation from the powers of evil and an integration with the spheres of life in an effort to bring about constructive change. They provide us with the best example of the future relationship between church and world because they seek "to live an alternative life through a communal economic and financial behavior, a simple style, a spirit of joy, hope and mutual care while at the same time getting involved in national and international struggles together with the poor and the oppressed for a relative betterment of political and economic structures."[54]

Duchrow, like Luther, urges us to recognize the incarnational presence of Christ in the world through the church. The lordship of Christ, which the church knows by faith, is exercised in the world by Christians who seek to bring the structures of existence under justice and love. But neither Luther nor Duchrow see a time prior to the final consummation when the forces of evil will be sufficiently tamed or concerted so that the ideal society known as Christendom may be accomplished. The conversion of the structures of existence remains an eschatological hope.

9

CHURCH TRANSFORMS WORLD

We come now to the third Reformation model of the church, the transformational model. It presents a view of how to live under the two rules simultaneously in a way that differs significantly from both the church in antithesis to the world and the church in paradox to the world.

The major difference is this model's assumption that the structures of life can be converted and changed. The transformationalist's view is not that of withdrawal, as emphasized by the separatist; nor is it that of accommodation, into which those who emphasize paradox may slip. Instead, the transformationalist advocates an optimistic position toward the world as central to the Christian conviction about history and life.

This does not mean that all who believe in this model agree about how and when the church will change the world. There are decided differences of opinion about this. But the hope for a transformed society remains the same.

BIBLICAL BASIS

The biblical teaching on transformation is found not in examples as such but rather in the theological consciousness of the biblical writers themselves. Specifically this viewpoint is expressed in the theological teaching about creation, redemption, and eschatology. It is integral to the biblical theology of salvation that (1) the world, though created good, has fallen; (2) the fallen, human nature is expressed in cultural formation; (3) Jesus' death and resurrection reverse the fallen human condition; and (4) the Christian hope is for the ultimate release of humanity and the creation from the bondage of sin into a new and perfect creation. These teachings, which are central to all of biblical theology, were especially stressed in the eschatological hope of Israel, the redemptive work of Christ, and the eschatology of the New Testament.

The eschatological hope of Israel is particularly apparent in the prophetic literature. The prophets look for a time when the earth will be transformed. In that day the Lord will "create new heavens and a new earth" (Isa. 65:17) and "the wolf and the lamb will feed together, the lion will eat straw like the ox; but dust will be the serpent's food" (v. 25). And in that day "the mountains will drip new wine, and the hills will flow with milk; and all the ravines of Judah will run with water. A fountain will flow out of the LORD's house and will water the valley of acacias" (Joel 3:18). Passages like this, which can be multiplied from the writings of the prophets, continually bring together creation and salvation. That is, the future salvation of Israel is not merely spiritual but earthly. The whole creation will be changed. Culture will someday be what it could have been before the Fall.[1]

The redemptive work of Christ is central to this restoration of creation. Paul sets forth this theme in his epistles. In Romans 5:12–21 he compares the first Adam with the second, Jesus Christ. The first Adam did something *to* the human race: he brought sin, death, and condemnation. The results of his action are seen within the created order, which is marked through and through with signs of death. Thus culture is under the judgment of God (Rom. 1:18–32). But the second Adam reversed the human situation. He did something *for* humanity. He brought righteousness, life, and justification. The point is that what Christ did, He did in a cosmic sense. He called into being a "new creation" (2 Cor. 5:17). Consequently, the whole created order now anticipates its ultimate release and renewal. As Paul states, "The creation waits in eager expectation for the sons of God to be revealed. For the creation was subjected to frustration, . . .

the creation itself will be liberated from its bondage to decay
. . . the whole creation has been groaning as in the pains of
childbirth right up to the present time" (Rom. 8:19–22). This
future hope of creation is rooted in the redemption of Christ,
even as creation and redemption were connected in the Old
Testament prophetic consciousness.

But creation and redemption are not complete without
eschatology. The redemption of the creation in the ultimate
and complete sense is in the future. The church *now*
participates in the redemptive process toward the future. But
the complete redemption of the creation has not yet been
finalized. The eschatology of the New Testament recognizes
this and looks beyond the present order to the completion of
Christ's redemptive work. Peter speaks of such a day, "the
day of God, because of which the heavens will be kindled
and dissolved, and the elements will melt with fire! But
according to his promise we wait for new heavens and a new
earth in which righteousness dwells" (2 Peter 3:12–13 RSV).
This passage points to a cultural change, a passing away of
evil and the release of the created order from its bondage to
decay. And like the apostle John, it looks for a "new heaven
and a new earth" (Rev. 21 and 22), an expression which may
represent what this earth will look like after God's salvation
has been accomplished within it.

Having surveyed the general biblical basis from which
the transformationalist works, we turn now to the classic
example of the transformational position in the sixteenth-
century reformer John Calvin.

JOHN CALVIN

One of the major changes that occurred during the social
and political upheaval of the sixteenth century was the final
breakdown of the medieval church-state synthesis. By the
sixteenth century (and especially after the Reformation
movements were solidly underway), it was obvious that a
unified world society under church and state was no longer a
possibility. Nevertheless, the idea persisted that church and
state could act in partnership in small units such as a nation,
a territory, or even a city. Among the Reformers, only the
Anabaptists abandoned this concept entirely, advocating
complete separation between church and state. In order to
understand Calvin's view of the Christian in the world, we

must remember that he came out of this church-state milieu and thus presupposed a kind of unity between church and state. Calvin believed that both those who govern in the church and those who govern in the state are called to function *under* the Word of God. With this thought in mind, we begin our study of Calvin by examining the principles that are basic to his understanding of the Christian in the world.

The Sovereignty of God

In the first place, Calvin insists on the absolute sovereignty of God. In short, this means that God superintends the entirety of the world He has created. Calvin insists that God is not only Creator but also "a Governor and Preserver, and that not by producing a kind of general motion in the machine of the globe as well as in each of its parts, but by a special providence sustaining, cherishing, superintending, all the things which He has made, to the very minutest, even to a sparrow."[2] God's sovereignty extends to every phase of human life, not just a person's private and devotional life.

One immediate application of this view of sovereignty may be seen in Calvin's insistence that religion and daily life are unified. If God is sovereign over His entire creation, then there can be no separation of religion from our daily affairs. Religion is not something that runs alongside the rest of life. All of life and all human actions bear a religious character, because God is sovereign in every aspect of life. As Henry Van Til expresses it, "God's sovereignty is the atmosphere in which the Calvinist lives, the milieu in which he acts as a cultural being. It means that religion is not of life a thing apart, but the end-all of man's life under the sun."[3]

The sovereignty of God which extends over all things may be especially articulated in the threefold schema of creation, fall, and redemption. In regard to creation, Calvin affirms that all of life is under God and the lordship of Jesus Christ. All institutions—such as government, economics, family, education, work, and so on—are a result of His creative act. Consequently, Calvin can refer to the world as the "theatre of his glory,"[4] and admonish his readers that "wherever we cast our eyes, all things they meet are works of God."[5] Essential to Calvin's theology is the conviction that these works of God which find expression within creation are not chaotic but ordered. "Nature," he says, "is the order prescribed by God."[6] Consequently, "we ought in the very order of things to contemplate diligently God's fatherly love toward mankind."[7] Here Calvin gives us insight into his commitment to the orders of creation (what we have called *structures of existence*). They have been created by God to serve His purposes for humankind. They express His sovereign benevolence and they have been given to us for the rightful ordering of our lives.

Calvin's view of history is deeply rooted in his conviction that God is Lord of the entire creation. History is the dynamic but ordered context in which God's will is being worked out. God is moving within history through a series of meaningful events toward the eschaton. Calvin's emphasis on the covenants are to be seen in this light; the content of each historical covenant is Jesus Christ, who has been progressively made known and who is yet to be known finally in the end of history. Consequently, history is involved in the redemptive process. One who sees creation and history in this way, from the vantage point of God and His purposes, will not deny the role of the human element in the unfolding process of history. History is not the Devil's terrain, but God's. Thus to participate in history, to move it in the direction of its eschaton, is to be able to do the work of God.

Second, Calvin has a sensitivity to the powerful impact of the Fall in the created order. He believes the Devil to be the leader of an "empire of wickedness," set up in opposition to God and His kingdom of righteousness. Although the Devil is under God and may only do what God permits, the Devil and his emissaries are "instruments for the ruin of others,"[8] because "he seduces man from the obedience owed to God."[9] Thus, the Fall represents the introduction of disorder into the creation. Commenting on Satan's work, Calvin says, "he attempted to subvert the order established by Him, and because he could not drag God from His throne, he assailed man, in whom His image shone. He knew that with the ruin of man the most dreadful confusion would be produced in the whole world."[10] Consequently, Calvin can speak of "great armies, which wage war against us."[11] These armies of evil subvert, pervert, distort, and destroy the true function of people and the orders of existence.

According to Calvin, people are made in God's image, and as image-bearers they have a divine calling to do God's will in creation. As image-bearers, people are social beings and find fulfillment in life through relationships with others, particularly in marriage, in the family, and in work. Within these relationships people have the opportunity to do the will of God and to express in concrete and tangible ways their obedience to the Creator.

But the Fall, which is a human choice not to do the will of God, demonstrates that human affection and commitment are not toward God but toward self. Rather than being a slave to God's will (which would be good, since God's will is for a human's good), people become enslaved to those passions and desires that tend to pervert their character as divine image-bearers. Consequently, people do themselves a disservice. They become less human. They no longer live up to the image of their original creation. They are less than what they could be.

The consequences of this perversion of the self-image are expressed in human social relationships. Since marriage, family, and work are integral to human welfare, they cannot escape the effect of a personal decision to turn from the will of God. Bieler in his work entitled *The Social Humanism of Calvin* comments:

> Thinking to save his liberty, man has separated himself from God, thereby not only destroying his individual self but also changing the nature of social relationships. Man has distorted social life and economic exchanges. Thinking to find his freedom outside God, man in fact ends by foundering in a combination of slaveries. He becomes a slave of his own nature, of his sexual and emotional life, and of his work. He becomes the tyrant of his neighbor each time that he avoids being his neighbor's slave. All natural hierarchies are corrupted.[12]

But Calvin is no pessimist. He believes the situation is not hopeless, for a new person has appeared. Jesus Christ is not only the Son of God but also truly man. He perfectly reflects the image of the Father. What this means for human beings is a new beginning—for them and therefore for the world. Faith in Christ changes a person by conversion. As a result, a person no longer looks to self as the basis of life but now looks outward toward God and puts self under the authority of the Word of God. A person becomes submissive to Christ and through Him to the will of God. A converted person now more perfectly bears the image of God.

Through the work of Christ the distorting influence of the Devil is destroyed and creation is restored. Commenting on Ephesians 1:8, Calvin stresses this work of restoration in Christ. He says, "Paul wants to teach that outside Christ all things were upset, but through Him they have been reduced to order."[13] Later he writes, "Such [a recapitulation] as would bring us back to regular order, the Apostle tells us, has been made in Christ."[14] In this comment we may see how strong is Calvin's emphasis on order. He believes that creation reflects order, the Fall disorder, and redemption returns us to that order.

The Church

These three concepts—creation, fall, and redemption under God's sovereignty—form the basis for Calvin's doctrine of the church in the world. The church is that divine institution in society where God especially dwells. Thus, the church is the instrument of God's universal purpose and the focus of history. The church understands God's order and therefore promotes and preserves it. So Calvin can say, "The whole order of nature will be thrown into confusion, and creation will be annihilated"[15] without the work of the church in the world. God's will for the world is accomplished primarily through the church. No other institution in the world is so endowed with God's blessing and favor. For this reason, Calvin acknowledged that the work of the church is the ceaseless activity of bringing order out of chaos. Calvin refers to the whole world without Christ as "a shapeless chaos and frightful confusion." Christ alone "gathers us into true unity." And this gathering takes place through the work of the church which brings order back into the world out of chaos.[16]

Since God intends to bring order back to the creation through the church, He begins His work of restoration in the church, so that the church in the world is a sign of the future. Thus, the church's understanding of itself involves a tension between order as a present task and order as a final goal.[17] Calvin's concept of order accounts for his emphasis on the inner order of the church. He believes the minister is a servant of the Lord, committed to serving the church in such a way that his leadership expresses the rule of Christ, preserving decency and order in the church. The motive behind Calvin's strong emphasis on discipline in the church is the maintenance of order; and Calvin's rejection of Roman Catholicism arises out of his concern to restore the ancient order of the church. Nevertheless, Calvin "never expected that an institution would emerge which would be in complete conformity to God's will. While the making visible of the ordering work of God is the church's present task of obedience, this task is never complete, but remains an eschatological goal."[18] Nevertheless, now in this world the church exists in the midst of the larger society as, in the words of Bieler, "the small priming for the social restoration of humanness."[19] In a sense the church "is the embryo of an entirely new world where the once perverted social relations find anew their original nature."[20] This restoration of a new society is still fragmentary, of course, because of the persistence of sin in the life of the world.

In Calvin's thought the emphasis on order moves from order in the church to the task of the church bringing order to the world. Calvin believes that whenever order is brought to the world, the kingdom of God is expressed. And the work of the church is to fill the whole created order with the kingdom of God, the rule of Christ over all things. Consequently, Calvin asserts that the role of the church in the world is to extend its rule over the whole of society, bringing society into conformity to the rule of Christ as expressed in the Word. Commenting on Daniel 2:40, Calvin writes, "We see how the prophet here predicts the beginning of Christ's Kingdom, as contemptible and abject before the world. It was not conspicuous for excellence . . . hence, Christ appeared cast down and lowly; but the branch increased wonderfully and beyond all expectation and calculation, unto an immense size, till it filled the whole earth."[21]

Calvin's eschatology is not an abrupt apocalypticism as in Luther or the Anabaptists. Rather, he sees the kingdom coming gradually as the creation is slowly brought back to its pristine state. There is a progress of the church in the world as it accomplishes its mission of routing out the chaos introduced by evil and establishing the kingly rule of Christ over all the world. So Calvin can say, "The nature of the Kingdom of Christ is that it every day grows and improves, but perfection is not yet attained, nor will be until the final day of judgment. Thus, both are true—that all things are now subject to Christ, and yet that this subjection will not be complete until the day of the resurrection, because that which is now only begun will then be completed."[22] Calvin looks for the renovation of the world. All evil and its influence through the orders of creation will be put away, and the whole created order will be renewed and recreated. This renewal, which began at the Incarnation and finds expression through the church, will be completed at the end of time.

What Calvin says on these themes, then—the sovereignty of God, creation, the Fall, redemption in Christ, and the church—provides us with the biblical and theological keys to Calvin's view of the church and world. We now turn to Calvinists' application of these thoughts in politics, in economics, and in work.

Politics

We have seen that Calvinism views all aspects of life as being under the sovereignty of God and His Word. Let us see what this means in the political order. Lutheran scholar William Mueller comments, "The church and the state are both subject to the sovereign rule of God, *the regnum Dei et Christi*. The authority of both spheres inheres in the will and purpose of the living God."[23] Although the origin of the state ultimately lies in the will of God, who decreed it into existence, we may speak of three earthly reasons for the state's existence.

> First, the fact of sin: Because sin expresses itself in a human's desire to develop culture away from the will of God, the state as an institution that holds sin in check has been instituted by God.

> Second, the goodness of God: The creation of the state may be seen as an act of God's goodness toward people. Sin unchecked by some external restraint would destroy humanity.

> Hence the third reason, the preservation of human life.

These reasons for the origin of the state suggest the purpose of the state. Calvin writes that its purpose is "to foster and maintain the external worship of God, to defend sound doctrine and the condition of the church, to adapt our conduct to human society, to form our manners to civil justice, to conciliate us to each other, to cherish common peace and tranquility."[24] He insists that magistrates have "a commission for God, that they are invested with divine authority, and in fact, represent the person of God, as whose substitutes they in a manner act."[25] They are the "ordained guardians and vindicators of public innocence, modesty, honour, and tranquility, not that it should be their only study to provide for the common peace and safety."[26] In this we see again Calvin's strong commitment to order in society.

Both the origin and purpose of the state in Calvin's thought point to the necessity of Christian involvement in the affairs of state. The effect of the involvement of Christians in government is obvious. If the Christian submits to what he or she understands the will of God to be in the state, the order of society will be stable and sin will be held in check. Involvement in government is therefore a Christian calling.

In this respect, the church as a body has a particular role to play toward the state. In the first place, the church ought to be "a leaven inspiring and generating social, political, and economic life."[27] A dead church will make no impact on society. But a church that is alive to the Spirit, one that is constantly being regenerated by the Word of God, will be acting redemptively toward the social order.

Second, the church has a reforming role to play toward the state. W. Fred Graham sets forth four tasks that Calvin enumerates for the church in regard to the state; these all have to do with a kind of continuing reform by the church. The church is called upon to "pray for the political authorities." It is to "encourage the state to defend the poor and weak against the rich and powerful." The church must also "ensure its own status by calling on the political authorities for help in promoting true religion and even enforcing ecclesiastical discipline." And finally, the church has a responsibility "to warn the authorities when they are at fault."[28]

In order that the relation between the church and state may work properly, Christians within the church must be obedient to the state. Obedience to the rulers is willed by God, for God has instituted the offices of the state. Furthermore, obedience is pleasing to God and helps to maintain the order and tranquillity of society, which brings glory to God.

Nevertheless, there are times when Christians have the right and duty to resist the state. Whenever the state demands something that opposes the will of God, the Christian has the right to resist compliance. The point is that the absolute authority over the Christian is Jesus Christ. For this reason, Christian obedience to the government is always conditional. But Calvin never teaches a radical revolutionary stance; he does not believe that it is right to uproot the social order. What Calvin does advocate is a prophetic witness that takes a firm stand for truth and justice, but does not seek to take matters into its own hands. God himself will sooner or later deal with evil rulers.

Economics

To assess Calvin's view of economics, we must remember that economic life and social life in his day were in upheaval. A rapidly growing capitalism had the effect of increasing the cost of living while at the same time decreasing the value of human labor. Consequently, a few were able to amass large fortunes while the masses were burdened with an increasing poverty.

Because Calvin did not separate the world into the secular and sacred domains, he understood that material goods belong to God. His positive attitude toward material possessions may be seen in what he thought about money. As Bieler points out, for Calvin "money is a sign with a twofold meaning: it is a sign of grace for him who through faith acknowledges that all his possessions come to him from God, but it is also a sign of condemnation of him who gets the goods of his living without discerning that they are the gift of God."[29]

Calvin believed in a mutual communication of goods. His model was the redistribution of the manna among the people of Israel, in which Paul observed that "he who gathered much had nothing over, and he who gathered little had no lack" (2 Cor. 8:15 RSV). Calvin did not oppose the unequal distribution of goods as such. Instead, he believed that this unequal distribution would provoke the redistribution of goods from the rich to the poor, motivated by Christian love. Anyone who really loves other people cannot be selfish. Thus, the rich have a mission to the poor. They can share their wealth so that the poor will no longer be poor and the rich will no longer be rich. By the same token, however, the poor have a mission to the rich: They provide the opportunity for the rich person to be rid of wealth and therefore to be free from becoming a slave to it. Unfortunately, however, the sin of greed prevents this redistribution, maintaining and encouraging an inequality in society.

In the heart of sinful people, money may become a god. Satan persuades people that money, not God, is what assures them of daily bread. Furthermore, Satan persuades people that there are two domains—the secular and the religious—and that people can serve money in the secular domain so long as they serve God in the heart and in devotional practice. Consequently, both society and the church become perverse. By failing to speak out against the service of money, the church fails to fulfill its prophetic role within society. As a result, the evils produced by the worship of money rage on unchecked.

The answer to this unfortunate situation is found in the voluntary poverty of Jesus Christ and in the common grace of God, by which the goods of creation are meant to be freely dispersed to all. The church must put these remedies into practice, for God's people have a proper understanding of money and its use in society. The act of sharing, then, is essentially a spiritual act. By giving money for redistribution, people dethrone money and put it into proper focus and use.

A rediscovery of the proper use of money has immediate social repercussions. The church rediscovers the spiritual nature of the mutual communication of goods; and through its obedience to the will of God in this regard, the church is able to point the way toward an economic equilibrium. For this purpose Calvin instituted the deaconship and stressed the importance of giving and sharing in the Christian church.

Calvin also insisted that the state has a responsibility to the poor. It is the state's task to "guard against business interests milking the life of the people by unjust methods" as well as to guard itself against becoming an "economic liability to its citizens."[30]

Work

Calvin's view of work, like his view of other aspects of life, is rooted in the will of the sovereign God. Work is not a meaningless activity, for it is the doing of the will of God in His creation. It is the means through which God's mandate for the maintenance and the unfolding of His creation is accomplished. As Bieler states, "The work of man has a meaning because, when rightly accomplished, it is the very work of God by which God supports the life of His creatures."[31]

Like everything else, however, work is affected by sin. It now participates in the chaos introduced into the created order. People free themselves from doing the will of God and seek instead to work autonomously. Human activity therefore frequently produces pain, disruption, inequality, injustice, and the like.

In order to restore work to its original meaning, people must be realigned with Jesus Christ, and through Him brought back to obedience to the will of God.

Calvin believes that the Sabbath as a day of rest points to the recovery of the meaning of work. Rest has no meaning in and of itself; its purpose is to put people back into the condition of being able to work. In the freedom of rest, our minds and bodies are able to recognize again the Creator and our relationship to Him. To misuse the Sabbath by not observing it as a day of rest results in the corruption of work.

Because people are created to work, all forms of idleness are a curse. To be lazy, or to accumulate wealth through the sweat of another person's brow, represents a rupture with God and His calling in work. Consequently, unemployment is a social scourge to be fought against, "for to deprive man of his work is truly a crime. As a matter of fact, it is equivalent to taking away his life."[32] To abuse another person's work or to exploit workers is also a crime.

Since work is doing the will of God, workers ought to recognize that their pay is the result of the grace of God. Rich and poor alike receive their wage from God. Therefore, for an employer to withhold an employee's fair share is to withhold what God intends for him. "The master," as Graham points out, "is simply 'paymaster' for the heavenly master."[33]

The real point is that everything belongs to God.

Whether a person is an employer or an employee, a person is simply a steward of God's creation. And since people live in solidarity with others, they must remember that there is one "master" over all—God. Salary must be seen, then, to use Bieler's words, "in relation to the real needs of the working man considered in their new dignity as children of God. This does not forbid, but on the contrary, it commands the state to exercise a certain control over salaries. Salaries must be guaranteed by contractual regulations. Finally, in case of conflicts, one must recur to arbitrations."[34]

All of this must be seen in the context of Calvin's world view. Because this is God's world, the purpose of economic goods and work is the service of God in society. What serves the best interests of society in terms of fairness and equal distribution of goods serves God. What creates an imbalance in society and produces poverty and suffering does not serve God. Commerce, then, "must relieve the pain of man and render his existence pleasant. In order to respond to the purpose of God, commerce always must tend to this goal."[35]

EVALUATION

First, John Calvin's attempt to understand the relationship between church and world against the backdrop of creation, the Fall, and redemption is commendable. Rather than isolating certain teachings within Scripture and building a view of church and world that is inattentive to the broad sweep of biblical teaching, Calvin constructs his view from the main lines of thought that run from Genesis through Revelation. Like Paul, Irenaeus, Athanasius, and Augustine, Calvin seeks to see things whole. His view of creation leads into history and providence; his view of the Fall leads into the redemption gained by Christ; and his understanding of the church is incomplete without eschatology. He therefore does not see the church and the world as static objects unrelated to each other. Rather, he grasps the dynamic interrelationship that exists between them and sees things whole. Yet, in seeing everything at once in its complexity, Calvin never loses the vision of the goal of God's work, the redemption of the entire cosmos.

Second, the thoroughness with which Calvin understands the effect of the Fall and the scope of the redemption lends itself to the cosmic implications of the church in the world. For example, the Fall and the subsequent sinfulness of human beings is not seen in terms of individual acts alone, but in the broader impact which sin makes on the creation and human work. Calvin speaks of the consequence of the Fall as a perversion of "the whole order of nature in heaven and in earth." The whole creation is "bearing part of the punishment deserved by man."[36] Calvin treats the impact of the Fall on creation more thoroughly in his comments on Romans 8:18–25. Commenting on the "subjection" of the creation, Calvin says, "The whole machinery of the world would fall out of gear at almost every moment and all its parts fail in the sorrowful confusion which followed the fall of Adam were they not borne up from elsewhere by some hidden support."[37] In spite of the continued providence of God, "the condemnation of the human race is thus imprinted in the heavens, the earth, and all creatures." [38] Calvin recognizes that the Fall unleashes the "principalities and powers" and the "rulers of darkness" (Eph. 6:12). He claims that Paul "means the devil reigns in the world, because the world is nothing but darkness. Hence it follows that the corruption of the world is nothing but darkness."[39] Elsewhere Calvin refers to Satan as "the prince of darkness, under whose tyranny we are held captive until we are set free by Christ's hand."[40] For Calvin, the whole world including human beings and the orders of creation such as the state, economics, and all vocations are adversely affected by the Fall.

The parallel to the cosmic effect of the Fall is found in the redemption of mankind. The work of Christ on the Cross—which reverses, renews, and restores the human condition—is extended to the creation as well. Calvin comments on Romans 8:21, which says that the creation itself will be liberated from its bondage to decay, by observing that "God will restore the present fallen world to perfect condition at the same time as the human race."[41] He warns his readers against too great a curiosity with regard to the nature of this perfection, and asks them to be content "with this simple doctrine—their constitution will be such, and their order so complete, that no appearance either of deformity or of impermanence will be seen."[42] In answer to the meaning of 2 Peter 3:10, Calvin says, "I shall say just one thing about the elements of the world, that they will be consumed only in order to receive a new quality while their substance remains the same, as can easily be concluded by Romans 8:21 and other passages."[43] Here Calvin gives us further insight into his eschatology. He does not expect the created order to be annihilated. Rather, he anticipates the destruction of those evil powers which have corrupted the human element and the creation, setting God's creation free of its subjection to the powers of evil, so that it can function according to its original intent.

A third strength of Calvin's thought is his thoroughgoing concept of the church, as it is seen in relation to the Fall and the redemption. He believes the church is no mere collection of people; it is a people who have as their task the restoration of the creation under God. By connecting the church with the creation, the Fall, redemption, and eschatology, Calvin gives the church a strong sense of mission. Its work is the transformation of human persons and the ultimate transformation of the structures of creation. And its work is not done in vain. Rather, the church works for the redemption of the whole world in the light of "the triumphant resurrection hope which embraces the whole creation and promises transformation of the present order."[44]

While Calvin's understanding of church and world holds promise for our understanding of church and world today, it does contain several weaknesses. First, it tends toward a theocracy. Unlike the Anabaptists who hold church and world in antithesis, or the Lutherans who see the church and world in paradoxical tension, the Calvinist tends to blur distinctions between the two kingdoms, and fosters the notion that the kingdom of the church and world may become one. What is central to Calvin's understanding of this issue—i.e., gradual change of the world through conversion to Christ—may be subject to interpretation depending on one's millennial view. In particular, Calvinists who are postmillennial will work toward the establishment of God's theocratic kingdom in the here and now. Calvinistic attempts to alter civil government, such as the Puritan experiment, have sought to establish God's rule on earth. The ideal was that "the elect of God who formed the church would also rule the nation."[45] While this notion has much to commend it, the failures of such experiments suggest that it is too idealistic, without a realistic view of the permanence of sin in the human nature.

A second weakness in Calvin's view is related to the

first. The implicit teaching of a gradual transformation of the world by the presence and permeation of the church does not appear to fit the facts. While the postmillennial Calvinists argue that sufficient time is available (an argument that is difficult to oppose), the time since the Reformation seems to contradict the gradual conversion of the world by the church. If anything, the historical convictions of the premillennialist or amillennialist, who argues that the world is becoming progressively more wicked and that change will not occur until the consummation, seem to be more in keeping with the fact of secularization, increasing technology, and the threat of totalitarianism from both the right and the left. But then we must admit that four hundred years is a short period of time from the long-range view of history itself. In sum, then, Calvin affirms the incarnational presence of Christ through the church as well as the lordship of Christ over the structures of existence. But this view of the lordship of Christ over the world may lead the church to attempt a Christianization of the powers, resulting in the dominance of the church over the structures of existence.

A CONTEMPORARY INTERPRETATION

Since the Reformation, Calvinists—more than the Anabaptists or Lutherans—have consistently written articles and books about their view of church and world. For that reason, the Christian social thinkers from which I could choose a representative of contemporary Calvinist thought is quite broad. Perhaps the most significant thinker in America in the Calvinist tradition is Richard J. Mouw, professor of philosophy at Calvin College.

In a recent work, *When the Kings Come Marching In*,[46] Mouw clearly demonstrates how he stands in continuity with the Calvinist tradition. The book is primarily an exposition of Isaiah 60, which Mouw takes to be "a revelation in which God tells his people what will happen in the future."[47]

Mouw stands in the Calvinistic affirmation of creation as good. But he is more specific than Calvin in regard to the way the structures of existence have been perverted through evil and can be put to an evil end. For him, the history of human cultural formation is one of "perverting the good creation."[48] For example, he says, "Many human ills and wrongs are rooted in political life. Sometimes political systems are directly responsible for evil—as when totalitarian governments deliberately enforce unjust laws and practices."[49] This power of evil working through structures of human existence actually began immediately after the Fall, when "God told the woman that she would be ruled by the man (Gen. 3:16)—thus began the patterns of the sinful domination of one human by another."[50] The problem is that sinful, rebellious persons pervert the cultural mandate to subdue and have dominion over the world. Consequently, "the cures of sin touch thrones and principalities, constitutions and legal systems. Tyranny, oppression, and manipulation are distortions of the good administrative patterns which God originally willed for human creatures."[51] Thus, "human rebellion *institutionalized* sin" and "evil has become a part of the very fabric of human sociality."[52] Nevertheless, Mouw does not give up on these structures. Rather, he would acknowledge that these structures, although perverted by sin, are still under God and are socially significant areas of human work. For example, governments "invested with the power of the sword are necessary. They are in an important sense, a curb on human wickedness, a divinely ordained remedy for our fallenness."[53]

Like Calvin, Mouw acknowledges that God's work in Jesus Christ is "cosmic in scope."[54] God in Christ reconciled the whole world to himself. For "God has not abandoned his good creation, even in its presently distorted form. . . . He sent his own son to rescue the entire cosmos from the effects of sin."[55] He "dies on the cross to liberate his creation."[56] This "redemption restores the work of creation, and in doing so it also repairs the damage done by sin."[57] The work of Christ on the cross reaches "not only into the hearts and lives of individuals, but into every corner of the creation which the curse has affected."[58]

Mouw also recognizes the special role of the church in God's work of redemption. The church "stands between the Old Testament age and the coming manifestation of the eternal order of things."[59] The church is rooted in the historic work of Christ on the cross which dealt a decisive blow to the powers of evil, and it anticipates the end times when the work of Christ in putting away evil will be consummated. Consequently, the church is that place where we may see "present signs"[60] of the future. For example, in the church Christ calls us to cast our lot with the lowly ones, to identify with the poor and the oppressed of the earth. To live in this manner is to anticipate the coming political vindication when "the least one shall become a clan, and the smallest one a mighty nation (Isa. 60:22)."[61] Christians are not to sit idly by, waiting for the consummation to take place. Rather, they are to "actively work to abolish patterns of ethnic and racial discrimination *within* the Christian community."[62] In the matter of racial, economic, political, social, and moral issues, the church is to be "a model of, a pointer to, what life will be like in the Eternal City of God."[63]

Mouw also stands in the Calvinist tradition when he recognizes that what the church is expecting in the end of time is not the destruction of the creation and its structures of existence, but the *release* of the creation from the disabling and perverting powers of evil and the havoc they create throughout God's good world. In Isaiah's vision, Mouw suggests "there is no need to read the negative passages as insisting that these pagan entities *as such* will be destroyed. . . . My own impression is that the judgment that will visit the ships of Tarshish is of a purifying sort . . . the judgment here is meant to *tame*, not destroy. . . . It is not, then, the ships *as such* that will be destroyed; it is their former *function* that will perish."[64] But this taming, redemption, and release will occur only at the end of time. It is not the goal of the church to accomplish this taming; rather, it is God's work alone. But the church which now awaits this day does so "actively, not passively." It must "*seek* the city which is to come," and it does so by calling "human institutions to obedience to the creator."[65] Thus, Mouw's church-and-world view is drawn both from an incarnational and a lordship christology, with a strong emphasis on Christ's lordship over the structures of existence, finding expression through the work of the church.

C. The Changing Circumstances

10

THE CHURCH AND SECULARIZATION

The general relationship of the church toward the world between Constantine of the fourth century and the Reformers of the sixteenth century can be interpreted as an attempt to Christianize the Powers. The opposite may be said about the time span between the sixteenth and twentieth centuries. During this period, the church lost its control and influence over the political, economic, scientific, and moral spheres of human life. The process by which this happened is known as *secularization*. Secularization, as it is being used here, may be defined as the movement away from the influence of Christianity in all spheres of life toward the differentiation between the Christian faith and the structures of existence. An autonomy is thus given to powers that operate in various arenas, such as political and economic life, allowing them to exist outside the influence of faith. Christian experience is relegated to the private life, concentrating on personal piety and holiness. It is the purpose of this chapter to illustrate the shifts in thought which brought about the differentiation of the Christian faith from the spheres of human activity in the modern era.

RENAISSANCE HUMANISM

The Renaissance and Reformation of the sixteenth century provide us with a basic background for the study of contemporary society. These two movements which unleashed such powerful new forces into society were the formative principles for a Christian world culture on the one hand and for a humanistic world culture on the other.[1]

The Renaissance is recognized as the movement which marked the transition from the medieval to the modern era.[2] Gradually expanding from the fourteenth through the sixteenth centuries, it spread over Western Europe and contributed greatly to the end of the domination of the world by the church. It infused philosophy, religion, politics, and art with a new spirit of human freedom. The Renaissance resulted in a shift in human interest from the church to the world, from God to humanity. The ideal of religious life was replaced with the joy and affirmation of life in the here and now. Human beings' relationship with nature was rediscovered, and the Renaissance thinkers' concern to explore this relation expressed itself in a newfound interest in individualism and subjectivism. No longer subjected to ecclesiastical jurisdiction and dogmatic creedalism, the human person was elevated to the center of the universe. The Renaissance exalted the power of human reason and sought apart from the strictures of traditional thought to interpret and understand this world. It is in this consideration that the significance and the importance of Renaissance humanism is found. Perhaps we could summarize it as a *human attempt, unaided by anything outside, to interpret and control the world—a spirit of total self-sufficiency.* It was this spirit that called for and generated a human-centered culture.[3]

Renaissance humanism is a world view that may not be called a product of the medieval era nor the Enlightenment.[4] It stands somewhere between. It may be seen as a reaction against medieval habits of mind, ideals, cosmology, and religion; yet it did not have the new habits of mind, ideals, religion, and cosmology that were to be developed in the Enlightenment age.[5]

Renaissance humanists, as scholars of the Greek and Roman culture, expressed their yen for learning in art, architecture, sculpture, and painting. In this respect they were more closely connected with the past than with the more scientific future. Renaissance humanists were also rebels. They were rebelling against a decaying scholasticism and the authority of a weakened church. They found the medieval way of life unlovely, untrue, and very dull and now wanted to open the intellectual windows and let in the fresh air. Some of the humanist rebels were extremists who went so far as to engage actively in the destruction of the medieval political and moral order. The majority of Renaissance humanists, however, were simply obsessed with the joy of living and were primarily concerned with the gratification of their earthly desires.

While the secularization of the West may be traced back to the humanistic spirit born in the Renaissance, the daughter of the Renaissance—the Enlightenment— spawned the specific movements that drove a wedge between the church and the world. Specifically, two movements accelerated this cleavage, forcing religion into an ever increasing privatism: (1) the rise of reason over against the authority of divine revelation, and (2) the emergence of a naturalistic world view as opposed to a supernaturalistic world view.

The Rise of Reason Over Revelation

First, we must note the ascendance of reason over revelation. Renaissance humanists gave birth to the rationalistic spirit that dominated the Enlightenment era. The basic difference between the humanists and the rationalists can be understood in a comparison between artists and scientists. The humanists were artistic dreamers, while the rationalists and the scientists were able to fulfill their dreams to some extent. The humanistic emphasis on nature led the rationalists into an investigation of nature. The humanistic artists' emphasis on detail conceived of the universe as a machine-like structure, which led the rationalists to discover the laws through which they demonstrated that the world ran like a machine. The humanistic political theory of Machiavelli, which conceived of the state as an end in itself, was implemented by the rationalists in the French Revolution. Thomas More, in his *Utopia*, dreamed of a world in which people living according to their good nature would deal virtuously with each other; the rationalists attempted to fulfill this dream through the doctrine of progress, which looked forward to creating a utopian world.[6]

The rise of reason over revelation was aided by two

movements: the development of a new cosmology and the discovery of a new epistemology. The discovery of a new cosmology necessarily involves the breakdown of the old medieval cosmological concepts. Basically, the medieval cosmology was moral rather than scientific. It was believed, on the authority of the church, that a love affair existed between God and the world. The world was viewed as the center of all things, since it was the center of God's attention, and medieval thinkers assumed that heavenly bodies moved around the earth. Copernicus raised the first note to question the voice of the church in the area of science. He taught that the earth swings around the sun once a year, and at the same time the earth turns on its own axis once every day. The spread of Copernicus' discovery was insured by the appearance of three new stars in the intellectual heavens: Johannes Kepler was able through observation to chart the movement of the heavens. This set the stage for the notion of a mechanical universe. Then Galileo Galilei, the father of modern empiricism, discovered the basic laws for the mechanics of motion. By joining logic to experiment, he was able to overthrow many medieval ideas and shake the authority of the church in the area of science. Finally, Sir Isaac Newton provided the capstone of the cosmological concept of change. In seeking a law that would have universal application, he discovered and propounded the law of gravity. Thus, what has become known as the "Newtonian world machine" was born. Everywhere mechanistic laws were sought which would apply not only to the natural world but also to the religions of the world. The idea of truth derived from revelation was breaking down and the conception of life rooted in reason and science was assuming an ever-increasing influence.[7]

The second contribution of the Enlightenment rationalists toward a world view based on reason was in the area of epistemology. Medieval epistemology looked to the authority of the church, while the Reformers sought their authority in the Scripture. In either case, final authority was thought to come from outside the world. The Enlightenment's epistemology shifted to the authority of science, experience, and reason.

First, authority was located in science. Francis Bacon contributed greatly to the rise of the scientific attitude. In his book *New Atlantis*, he proposed a new society based on the principles of science. The community was to contain a house of science and technique, a laboratory, a bureau of planning, and a workshop.

Next, authority was located in experience. John Locke, having overthrown the concept of innate ideas, suggested that people are shaped entirely by their environment. This view was to have its full effect later when people became convinced that the manipulation of the environment could result in a good human nature and a peaceful utopian society.

Finally, René Descartes located knowledge in reason. Descartes held that if a thing is proven, it will be believed. The view that knowledge derives from science, experience, and reason naturally contributed to the breakdown of a supernatural concept of life and gave rise to the naturalistic way of viewing things.

EMERGENCE OF A UTOPIAN WORLD VIEW

The rationalists combined their naturalistic world view with their authoritarian structure of belief drawn from science, experience, and reason to address the questions of religion, politics, and society. Each succeeding generation in the eighteenth century carried the Enlightenment views to more radical conclusions. In religion they went from deism to atheism and materialism. From the innocent beginnings of psychology in John Locke, they went on to attempt an explanation of human nature from a psychological point of view. In economics they went from a state-controlled program to one of absolute free economic competition. In politics they reacted against forms of absolutistic government and brought about the French Revolution.[8]

The eighteenth-century rationalists were enthusiastically utopian. They were convinced that human nature was basically good and that evil lay in the environment. They felt that if they could change existing laws and institutions, and encourage education, human beings could get along and society would reach its utopian ideal. The first step in changing the environment lay in changing the government. The authority of the government over the people kept them in conditions of poverty. So the existing government had to go. The grand rationalistic experiment was the French Revolution. The French revolutionaries believed that utopia was around the corner.

The French Revolution failed, but the utopian hope did not die. However, the events of the nineteenth century drastically modified the utopian concept. During the nineteenth century the environment improved as a result of the industrial revolution, which brought an increasing wealth for some and worse conditions for others. Nevertheless, confidence that life was improving permeated the culture.[9]

The idea of an immediate utopia was revolutionized by several developments of the nineteenth century.[10] First, it was changed by the writings of biologists, especially Charles Darwin. Darwin's geological research indicated that life had been here for thousands of years. He discovered fossil remains which suggested that life moved from the simple to the complex, with life progressing on an ascending scale. Human beings came to be viewed as the final triumph of living organisms. The immediate result of Darwin's idea of evolution seemed to be a mitigation of the idea of obtaining an immediate utopia. The change from the old social environment was now viewed as a transition instead of a leap. Second, the rise of nationalism challenged the idea of an immediate utopia. For example, the evolutionary idea of a struggle for existence between the lower orders was sublimated now into the idea of a struggle between organized groups, nation states, or classes of people. Nationalism tended toward an ethnic or regional utopia rather than a worldwide utopia. Finally, the eighteenth-century hope of an immediate utopia was modified by romanticism. Romantics looked on the rationalists with a certain amount of contempt, regarding rationalism as a shallow approach to thinking. The romantics emphasized knowledge through intuition. They believed that only emotion could touch the depth of life. Romantics were much more religious. They were not traditional theists, but neither were they atheists. They thought of God as being imminent within the structure of life itself. He was the principle at work in nature, producing the movement of history and generating the process of evolution. Drawing from the Hegelian concept of God as the spirit within history, the romantics did not differ from the rationalists in their hope for a utopia. What marked the difference was the way in which the utopia would come about. The romantics looked to a force (God) working in harmony with people; whereas the rationalists looked to people, apart from any principle or force in nature, for the creation of a utopia.

Twentieth-Century Utopianism

The twentieth century opened on the romantic notion of a utopia based on the progress of people through science, reason, and a principle at work in the universe, through which the ideal would be achieved. The optimism of the early decades gradually gave way to a pessimism about the future. World War I, "the war to end all wars," was rapidly followed by the Depression and World War II. The atrocities of World War II challenged the whole structure of utopianism. The idea of process and progress was shattered; the concept of the goodness of man could not stand in the face of the facts. Industry and science which were to have served the needs of humanity were now turned against people and used as instruments of their destruction. Despair rather than hope became the byword. After the war, conditions did not improve. A new kind of archetypal person emerged. Rather than being characterized by the free, autonomous spirit of utopia, modern man became dominated by mass movements and conformity, typified by the ideal lifestyle of suburbia. Some argued that human beings were not free; they were trapped like animals in an unhealthy environment, threatened by poisonous air and water, as well as by overpopulation. Psychological stress became dominant as the future of humanity's very existence began to be questioned. Out of this present situation two attitudes emerged.

The first, the attitude of *despair*, expresses itself in an absurdist philosophy of life. Absurdity, which is the logical conclusion of atheistic humanism, regards life as totally meaningless. People are thought to be animals, produced by biological chance, with no purpose in life except death—the ultimate in absurdity. Released from all religious, moral, or societal norms, humans become their own final reference point. Only the restraints of society keep the world from total chaos in this situation. The significance of the attitude of despair is that these people no longer hope for a utopia.[11]

The second twentieth-century attitude which is still somewhat utopian is reflected in the *new intellectualism*. The new intellectual describes our present ills as a result of our inability to keep up with the development of science. While science has produced a new world, human beings have not significantly changed for the new intellectual. The hope of the world lies in the control of people and of the environment. Human beings can and should be controlled through the behavioral sciences. New creatures can be produced through scientific advancement. Patterns of behavior can be introduced by introducing new drives in the unconscious and new ideas of right and wrong in the super-ego. Thus, by conditioning, people can be made better. The planning for this society may be executed by a few elite who will decide what kind of a society and what kind of a human being is most desirable. The significance of the world view of the new intellectuals is that the utopian concept is still strongly believed, but the romantic ideal of process has been replaced by the idea of utopia resulting from the manipulation and control of environment.[12]

THE CHURCH AND SECULARIZATION

Reformation Christianity and the subsequent seculariza-tion of the Christian world view must be understood in the context of the medieval world of thought from which it developed. The medieval world was first and foremost a church civilization. It was based on the assumption of divine revelation embodied in the church which by divine right executed authority in both spiritual and temporal affairs. In the second place, therefore, medieval civilization was a civilization of authority *par excellence.* This authority extended over all of life, not only over the birth-to-death cycle of the individual, but also over the various spheres of the natural order, as well as academic pursuits. The ideal of the medieval world was simply that the natural order was to be brought into harmony with the divine order, regulated under the authority of the church.

The ideal of a church-ordered society ended with the Reformation. But the Reformers Luther and Calvin were not secularists. Their ideal was not a secular world in which the church was at work redeeming people out of this world. Nor were they other-worldly. In this respect, the Reformers had their feet planted firmly in the medieval ideal—a world in which the divine law and the natural law were one. The difference between the Reformers and the Catholic church of the medieval world was not in their hope for a Christian world but in the authority by which they felt the world should be guided and the means by which this authority should be executed.[13]

Of primary concern for both Luther and Calvin was the authority of the Word of God which replaced the authority of the church. While the Reformers maintained that each individual was to stand under the authority of the Word of God, they cautiously avoided the modern doctrine of individualism through their emphasis that nations as well as civil authorities stood under the authority of the Scripture. In this respect, a Christian civilization under divine authority still remained their ideal. The Reformers did not regard the church and the state as two distinct organizations any more than the Catholic church did. Both church and civil powers under the authority of the God of Scripture were destined to serve each other in love.[14]

The great significance of the Reformers lay in their concept of a Christian world. They were not secularists. However, in assessing either Luther's or Calvin's understanding of the relation between church and world, we must take into account the Constantinian basis of their thought. They lived in a time when Christendom was still the ideal; the Christianizing of the world order still seemed possible. The process of secularization had not yet taken place.

As the Reformation shattered the medieval world view of a church civilization, so the Enlightenment era brought an end to the Reformers' concept of a civilization ruled by the authority of the Word of God. The ascendancy of reason, the replacement of supernaturalism by naturalism, and the hope of a humanistic culture gave rise to a more pluralistic society. Consequently, the idea of the church's controlling or even influencing the structures of existence became increasingly irrelevant.[15]

The inability of the church to counter the forces of secularization aided the differentiation between the church and world of politics, science, economics, and the like. The church, rather than claiming the lordship of Christ over all areas of life, accommodated itself to the modern spirit. It allowed a complete separation between private faith and public policy. Many Christians were content to cultivate their personal holiness while all manner of evils were being perpetrated against people through industrial exploitation, racial and sexual discrimination, destructive wars, and oppressive and unjust governmental policies.

The twentieth century which, according to the nineteenth-century utopians, was to be the century when evil was eradicated, has been quite the opposite. The wars of the first half of the twentieth century jarred the idea that society could progress toward utopia. The concept of the basic goodness of man seems absurd in the face of modern atrocities. People have begun to feel alienated from self, from nature and from neighbor. The problems of depersonalization, persistent wars, the dissipation of energy resources, the starvation of millions, the potential of a nuclear holocaust, widespread abortion, apartheid, environmental imbalances, and the problems created by overpopulation are all evidence of the continuing presence of evil working through the structures of existence.

EVALUATION

In sum, the rise of reason over revelation and the emergence of utopia based on reason, science, and experience—trends which have dominated the Western world culture from the sixteenth to the twentieth century—have effected a differentiation between the church and world. The synthesis between church and world of the medieval period and the desire of the Reformers for both church and world to be equally under the Word of God have been shattered. By the twentieth century the world of politics, education, humanities, science, industry, economics, psychology, sociology, and life in general was no longer informed by either the church or the Word of God. The cosmological, epistemological, and scientific revolutions of the preceding four hundred years have established a new basis of authority for the life of the world. It is a secular, atheistic, and humanistic spirit. It is an authority based within the created order that does not recognize any validity to the supernatural world view claims of the church.

Church and world are now thought to be built on two different foundations. To some observers, it appears that history has come full cycle, the relation of the church to the world being similar to what it was in the first three centuries. We turn now to see how the church during the modern era has related to the process of secularization through which the church has been continually pushed away from its influence over the social spheres of life.[16]

11

THE RISE OF
THE SOCIAL GOSPEL

Although the process of secularization resulted in a differentiation of the church from the structures of existence and thus the privatization of Christianity, there were throughout modern history pockets of resistance to the exclusion of the Christian faith from public life. This movement of Christian resistance to the autonomy of the spheres of life has been dubbed *the social gospel*. While the term is more frequently applied to liberal Christianity, it is nonetheless applicable to more conservative movements as well.

The term *social gospel* may be defined as "the application of the teaching of Jesus to society, especially to the economic life and social institutions such as the state and the family." Although the social gospel is usually associated with Horace Bushnell, Washington Gladden, J. F. D. Maurice, and Walter Rauschenbusch, the social concern of the Pietists and Evangelicals of the seventeenth and eighteenth centuries laid the ground work for a Christianity that related to all of life.

THE EVANGELICAL BACKGROUND
TO THE SOCIAL GOSPEL

Pietism, a movement of the seventeenth and eighteenth centuries, was molded by the social context in which it had appeared. The Thirty Years' War which had devastated the German people produced a crisis in morality as well as in morale. It was a situation of despair. Furthermore, the religious influence of the time was at a low ebb. Protestant scholasticism, influenced by the rationalism of the Enlightenment, preached a faith by way of intellectual assent. For a people emotionally and physically deprived, the intellectual appeal of the gospel was unsatisfactory. Besides, the churches (being state churches) produced an atmosphere of coldness and impersonalism in which it was thought that to have one's membership in the church was enough.

In this context Pietism emerged as a gospel of the heart, not the head. Pietist leaders—notable among whom were William Law (1696–1761), Philip Spener (1635–1727), and August Francke (1663–1727)—thought reason was the chief enemy of the gospel and the source of all disorders in the heart. They called Christians to take their religion seriously. William Law urged that if Christianity was true, then all of one's life should be devoted to following Christ.[1] He masterfully applied the principle of piety to every aspect of life—to vocation, family, personal affairs, education, and the whole of existence. He called on people to renounce the world and to resist the spirit of the world. The Christian was to renounce its goods, reject its joys, and place no value on its happiness. Christians were to live as pilgrims in spiritual watching, in holy fear, and heavenly aspiring after another life. They were called to take up their daily cross, deny themselves, and seek a poverty of spirit through forsaking pride and riches and by living in a state of humility, while rejoicing in the sufferings of the world. Law made the principle of separation foremost when he insisted that one's common life must be one of humility, self-denial, renunciation of the world, poverty of spirit, and heavenly affection. Otherwise, Law argued, one does not live the Christian life.

In 1716 August Francke published *Three Practical Discourses*, in which he urged Christians to assume responsibility for the poor, based on the love demonstrated by God in Jesus Christ.

In his "twenty-four motives to a faithful discharge of the duty of bounty to the poor," his first motive (as described below) is incarnational, for it is rooted in the gospel, in the love of God demonstrated in Jesus:

The first motive to Christian bounty and charity is the 'unspeakable and incomprehensible love and mercy of God towards mankind.' This love is explained to us by our Lord, John 3:16, telling us, that God loved the World. And in what manner did he love it? 'That he gave his only begotten Son.' To what end? 'That all who believe in him, might not perish, but have everlasting life.'

The same love of God towards men is plainly set forth by the Apostle, Eph. 2:4 and Rom. 8:32 . . . . God delivered his own only begotten Son to the most infamous death of the cross and thereby redeemed us from eternal death and damnation. There is no doubt that whoever ponders this love, whoever lets it revolve again and again in his mind, will be excited thereby to bestow a like love on his poor and indigent neighbor. This divine love, seriously weighed and laid to heart, will stir up in him these and like considerations: 'Has this infinitely great God been so merciful unto me, as not to spare his only begotten Son, but to give him up freely for me? Then, why should I be so stingy, as to spare my worldly estate and income, while I see so many miserable objects about me, who stand in need of my help and assistance? Nay, if I should bestow all that I have on the poor, what an inconsiderable proportion would it bear to that love, which the Lord has conferred on me?' . . .[2]

The Evangelical Revival of the eighteenth century under the leadership of John Wesley in England and George Whitefield in America emerged from a situation similar to that out of which Pietism came. Rationalism had taken hold in England and produced a sterile religiosity in the established church. Furthermore, the effects of the industrial revolution were beginning to be felt in the crowded and poverty-ridden conditions of the city.

The effect of Evangelical revivalism was much like that of Pietism. It renewed a heartfelt, Bible-centered religion which motivated people toward the communication of the gospel and good living. It produced numerous missionaries, pastors, and Christian workers who were responsible for the rapid growth of Protestant Christianity in the nineteenth century throughout the world. It also produced, as a direct result of its preaching, a social concern for the underprivileged and the poverty-stricken as well as an insistence on justice and equity in society.

John Wesley (1703–91), George Whitefield (1714–70), and other leaders of the revival held what is known as a holistic view of salvation. They did not separate the body from the soul, the material from the spiritual, or the personal from the social. Rather, their approach to revival stimulated the improvement of social conditions and the bettering of human life.

Wesley himself was in the forefront of social change. In 1746 he opened a free medical dispensary for the poor of Bristol, England. In 1785 he organized a Friends Society to aid strangers and those in need. He wrote against bribe-taking and smuggling. He supported the rise of education, particularly the Sunday school movement. He fought against the slave trade. He supported prison reform. And he freely gave his money for the support of these various reforms. It is estimated that he gave more than £30,000 during his lifetime to such causes.

Wesley was not unique. Many other Christians, including members of the upper classes such as wealthy politicians and businessmen from Clapham Commons, a village near London, were involved in social reform. Although they were derisively nicknamed "the saints" by their opponents in Parliament, these benevolent Christians are better known as the Clapham sect. They gave away large portions of their income for the support of social change. Among them were William Wilberforce (1759–1833), who led the fight to stop the British slave trade, and Granville Sharp (1735–1813), who brought about the judicial decision to free the slaves in England.

Among the numerous social movements that resulted from the influence and leadership of the Evangelicals, we will look at three major ones: the abolition of slavery, prison reform, and the improvement of working conditions.

The abolition of slavery became the life interest of Granville Sharp, a grandson of the archbishop of Canterbury during the reign of Queen Anne. His study of the Old Testament convinced him that slavery was a sin. Setting out to destroy this evil in England, he found out that he had the support of most of the clergy of the Church of England.

One of the many persons influenced by Sharp was William Wilberforce, a member of the Clapham sect, an Evangelical, and a member of Parliament. Wilberforce worked with other Evangelicals who gathered information for him and actively agitated in Parliament for the abolition of slavery. His move for abolition was defeated in 1792 and again in 1796. Rather than giving up, the Evangelicals became even more active in pressing for abolition. In 1802 they began publishing the *Christian Observer*, an anti-slavery magazine that spread their ideas further and gained support for the cause. In 1804 Wilberforce introduced another bill for abolition, and it eventually passed.

But the abolitionists did not stop with their victory in England. They carried their cause to other countries and were influential in stopping the slave trade in Denmark, the United States, Sweden, Holland, and other countries.

The same kind of energy was put into prison reform. John Wesley and some of his fellow members of the Holy Club had visited prisoners in the jail at Oxford. From that time on, Wesley took an interest in prisoners. He publicized the poor conditions in prisons and advocated reform. John Howard (1726–90), who became the foremost leader in prison reform, freely acknowledged his indebtedness to Wesley. Howard, who had experience in a jail in Portugal, sought through the accumulation of evidence to change the laws that treated prisoners unjustly. As a result of his work, a number of improvements were made, including the development of more just penal laws, the ending of the unfair practice of jailors' fees, and the improvement of sanitary conditions in prisons.

Similar efforts were made to improve the lot of workers through changes in the laws. The most ardent champion of the working class was Anthony Shaftesbury (1801–85), a committed Evangelical and a member of Parliament. Comments Earle Cairns: "He was of the opinion that what was morally right must be politically right and what was morally wrong could never be politically right. He would use the law to restrain those who were vicious and to protect the oppressed."[3] Shaftesbury worked tirelessly for shorter hours, better working conditions, and better pay for workers. As a result of his spirit and leadership, laws were eventually passed that reduced the length of the working day, restricted and regulated the employment of women and children, and reformed such occupations as mining, chimney sweeping, and the operation of lodging houses.

One of the most notable evangelical leaders in the campaign to apply the gospel to social conditions was William Booth (1829–1912), the founder of the Salvation Army. Booth, originally a Methodist, left that church to devote full attention to street preaching and mission work in London. By 1875 he had established thirty-two centers for evangelism and social work in London. Within ten years, more than one thousand Salvation Army centers were established in various parts of the world including Russia, the Orient, and North America.

In 1890 Booth published his well-known work, *In Darkest England and the Way Out*. He described England as "a population sodden with drunks, steeped in vice, eaten up by every social and physical malady." He compared England with darkest Africa and claimed, "The foul and fetid breath of our slums is almost as poisonous as that of the African swamp."[4] He noted that in London in a single year 2,157 people had been found dead, that suicide brought death to 2,297, that there were 30,000 prostitutes, 160,000 people convicted of drunkenness, and 900,000 paupers in the city. Booth called for the foundation of the rescue mission, shelter stations, food centers, and city and farm colonies as well as the continued preaching of the gospel. His work and ministry had a momentous effect on succeeding generations of evangelicals and has the distinction of being one of the most enduring social outreach programs in the West.

We may conclude from these examples that William Booth, John Wesley, Lord Shaftesbury, and other early Evangelicals understood the "cosmic" dimension of Christianity—that it extended to the whole person and to one's entire existence under the sun. Theirs was no reductionistic, anti-material, "soul-only" salvation.

Social Change in America

At the same time that these social changes were occurring in England, similar changes were being made in America, and for the same reason: revival. In an interesting book entitled *Discovering an Evangelical Heritage*, Donald Dayton looks back into the roots of his own denomination, the Wesleyan Methodist Church, and Evangelicalism in general. Happily, he discovers that his denomination "was a product of the closest parallel to the civil rights movement in American history—the abolitionist protest against slavery in the pre-Civil War period."[5] Further research leads him into the "sweet irony that this denomination was not unique, but shared a reformist heritage with other aspects of Evangelicalism."[6] Dayton discusses some of the major reformers and movements that gave shape to an evangelical social conscience. Three persons—among many—who illustrate the social roots of Evangelicalism are Jonathan Blanchard, Charles G. Finney, and Theodore Weld.

Jonathan Blanchard was the founder of Wheaton College. By today's standards he would be considered a radical. A plaque in Blanchard Hall on the Wheaton campus contains a quotation from an address by Blanchard entitled "A Perfect State of Society." The plaque reads: "Society is perfect where what is right in theory exists in fact; where practice coincides with principle, and the Law of God is the Law of the Land."

Blanchard did not separate his theology from practice. Unlike those who are concerned with right doctrine and a private ethic, Blanchard's concern was for right doctrine and a *public* ethic.

For example, the doctrine of man made in the image of God was not a matter for pure speculation for Blanchard; it was basic to his convictions against slavery. And it was not enough for him merely to have an anti-slavery position in his heart. Rather, his theological conviction gave rise to an active engagement within society against the evil institution of slavery. Blanchard worked against many odds—and with no little opposition from some Christians—to abolish slavery. His concern (and the motto he left for Wheaton College) was "For Christ and His Kingdom." By this he meant the rule of God in the life of society, which could bring about a gradual transformation of culture.

This was also true of Charles G. Finney (1792–1875), another founding father of American Evangelicalism. Although Finney is best remembered as a preaching evangelist, he also exercised a strong influence in America through his writing, particularly his *Lectures on Revivals of Religion*. In this work he argued that "revivals are hindered when ministers and churches take wrong ground in regard to any question involving human rights."[7] These were no idle words. Finney practiced what he preached in regard to slavery and insisted that the church must face that issue. "One of the reasons for the low estate of religion at the present time," he said, "is that many churches have taken the wrong side on the subject of slavery, have suffered prejudice to prevail over principle, and have feared to call this abomination by its true name."[8]

Theodore Weld, converted under the ministry of Finney, became the most important anti-slavery worker in America.

For some time after his conversion he worked in the "Holy Band," a group of Finney's assistants. Throughout the years, Weld continued to apply to social issues the principles taught by Finney. He was a major influence in opening the door for women to speak in mixed gatherings, which, says Dayton, "foreshadowed the later practice of women taking to the platform in defense of abolitionism and the consequent birth of feminism."[9] But his greatest work was done in the anti-slavery movements, as recognized by the *Dictionary of American Biography*, which calls Weld "the greatest of the abolitionists."

These examples illustrate the extensive nature of the evangelical impulse as it took shape in the nineteenth century. Evangelicalism in its best form is no stranger to social concern; such concern is, in fact, close to the center of what evangelical Christianity is all about. Nor does it appear that eighteenth- and nineteenth-century evangelical social concern was relegated to private and personal morality. It was deeply concerned over the structures of existence and the way in which evil is perpetuated through them. But it was the more liberal social gospel that became the stronger advocate for the conversion of the social structures in the nineteenth and early twentieth century. We now turn to that story.

THE SOCIAL GOSPEL
OF THE LIBERAL CHURCH

The rise of the so-called liberal approach to the social gospel must be understood in the context of evangelical history. In the late nineteenth and early twentieth centuries, Evangelicalism as a whole became less involved in social issues. There are several readily discernable reasons for this shift. One reason was the impact made by the Civil War, which dampened the utopian hope for a world changed through the betterment of society. The war was a slice of realism interjected in the midst of many dreams. It had the effect of bringing people back into the reality of this world and thus it diluted the reformers' vision.

Another influence was the shift that occurred in eschatology. Nineteenth-century Evangelicalism was largely optimistic and postmillennial. With the rise of dispensationalism (which accented not so much the vision of the kingdom as teaching about the end times), and with the catastrophe of

wars and depression in the early twentieth century, Evangelicalism shifted toward a pessimistic mood. It began to look
for the "life beyond" as the better state and became less
concerned about making this life better. The emphasis then
fell on "rescuing" fallen souls from the sinking ship of this
world. Consequently, evangelism lost some of its social
emphasis.

More importantly, the fundamentalist-modernist controversy of the early decades of the twentieth century resulted
in a strong shift toward the defense of doctrine among
Evangelicals. The subsequent split of fundamentalism from
the mainline churches caused the energies of the fundamentalists to be expended on the formation of new denominations, mission agencies, and educational institutions. While
fundamentalists continued to actively support rescue missions, prohibition, and local social causes, the most visible
social activists were in the mainline churches. These activists
for the social gospel were dubbed "liberals," along with their
theologically liberal friends in the mainline denominations.
The implication was that the social gospel was a poor
substitute for the redeeming gospel of Christ. The liberal
social activist, who had no redemptive gospel, substituted
humanitarian concern in the place of truth. The extreme
liberal point of view was at best a humanitarian theism. The
supernaturalism of the Bible was rejected for a rationalistic
view of the world. In this framework, Christianity was the
espousal of love and Jesus was its main proponent. Doctrines
such as the incarnation of the Son of God in the womb of the
virgin Mary, the substitutionary death of Jesus Christ, His
resurrection, His ascension, the coming of the Holy Spirit at
Pentecost, and the preaching of repentance toward faith in
Jesus, were dismissed as creations of a Hellenistic metaphysical mind set. The real Jesus was thought to be found beyond
all the supernatural myths of Paul in the teaching of love—
Love God and your neighbor. The liberal thinkers believed
the message of Jesus was social, not supernatural. Consequently, all forms of social concern became suspect among
fundamentalists; a distinction between evangelism and social
action was born.[10]

The modern roots of the more liberal social gospel go
back to the middle of the nineteenth century and to the
emergence of the industrial revolution. Rapid urbanization
and industrialization threatened to isolate Protestantism

from the working class. In this context, Christian leaders voiced new concerns for social justice. Indictments were leveled at capitalism for creating a situation in which very few were rich and many, especially those of the inner city, were extremely poor.

The Christian socialist movement was founded in England in the middle of the nineteenth century. It was led by J. F. D. Maurice, an influential Anglican theologian who sought to make the established church more relevant to the social conditions of people. The Christian socialists rejected all theological notions that tended to devalue human life on earth and advocated the universal sonship of all people with God. They succeeded in initiating legislation for working people, particularly tradesmen, alleviating the dour conditions of their working life.[11]

In America the most significant proponent of the social gospel was Walter Rauschenbusch, author of the highly acclaimed and classic work, *A Theology of the Social Gospel*.[12] The emphasis of Rauschenbusch's social gospel was on the corporate nature of the Christian commitment, in distinction from individual salvation. God, he argued, is immanent within the created order, working out His purposes to bring about the era of brotherhood and peace. The establishment of a just social order, which was the work of the church, was seen as a preparation for the coming of the kingdom of God.

More than anything else, the kingdom of God on earth was the vision of the social gospel advocates. It was the dominant motif from which the social agenda of the mainline churches was derived. This kingdom vision implied a social ethic, as opposed to an ethic of the individual alone. Furthermore, sin was seen not only in individual terms, but in its larger scope as the evil expressed in society through societal structures. Consequently, the liberal social gospel sought to convert the structures of society, to change the environment so that God's principle of justice would reign in politics, economics, and industry, as well as in every sphere of life.

Since Walter Rauschenbusch and his book *A Theology for the Social Gospel* are hailed as the epitome of the entire social gospel movement, we may summarize the salient features of the social gospel by reviewing the fundamental argument of his book. Rauschenbusch's doctrine of sin and his concept of the kingdom of God will bring us into the heartbeat of the message traditionally understood as the social gospel.

Rauschenbusch defines sin as selfishness. The sinful mind is the "unsocial or antisocial mind." The climax of sin is not found in the man who "swears or sneers at religion," but in the "social groups who have turned the patrimony of a nation into the private property of a small class, or have left the peasant labourers cowed, degraded, demoralized, and without rights in the land."[13] Sin, being social, is transmitted through social institutions. Sin, being socialized into a hereditary social force, becomes "lodged in social customs and institutions and is absorbed by the individual from his social group."[14] It then becomes a super-personal force, a power of evil that works through the society of humanity and through the structures of existence. These evil collective forces become "the most powerful ethical forces in our communities."[15] Consequently, they create what Rauschenbusch calls "the kingdom of evil." This is "the power of evil behind all sinful human action"[16] which gains control of "legislation, courts, police, military, royalty, church, property and religion."[17] Rauschenbusch, after giving a history of these demonic forces throughout the various stages of church history, concludes that the ancient concept of demonic powers and the modern social-gospel concept of an evil kingdom are not alien to each other at all; they are "blood kin."[18]

The second motif in the theology of the social gospel is the kingdom of God. The kingdom of God, which is the opposite of the kingdom of evil, is the "realm of love and the commonwealth of labour."[19] This reign of love, which confronts the selfishness of evil, seeks to make the institutions of life "fraternal and cooperative' so that the sinful exploitation of institutions which results from selfishness will be turned around, allowing institutions to serve humans rather than to exploit and destroy them. This unselfish service of one human to another is expressed in cooperative labor. Sin, which "shirks its own labour . . . increases the labour of others."[20] But love seeks to serve the other and to work cooperatively toward the good of the whole society. The church, which serves the interests of the kingdom of God, becomes the other super-personal force whose work, in part at least, is to "bring social forces to bear on evil." But the church must never take the place of the kingdom of God as the purpose of the Christian's labors, for the ideal of the church (and thus the "test and corrective" of the church) is the kingdom of God.[21] Whenever the church loses sight of the kingdom it becomes a power, an end in itself, and joins the powers of evil in suppressing the people. Consequently, the church must always see its task as that of serving the kingdom by "saving the social order."[22]

The kingdom of God is variously described as the goal of history, a historical force,[23] the teleology of the Christian religion,[24] the energy of God realizing itself in human life,[25] humanity organized according to the will of God,[26] the supreme end of God,[27] and thus the purpose for which the church exists. Further, Rauschenbusch says that the kingdom of God goes beyond the limits of the church to embrace the whole of human life and to ultimately transfigure the social order.[28]

While not all theologians agree with every point in the theology of Rauschenbusch, it is eminently clear that he had a sense of the power of evil working through the structures of existence. In this, he stands in the best tradition of Christian theology, which recognizes that sin and its effects are not only individual and personal but social and institutional.

In this chapter I have attempted to show that the idea that evil works through the structures of existence remains a modern Christian conviction. The Evangelicals of the eighteenth and nineteenth centuries directed their social action not only against personal sin but social sin as well. And the social gospel proponents of the late nineteenth century turned the issue of the power of evil into a theology of two kingdoms, evil and good, in conflict with each other.

Although the early Evangelicals and the later social gospel activists had differences of theological opinion, it is clear that both opposed a secularization that sought to make the church irrelevant by isolating it from the spheres of human activity. They both advocated the rule of God over all of life and insisted that the church, the servant of God's kingdom, must strive to meet the needs of the whole world.

Yet both camps did not have a theology of church and world that was as well formulated as that of the sixteenth-century Reformers or the theology which was to be developed in the later twentieth century. We turn now to those later developments.

III

CONTEMPORARY MODELS
OF CHURCH AND WORLD

12

THE NEW DEMONS

The title of this chapter is taken from Jacques Ellul's book entitled *The New Demons*. Ellul based this phrase on the observation that "the world is abandoning the religious idea that it had of itself"[1] and has subsequently turned toward new gods. These are not transcendent gods, but secular gods who provide salvation from within, not from without.

The "Pastoral Constitution on the Church in the Modern World" proclaims that "the church carries the responsibility of reading the signs of the time and of interpreting them in the light of the gospel."[2] Perhaps it can be said that the signs of our times are new demons with which we must wrestle. What is most strange is that these new demons are gods, idols of our time which promise a new messianic era, a new secular salvation.

The context in which these saviors have emerged is our present changing world; a world of industrialization and technology; urbanization and poverty; mass media and violence, emigration and homelessness; an overabundance of food and starvation; human rights and abortion; disarmament treaties and nuclear build-up. In this world people look for a center, a unifying principle that provides meaning, authority, and leadership. Consequently, today's church is seeking to apply the Christian vision of reality in an altogether new context, a situation unique to the twentieth-century church. It is in the context of this new situation that we must think about the church and world today.

Current models of church and world need to be interpreted against the background of secularism, scientism, nationalism, and economic utopianism. These four issues do not exhaust the modern situation. Rather, they point to several unique powers of the twentieth century through which modern people define themselves, their lives, and their work. Consequently, they are matters of particular importance to the church. In this chapter a brief explanation of each of these four issues will be set forth; and in succeeding chapters, how the church relates to these issues will be made more clear.

SECULARISM

Like biblical supernaturalism, secularism sets forth doctrines having to do with origins and the meaning of life, history, salvation, and the like. While secularism is not a formal religion (because it has no cultic practices), it addresses religious questions and requires faith by asserting the nonexistence of God and the sufficiency of naturalistic explanations.

The origin of secularism in the Western world, as we have seen, is connected with certain strains of the Renaissance. The Renaissance initiated a movement away from the particular Christian mind set established by medieval Catholicism toward a new mentality which eventually discounted a supernatural world view, replacing it with the secularism of the modern era.

Since the Renaissance, several movements have been responsible for the process of secularization (which can be described as the movement away from a Christian mind set toward a secular mind, together with those convictions and values which proceed from its presupposition). One movement which has contributed significantly to the shaping of the modern mind is the Enlightenment.

One of the most powerful aspects of the Enlightenment was its leaders' rejection of the Christian vision of sin and redemption. This rejection was linked with the positive vision of a society based on the inherent goodness of human persons and the possibility of human self-redemption. The principle set forth by Jean-Jacques Rousseau is that people are good and all evil is resident in society, not in people. Since society is the agent of evil, it follows that society can be reformed by exercising the good within humans until society, by becoming good, becomes the agent for salvation. In this way human beings are responsible for their own salvation—giving birth, as it were, to the new society in which evil has been eradicated. This superficial analysis of society has become the major impulse from which the secular vision of society derives. It has denied God and all supernatural considerations for understanding the nature of society. The responsibility for understanding evil as well as redeeming society has been placed on the shoulders of the human intellect. Humankind alone must answer to itself and create its own future.

A good example of this secular trust in human potential, a trust that denies the supernatural and affirms a materialistic concept of the universe, is found in *The Humanist Manifesto II*, a document written by a small group of world leaders in 1973. While many people are not aware of this document, it nevertheless expresses the humanistic and secular hope that pervades the world outlook of those who either consciously or unconsciously subscribe to the idea that the world has no meaning outside of itself or apart from those who shape its destiny. After setting forth seventeen proposals, it concludes with the following secular appeal for a world of brotherhood and peace:

> The world cannot wait for a reconciliation of competing political or economic systems to solve its problems. These are the times for men and women of good will to further the building of a peaceful and prosperous world. We urge that parochial loyalties and inflexible moral and religious ideologies be transcended. We urge recognition of the common humanity of all people. We further urge the use of reason and compassion to produce the kind of world we want—a world in which peace, prosperity, freedom, and happiness are widely shared. Let us not abandon that vision in despair or cowardice. We are responsible for what we are or will be. Let us work together for a humane world by means commensurate with humane ends. Destructive ideological differences among communism, capitalism, socialism, conservatism, liberalism and radicalism should be overcome. Let us call

for an end to terror and hatred. We will survive and prosper only in a world of shared humane values. We can initiate new directions for humankind; ancient rivalries can be superseded by broad-based cooperative efforts. The commitment to tolerance, understanding, and peaceful negotiation does not necessitate acquiescence to the status quo nor the damming up of dynamic and revolutionary forces. The true revolution is occurring and can continue in countless nonviolent adjustments. But this entails the willingness to step forward onto new and expanding plateaus. At the present juncture of history, commitment to all humankind is the highest commitment of which we are capable; it transcends the narrow allegiances of church, state, party, class, or race in moving toward a wider vision of human potentiality. What more daring goal for humankind than for each person to become, in idea as well as practice, a citizen of a world community. It is a classical vision; we can now give it new vitality. Humanism thus interpreted is a moral force that has time on its side. We believe that humankind has the potential intelligence, good will, and cooperative skill to implement this commitment in the decades ahead.[3]

For a Christian one issue of secularism is its denial of a transcendent point of reference for values. How, Christians argue, can the human race arbitrarily choose values of love and justice as norms for peoples and civilizations to live by when these values have no other origin than human consensus? There must be a higher source of authority from which values derive and to whom persons are held accountable. A related issue of secularism is the autonomy it gives to the structures of existence. How, it may be argued, can the evil which is perpetuated by people through social, economic, and political institutions be curbed? What is there to prevent the rise of totalitarianism, together with all the evils it perpetuates, when there is no higher power to rule over it? These questions and other similar issues have caused various groups of Christians to rise and reassert the role of the church in proclaiming and actualizing a Christian reclamation of the structures of existence. Christians have become increasingly impatient with a privative faith and express growing interest in making the structures of existence accountable to the Christian view of reality.

SCIENTISM

The misuse of science has also had its part to play in the process of rejecting the supernatural. In particular, an insistence on the knowledge of all things through scientific inquiry has resulted in the denial of mystery and revelation. This demystification of the world has hastened the assertion of human autonomy.

At the outset, a distinction must be made between science and scientism. It is a misunderstanding to set Christianity against science as though the two are natural enemies. Historically, the Christian world view has set the stage for the development of science. It is generally recognized that the medieval emphasis on the rationality of God paved the way for scientific inquiry. In the medieval world view, every detail of the world was supervised and ordered by God. Consequently, the search into nature was a positive way to discover more about the God who made the ordered universe.

Likewise, modern science is rooted in the Christian conviction of a rational universe characterized by order and regularity. Newtonian science operates on the conviction that the orderliness of the natural world is intelligible, and that human reason is a reliable means by which that order is uncovered.

But scient*ism* is something quite apart from science; scient*ism* is a theory about science—a *weltanschaaung* based on certain presuppositions which control scientific inquiry. Julian Huxley, an advocate of scient*ism*, put it succinctly. He set Christian faith and science in antithesis, calling the one dualistic supernaturalism and the other unitary naturalism. "In the first system," he writes, "the phenomenal universe and its evaluation are secondary to the central and eternal god, and are assumed to be products of or dependent on divine operation. In the second, gods are peripheral phenomena produced by evolution. In modern god-centered systems, human beings are supposed to possess a unitary and immortal spiritual entity or soul, capable of existence apart from the body. In the evolutionary system, man's spiritual capacities are taken to be part of the mental aspect or 'inner face' of the human organism."[4]

Scient*ism* has broken away from the Christian presupposition of God, providence, and meaningful purpose. It has developed an entirely new frame of reference in which and through which it interprets the data of scientific inquiry. It argues that the material world is all there is, that human nature is fundamentally good and capable of improvement, and that society can be perfected.

The success of modern scientism is rooted in two developments: (1) its break from questions of final cause and purpose, together with (2) the affirmation that it alone is the intellectual tool through which reality is ultimately known. From a Christian point of view, when science is made the only method of understanding reality—the only "real" explanation, the only legitimate avenue of human experience and knowledge—it is perverted from its God-given function as a structure of existence and is turned into a god. Ultimacy is attributed to it, and claims are made that it is the means through which all of life is to be interpreted.

A good example of this all-pervasive scientism is articulated by Dean Wooldridge, a research associate in engineering at the California Institute of Technology and former chairperson of the National Institutes of Health Study Committee. In his book, *Mechanical Man: The Physical Basis of Intelligent Life*, Wooldridge argues that "ultimately all aspects of the structure and behavior of living matter will be explainable in terms of exactly the same particles and natural laws as those we find underlying the load-carrying qualities of a bridge, the flight capabilities of a rocketship, or the color of a sunset. According to this magnificently *unifying concept*, there is but *one ultimate science*, and that is the science of the physicist"[5] (italics added).

In the next paragraph, Wooldridge articulates his thesis that "*all biological phenomena have physical explanations*" (italics added). What is of special interest in Wooldridge's book is his use of the words "unifying concept," "one ultimate science," and "all." What he has clearly set forth is a universal and ultimate claim of science, insisting that every aspect of human existence must be understood under physical science. This is scientism in its clearest expression. (This is not the view of all scientists, only that of those who make science a universal through which all things are interpreted.)

This universal claim for science is analogous to putting on one pair of glasses through which everything is seen. It is the presupposition out of which everything else is interpreted. But scient*ism* which rejects the notion of an all-embracing God makes a godlike claim for science and interprets all of life through that lens. Although it would be interesting to show how scient*ism* acts as a god over every aspect of life, limitation of space forces us to illustrate this thesis in the areas of religion and morality alone.

For example, scient*ism* as a system leaves no room for moral absolutes. In the system of scient*ism* materialism is all that is. Thus there is no afterlife, no religious compulsion toward acceptable behavior, and no religious right and wrong. Human beings are left on their own to discover and determine their own ethics.

Thus, within the system of scient*ism* the origin of religious and ethical concern are explainable physically. For example, Wooldridge asserts, "According to our mechanistic point of view, a tendency toward moral behavior is a genetically determined, evolutionarily developed physical property of the human animal, just like the number of fingers and the size of the brain."[6] According to this theory, the idea of right and wrong results from trial-and-error process. Thus the argument runs that through a social pressure, which approved of certain practices and disapproved of others, a social consciousness gradually developed in the nervous system. Consequently, the ethics that eventually developed in society resulted from the evolutionary process.

In this social system of ethics, human beings must act as the arbitrators of their own rules and destiny. Such a responsibility is overwhelming today because our complex technological society has raised new ethical dilemmas which demand the application of moral principle to issues which will determine the future of humankind. In today's situation it is altogether conceivable that a tyrant or a ruling elite could use technology to rule the world.

Technology has been described as the application of science. Science is concerned to know, while technology is concerned to make. More specifically, "Science is the combination of rational inquiry and empirical experiments in the investigation of the way in which the natural world functions. Technology is the theory of the use of practical skill to fulfill some human purpose. Technics is the use of that practical skill."[7]

Science makes its impact on the world in which we live

through technology and technique. For this reason the Christian is called to struggle against the theory of scien*tism* and the application of that theory in technology. Neither science nor technology is evil. But they may become tools toward evil ends when they are no longer understood and practiced *under God*. Both science and technology can be used to enhance or destroy life. When they are used toward destructive ends, they become oppressive and demonic. An example is in order.

A severe problem of a technology rooted in a scien*tism* is the alteration of human life, as is now occurring in the biological revolution. In the area of reproduction, technology can control fertility (birth control), family size (abortion), and human reproduction (artificial insemination, choice of sex in offspring, and so on). The possibility of artificial inovulation, cloning, and baby factories are within the reach of modern science. In the area of physical modification, science has made immense strides. It is now possible to transplant body parts, create artificial limbs, and regenerate certain parts of the body. The new process of *eugenics* (genetic engineering) could put the evolution of humankind into man's hands. In some quarters there is even talk of a synthesis between humans and machines. Mental modification of the human person is another creation of modern science. Such things as the electrical control of the brain or the chemical control of behavior, memory, and intelligence make some scientists project the possible scenario of disembodied brains, head transplants, and brain transplants; science has also produced the prolongment of life through the control of disease, and hopes eventually to control the aging process. These incredible advances have propelled the human race toward moral and ethical dilemmas which Christians believe cannot be judiciously handled without recognizing an accountability to a higher power and law. Consequently, applied science raises the specter of new demons and powers which will control and distort the life of humanity through the perversion of those newly discovered structures of existence that control our lives.

Scien*tism*, which is another form of secularism, thus threatens the Christian understanding of the human personality. If the human person is not understood in light of a transcendent point of reference, the unique quality of being human and all which that conviction entails from a Christian point of view may be conveniently disregarded. Actions and policies which dehumanize the person may be justified. In this context the church, which is the guardian of the transcendent understanding of personality, has risen to confront the powers of dehumanization and act in ways to protect human rights and interests. The war on abortion and the call for disarmament may be cited as two prominent examples in which the church now speaks and acts against the powers that dehumanize.

NATIONALISM AND POLITICAL IDEOLOGY

In the early church it was not long before the cry, "Caesar is Lord," clashed with the Christian confession, "Jesus is Lord." This clash, which occurred during the reign of Domitian, gave occasion for Christians to assess the state as a structure of existence in violent antithesis against the church. In this context the apostle John in the Apocalypse assessed the state as an enemy of God, a structure of existence under demonic influence, a power destined to destroy the people of God. Thus the attitude of the church toward the state in Revelation 13 appears to be the opposite of that in Romans 13. In Revelation, the emperor is the beast of the sea who asserts his power over the saint (13:7) and authority over "every tribe, people, language and nation" (13:8). Even the leadership of the church enters into an unholy alliance with the beast (13:11), so that many of the inhabitants of the earth are deceived (13:14), falling down and worshiping the beast.

In John's evaluation of the state, the negative side of the state as anticipated in Jesus and Paul is expressed. Here the state has overstepped its limitation. It assumes a godlike quality and, regarding itself as ultimate, it demands unquestioning loyalty and obedience. But the church, if it is to remain faithful to its Lord, cannot and must not serve the state under these conditions.

In the time of Jesus and Paul, the attitude of the state toward believers was such that the followers of Jesus could support the state. But by the end of the century, Christians were forced into a position of antithesis to the state because of its attitude toward the church. These two different perspectives toward the state suggest that the attitude of Christians toward the state may be somewhat relative to the attitude which the state takes toward the church.

Throughout history nations have asserted themselves beyond their God-ordained limitations, rearing their ugly heads in a demonic totalitarianism. A case in point is the German nationalism of the twentieth century. In a book entitled *The Church and the Political Problem of Our Day*, written by Karl Barth and published in 1939, Barth defends the attitude of the church in 1933 when it adopted a neutral attitude toward National Socialism; but by 1939 Barth claimed National Socialism was no longer a political experiment but a *religious institution of salvation* claiming to give to every person all that is needed "for body and soul, for life and death, for time and eternity."[8] For this reason, Barth insisted, "This dictatorship can no longer be understood as the carrying out of a divine commission, and that means that it can no longer be conceived as a 'higher power' in the sense of Romans XIII." The state had become "a hostile god, an evil god, and a hostile, evil service of god."[9]

Nationalism continues to assert itself in many parts of the world today. Unfortunately, nationalism often functions as a creed, a religion in itself which fosters devotion to the homeland as the one ultimate in life. It holds people in its grip and forces people to serve it as a god.

Today the church in many places must function under a hostile government. In all the countries of the communist bloc and in many parts of Africa and Latin America the church is up against a government that seeks to suppress and muzzle it. Even in the West, some argue that governments are becoming increasingly hostile to Christian values through permissive legislation that allows abortion on demand, permissive sexual behavior, and restrictions against the Christian church.

Due to the rise of nationalism and the political ideologies that accompany it, the church is forced today to think clearly about its relationship to the nation in which it finds itself, with particular reference to its political ideology. Can the church baptize national identity and move toward a synthesis of church and nation? Is there a particular political ideology taught within Scripture that must be espoused by the church? Or is the church a transcultural, transpolitical community of people? And, if it is the latter, how does it function in a particular national and political setting? While these questions are not unique to the twentieth century, they are more pressing than they have been in the past. This is heightened by the pluralism of ideology today, which encourages differences of opinion within the global church itself.

ECONOMIC UTOPIANISM

Another problem facing the church-and-world discussion today is the presence of economic utopianism, whether capitalist or socialist.

One of the most important and controversial structures of existence is the inescapable realm of economics. Economics as we know it today was formed in the radical break from the ancient agricultural society, together with the emergence of the Enlightenment and industrial revolution. The values of the modern era have so intertwined themselves with the modern developments of society that David M. Beekmann, author of *Where Faith and Economics Meet,* claims that the dominant culture of our time can be called an *economic culture.*[10]

Beekmann identifies the values of modern Western economics as this-worldliness, progress, reason, liberty, equality, and fraternity. These six values, Beekmann claims, are so deeply embedded in our social structure that they have gained a grip over us. They control us and run our economic lives and decisions in subtle and unconscious ways. They also represent the natural religion of a secularized culture, values which Western people vigorously defend as absolute. Even Christians have attached a quasi-religious meaning to these values in the economic sphere, politicizing the gospel in their support.

This-worldliness set in sharp contrast to otherworldliness stresses the importance of life in this world as though this is all that is. From this point of view, material abundance can be interpreted as the goal of existence. The idea of progress as understood in the Enlightenment emphasized a gradual economic abundance and security for all people, thus replacing the eschatological vision of Christianity with the hope of an earthly golden era. *Reason* has been the tool of social theorists, beginning with Hobbes, to improve economic institutions through the development of efficient use of time as well as inventions to accelerate production. In this way a this-worldly progress based on science and technology has gradually shaped modern structures of economics.

These three values—this-worldliness, progress, and reason—have been coupled with liberty, equality, and fraternity to give final shape to modern economic realities. Capitalism brought a *liberty* to personal lifestyle that was unknown before the Enlightenment. People were no longer locked into the economic station of their parents, but were free to risk movement toward new occupations and an upward mobility. Economic *equality* came to mean that all were free to compete for wealth and material prosperity, and economic fraternity was evidenced in the wider community of people, created through international trade and travel.

In the meantime the Protestant work ethic, coupled with the economic growth of capitalism, gave the new economics a religious sanction: Protestantism stressed worldly vocations as religious callings and imbued them with the values of hard work, frugality, and saving money. It emphasized the evil of idleness and material indulgence; it promised prosperity and the blessing of God on those who worked hard and lived right; and it foretold poverty and ship-wrecked lives for those who were lazy and indulgent. In this way, Protestantism ascribed a religious quality to different economic lifestyles. Prosperity was supposed to be evidence of God's reward for hard work, while poverty was the result of the failure to pursue one's life and work religiously.

However, in the twentieth century three shifts occurred in the Protestant work ethic, as the result of the expansion of the technological society: First, the frugality of the Protestant ethic was exchanged for pleasure resulting from prosperity. Second, prosperity became a mark of divine favor and poverty became the example of moral depravity and failure. What was once a work ethic now became a wealth ethic.

This shift toward a wealth ethic, coupled with the break from a Christian world view, resulted in the third shift—an evaluation of a person's worth in terms of wealth. The wealthy were thought to be worth more than the impoverished and therefore received more attention and acclaim. Thus, through the perversion of an economic structure, the nature of human work was changed from expressing the *imago dei* to expressing a material value. From a Christian point of view, this devaluation of personhood because of economics may be regarded as *economic idolatry*.

Capitalism became an *ism* (a structure perverted through the powers) as a result of the way in which Christians invested religious meaning in the capitalist system. Because its origins were connected with the Protestant work ethic, capitalism gradually became associated with the teaching of Scripture. Today, many Western Christians hotly defend capitalism as if it were an article of faith; they find its sanction in the seventh commandment, in the Book of Proverbs, and in the parable of the talents. In this way, the gospel is politicized; the Bible is twisted to support a particular economic system. Western Christians make the gospel a servant of the free enterprise system. They give capitalism a kind of religious authority and legitimacy through their religious sanctioning.

But the same thing occurs with those who advocate socialism. Socialism rose as a reform movement against the abuses of capitalism in the nineteenth century. Karl Marx advocated socialism because he saw that capitalism degraded the human person and was characterized by considerable social injustice. Unlike capitalism, which allows the means of production to be owned by private citizens, Marx's socialism advocates a collective ownership of the means of production, directed by the government. Socialism further differs from capitalism in the area of market transactions. In capitalism, people are free to market their goods in open competition with rivals; whereas in socialism the government rules the mechanism of marketing through central planning.

Some Christians who have taken a strong stand against the evils perpetuated by the capitalist system argue that socialism is the more biblical of the two. Drawing on the theological concept that God is the owner of His creation, that people are the stewards of the earth, that God instituted the Jubilee principle in the Old Testament, and that the church in Acts 2 practiced the communal sharing of their wealth and property, these Christians assert the biblical nature of socialism.

In each case, whether capitalistic or socialistic utopianism, we are faced with several issues the church must address. On the one hand, the church needs to confront the way in which people turn economic utopianism into a theory of human salvation. Faith in the economic system as the means of alleviating poverty, oppression, slavery of the masses, and the like ascribes to economic ideologies a near-religious status. People make an idol of their economic system, propagating it and defending it. On the other hand, we must recognize that economic ideology and practice is the source of much dehumanization, oppression, poverty, and human enslavement. Consequently, in our time economic systems are structures of existence through which evil is perpetuated in society. And the church, mindful of economic evil, must seek to address this evil.

CONCLUSION

In sum, the people of the twentieth-century Western world and much of the Third World hold a nonreligious secular view. Thus, the contemporary struggle with the powers seems to center around the ethical implications of a secularized world, modern technology, the policies of political nationalism, and the practical impact made on society through economic utopianism. While the relationship between church and world today may focus on these four areas, the issues which stem from them are broad and inclusive. Consequently, the four matters of secularism, scientism, nationalism and political ideologies, and economic utopianism provide an adequate (although not exhaustive) background for our study of the relationship between church and world within today's church.

In the next four chapters we will look at groups of Christians who seek to act out the relationship between church and world in the context of the modern world, a world that is characterized by the new demons of secular salvationism.

13

THE WORLD COUNCIL OF CHURCHES

The first meeting of the World Council of Churches (W.C.C.) took place at Amsterdam in 1948. At that meeting Dr. W. A. Visser't Hooft, the first general secretary of the council, spoke of this ecumenical band of Christians as "an emergency solution, a stage on the road, a body living between the time of complete isolation of the churches from each other and the time—on earth as in heaven—when it will be visibly true that there is one shepherd and one flock."[1]

The general secretary's vision of the church as one flock was not a new idea. In modern times this vision reached back to the early twentieth century, and now in 1948 it brought together several movements that envisioned a unified church.

The W.C.C. is made up of three preexistent movements which have come together under a single umbrella: The Faith and Order Movement which developed out of the World Missionary Conference in Edinburgh (1910); the Life and Work Movement which can be traced back to the efforts of Nathan Söderblom in the early twenties; and the International Missionary Conference which traces its beginnings back to 1921. In 1948 the Faith and Order Movement and the Life and Work Movement combined to form the World Council of

Churches. The International Missionary Conference joined them in 1961 at the assembly in New Delhi. Thus in 1961 the conferences on doctrine, social action, and mission were merged. From this convergence the modern concern of the World Council of Churches, which seeks a theological basis for social action among the oppressed, particularly those of the Third World, was born. Consequently, it is through the pronouncements and action of the World Council of Churches that continuance of the rise of the social gospel may be seen in mainline Protestant churches.

Prior to the Amsterdam conference of 1948, several pronouncements regarding church and world had already been made by the Life and Work Movement. For example, the 1925 Stockholm conference had as its slogan "Doctrine Divides, But Service Unites." Between 1930 and 1945 the Life and Work Movement advanced considerably in its social thought. The earlier identification which the liberal social gospel made between the kingdom of God and the ideal social order was called into question by the Depression, World War II, and the rise of neoorthodox theology. The stress was now on the development of a Christian view of justice drawn from Jesus' love commandment. Under the influence of Reinhold Niebuhr, a more realistic view of human sinfulness emerged within the Life and Work Movement, together with the argument that power had to be used to assure justice among sinful people. In the Oxford Conference of 1937, guiding principles for a more just society with regard to the political order, economics, and related matters were set forth.[2]

The concern of this chapter, however, is to describe the teaching of the W.C.C. on church and world after 1948. Therefore, we will first look at the church-and-world theme in the various world assemblies starting with 1948. Then we shall follow with a description of liberation theology, a major theological perspective of the W.C.C. pronouncements today.

WORLD ASSEMBLIES OF THE W.C.C.

The Amsterdam Council of 1948

Drawing on the guidelines for a just society developed previously, the next stage of social concern found expression in the Amsterdam conference of 1948. The theme for Amsterdam was "Man's Disorder and God's Design." The most controversial assertion of the assembly was expressed in the statement that "the Christian churches should reject the ideologies of both communism and *laissez faire* capitalism, and should seek to draw men away from the false assumption that these extremes are the only alternatives."[3] This statement must be understood in the context of the cold war tensions between the East and West.

More significantly the 1948 assembly published a statement on the responsible society, calling for the recognition of the centrality of freedom. It stated: "A responsible society is one where freedom is the freedom of men who acknowledge responsibility to justice and public order, and where those who hold political authority or economic power are responsible for its exercise to God and the people whose welfare is affected by it."[4] From a theological point of view, the freedom called for by the Amsterdam conferees is rooted in the doctrine of creaturely responsibility. Each person under God is responsible for his neighbor and his world. Unfortunately, this doctrine, not specifically christocentric, is not vastly different than the democratic ideal of the Enlightenment. It appears to be a humanitarianism accompanied by the veneer of religion.

Evanston, 1954

Six years later, at the second world assembly of the W.C.C., the concept of a responsible society began to be modified by the presence of an increasing number of Third World Christian leaders. Even the title of the section dealing with social issues gives evidence of this shift: "The Responsible Society in World Perspective." The emphasis is not in a particular kind of state as much as the responsibility all states have toward the people under their domain. In this document, the state is seen as a possible threat to freedom and is called upon to act as the servant of social justice, not its lord.[5]

One threat to worldwide freedom which Evanston addressed was the issue of disarmament. The assembly wrote, "It is not enough for the churches to proclaim that war is evil. They must study afresh the Christian approaches to peace . . . Christians in all lands must plead with their governments to be patient and persistent in their search for means to limit weapons and advance disarmament."[6] Political, economic, and peace issues were not the only issues at Evanston; resolutions were also made regarding racial injustice, interracial marriages, and civil disobedience. These issues were soon to engulf society in significant revolution and change. However, a strong biblical basis for social action does not appear in these documents.

New Delhi, 1961

Between 1955 and 1961 the social changes around the world were rapid and far-reaching in their consequences. Perhaps the most important change in the W.C.C. was the emergence of the nonwhite voices from Africa, Asia, and Latin America. The thinking of these younger churches, summarized below by Paul Abrecht, marks a significant new voice and emphasis in the W.C.C.:

> In contrast with the familiar ecumenical emphasis on gradual social change and reform, the inquiries in the new nations pointed to the rapid breakdown of old social systems and traditions and the need for a political and economic system supporting rapid development. In contrast with Western Christian thought which despite all its preoccupations with secularization was based on assumptions of a society still greatly influenced by Christian values and institutions, Christian social thinking in the new nations tended to emphasize the Christian contribution to a pluralistic social ethic which would promote human values in a national perspective. In contrast with the extremely critical attitude manifested toward nationalism in many of the Western Churches, the "younger Churches" stressed the creative role of the new nation-states in the work of development and in creating a new sense of dignity and self-respect. In opposition to the Western Churches, which still placed great confidence in the traditional structures of world political and economic relations, Christians from the new nations pointed to their inherent biases, and challenged the assumption of an "international law" developed by the Western powers and imposed on the rest of the world.[7]

In keeping with these changes the next W.C.C. conference was held in New Delhi, India, where direct exposure to the Third World played an important role in making the Western church more sensitive to the issues faced by Christians in developing countries.

One of the most important statements of New Delhi focused on the problem of human rights. Arguing from the central motif of love, the document calls Christians to "work for political institutions which encourage participation by all citizens, and which protect both the person's freedom of conscience and his freedom to express his convictions."[8] Nevertheless Christians were particularly warned against giving an ultimate loyalty to the state. Again, theological reasons for social action are lacking.

Uppsala, 1968

The period between 1962 and 1970 was one of revolution, developing technology, and secularism. In 1966 a conference met in Geneva to deal exclusively with social issues. Visser't Hooft caught the spirit of this conference when he said, "In Amsterdam the emphasis was too largely on economic justice *within* each nation. We have come to see far more clearly that the crucial issue now is that of *international* economic justice." He went on to suggest that the watchword for the future must be "responsible men participating responsibly in a world society in which all accept responsibility for the common welfare."[9] In the fourth W.C.C. meeting held in Uppsala, Sweden in 1968, the recommendations of the Geneva conference were given enthusiastic endorsement as the conference called for an increased awareness and sensitivity to worldwide social concerns by the church. The conference addressed such explosive issues as revolution, human rights, and religious liberty, the Middle East, the United Nations, China, the conflict in Nigeria, racism, and development of Third World countries.

In this 1968 conference one can detect a glimpse of a theological perspective that goes beyond the old liberal law of love and begins to move toward a christocentric approach to church-and-world issues. In the report on "World Economic and Social Development" there is evidence first of a deeper consciousness of sin as the report states, "in Christ God entered our world with all its structures and has already won the victory over the 'principalities and powers.' His kingdom is coming with judgment and mercy." Further, the document claims that Christians "who know from their scriptures that all men are created by God in his image and that Christ died for all, should be in the forefront of the battle to overcome a provincial, narrow sense of solidarity and to create a sense of participation in a world-wide responsible society with justice for all."[10] This more biblical basis for social action was to have a greater place in the next W.C.C. conference, held in Nairobi in 1975.

Nairobi, 1975

The growing attention to the Third World and its particular problems of political and economic oppression were in great evidence at the fifth W.C.C. assembly held in Nairobi, Africa in 1975. David Patton, in his book *Breaking Barriers*, captures the essence of this conference in his comments on a speech made by Robert McAfee Brown. Brown, speaking on Matthew 16:13-15,

> moved to an extended discussion of Jesus the Liberator, Jesus the Divider, and Jesus the Unifier. Negatively, he said, Jesus frees us from the false securities by which we try to make our lives secure; and positively, he frees us for the possibility of seeing the world through eyes other than our own. The eyes he gives us are those of the hungry, the exploited, the tortured—the nonperson whom the world ignores and discards. We do not live by bread alone, but Jesus never pretended we can live without it. His words and deeds were full of feasts, and he left a meal as sacrament of his ongoing presence. So he frees us also for struggle with and on behalf of those others, the poor and the dispossessed. But Jesus is also the Divider. He came to bring not peace but a sword. Talk about Jesus the Liberator seems to some to betray the gospel by making Jesus too political; but others feel that this Jesus in not political enough. Moreover, good news for the poor is bad news for the rich, and letting my people go from Pharaoh is not good news for Pharaoh.[11]

Because of the strong influence of Third World leaders in the Nairobi congress, one finds a new emphasis on Jesus Christ, His mission to the world, and the church's mission which grows out of the liberation Christ brings. In the document "Confessing Christ Today," both the personal and communal dimension of of this liberation are central:

Confessing Christ *today* means that the Spirit makes us struggle with all the issues this Assembly has talked about: sin and forgiveness, power and powerlessness, exploitation and misery, the universal search for identity, the widespread loss of Christian motivation, and the spiritual longings of those who have not heard Christ's name . . . .

When the Holy Spirit empowers us to confess Christ today, we are called to speak and act with concern and solidarity for the whole of God's creation. Concretely: when the powerful confess Christ, the suffering must be enabled to concur; when the exploited confess Christ, the rich should be enabled to hear in such confession their own freedom announced.[12]

The cental role played by the liberation theme in the Nairobi conference is evident in the sectional studies which addressed pressing issues of the day. Three examples will suffice.

First, in the study entitled "Education for Liberation and Community," the following excerpts indicate the role of Christian education in socio-political and economic liberation:

In obedience to the commandment of Jesus Christ to love our neighbor, we are called to work for the creation of a society in which humanity, justice, openness, and freedom reflect the will of God for his creation. It is Jesus Christ who gives us the vision and the promise of the new world, and provides the basis and the force for renewal in both personal and community life. To say that he is our hope and basis is not to claim that we are free from sin ourselves . . .

The link between school and society and the relationship between dominant economic and social values and the educational system leads many to hold the view that education cannot itself be reformed until the political and economic systems which it serves and which support it are also reformed or radically transformed. Education in too many societies is a consciously used instrument of power: designed to produce those who accept and serve the system; designed to prevent the growth of a critical consciousness which would lead people to want alternatives. In many places disenchantment with the system and with its unwillingness to reform itself leads groups to

infiltrate actively and consciously the educational institutions, to erode the structures so that they change more
rapidly, and incorporate more of the nonformal and the
informal in their methods. Where societies perpetuate
racism through separate systems of schools, churches
should actively combat such a system . . .

The aim of theological education is to contribute to
growth in Christ through community. Such growth takes
place through conscious intellectual reflection, the nurtur-
ing of spiritual awareness, the proclaiming of the good
news of human redemption, and the involvement of the
people in the total liberation process.[13]

The theme of liberation is even more clearly set forth in
the document entitled "Structures of Injustice and Struggles
for Liberation." Here the delegates speak to the issues of
liberation in human rights, sexism, and racism. The preamble to the document is of such importance that I have
included it in its entirety:

> 1. Structures of injustice and struggles of liberation
> pose a formidable challenge to the Church today. In
> striving to meet it, the Church has no other foundation on
> which to stand than it has in Jesus Christ. From him it has
> received its mandate: to witness to the truth which judges
> and to proclaim the good news which brings about
> freedom and salvation. In seeking its particular place in
> today's struggles for social justice and human liberation,
> the Church needs to be constantly guided by its divine
> mandate.
>
> 2. Whenever a Christian is confronted by structures
> of injustice and takes part in struggles for liberation, he or
> she is bound to experience the grip of destructive forces
> which are at work throughout the human family. Such
> forces give a taste of the "principalities and powers" of
> which Paul spoke.
>
> 3. The gospel brings us a message of God's total
> identification with humanity which is suffering under sin
> and other destructive powers. God's own solidarity with
> human beings is expressed in the reality of the servant
> Christ who humbled himself to take up human form, who
> was born into poverty, who accepted the path of rejec-
> tion, and who finally met his death on the cross. The
> vicarious suffering of Christ is the supreme manifestation
> of God's love. God in Christ took upon himself the whole
> burden of human sin and weakness.

4. God calls his Church, a community of forgiven sinners, to follow Christ on the same path committed to the cause of the poor, oppressed, and rejected, to declare the love of God by word and by the whole of life and to accept the cross.

5. The meaning of human suffering in itself is ambiguous. It both reflects the evils which plague the human race and it opens us to God's redeeming activity. In suffering for the cause of justice and for the sake of the gospel, the Church may participate in the vicarious suffering of Christ himself.

6. Is there readiness for suffering in our churches today? Or are our church structures built for our own protection and security and have they therefore become barriers which prevent us from sharing suffering in obedience to Christ and from receiving or reflecting God's redeeming love?

7. Christians who suffer together for the cause of justice and liberation find a deep experience of community with each other and with Christ. This community transcends differences of ideology, class, and Christian tradition. It is knit together by the power of forgiveness and love. It reflects the life of the ultimate community of the Triune God, and the expression of its deepest solidarity with the suffering and sinful humanity is the sharing of the Eucharist.

8. Suffering, however, is not the goal: Beyond the cross is the resurrection. Christ has overcome the power of sin and death and broken the grip of the principalities and powers now still seemingly self-reinforcing and outside the control of persons involved. The victory of Christ therefore brings a tangible and deepened hope to those engaged in actual struggles against oppression and dominance. Moreover, his victory promises that the vicious circle in which injustice breeds more injustice and one form of oppression gives way to another form is being broken.

9. We realize that those who operate the structures of oppression are dependent on the people they oppress and that both are equally in need of liberation and God's forgiving love. In this fallen world, however, it is far more likely that the will and strength to end oppression come from those who bear the brunt of it in their own lives rather than from the privileged persons, groups, and nations.

>   10. Structures of injustice and struggles of liberation
> cannot be separated from each other. For practical pur-
> poses, however, we have divided this Report into three
> main sections: Human Rights, Sexism, and Racism.[14]

A third study produced a document entitled "Human
Development: Ambiguities of Power, Technology and Quality of Life." This document, like the other two, stresses a
theology of liberation:

>   As Christians and churches we cannot speak about
> nor work for a new world order in the midst of situations
> of domination and structures of oppression without
> referring to the liberating power of Jesus Christ. He
> liberates us from sin, both personal and social. We
> recognize that the gospel expresses this liberating
> strength. The prophetic word of Yahweh's drawing near
> to the humble, to the powerless, finds an echo in
> fundamental passages of the Gospels (Luke 4:17–21;
> Matt. 25:31–46, etc.). The gospel *has been* brought to the
> poor, to the powerless, to the oppressed, to the captives,
> to the sick. In the person of Jesus, Yahweh has put
> himself decidedly in the place of the poor; he has searched
> for those who are "nothing" (1 Cor. 1:26–31). The word
> "nothing" refers not to intrinsic moral quality but to the
> very fact that the poor are marginal, leaving their very
> destiny to the powerful.

>   One implication is that Jesus is our liberator inas-
> much as:

>   1. he calls on us to follow him upon that role which
> brought him face to face with those who use religion as a
> means of domination;

>   2. he gives us a hope, i.e., he affirms the right to life
> and the triumph of life against cynicism and fatalism of
> the pure politics of power. To believe in him is not to
> renounce participation in the struggle for justice and
> liberation. It means, on the contrary, that in spite of our
> apparent powerlessness we must keep alive faith so that
> we hasten the day when "justice will flow like water";

>   3. he indicates to us that the way through which the
> community of believers is called to overcome the ambigui-
> ties of power is the way of love and the Cross. We are not
> faithful to Jesus Christ when we submit to the powers that
> be: At that moment we become captives of the powers
> that have been defeated by Christ.[15]

It is clear by 1975 that the early democratic ideal of 1948 and the liberal social gospel of love of preceding W.C.C. assemblies has been replaced by the dominant theme of liberation. This due largely to the presence and influence of the Third World church in the W.C.C.

Vancouver, 1983

The centrality of liberation theology seemed to be played down at the W.C.C. congress in 1983. There was a discernable shift in new efforts toward visible unity expressed particularly in worship. However, the efforts of the church in proclaiming peace and justice through a theology of liberation were still strongly present. Some, like German theologian Dorothee Sölle, wanted to denounce capitalism as the major oppressor; but the majority agreed with the perspective of Bishop James Armstrong, President of the National Council of Churches, who noted that in "every unrestrained earthbound system . . . sin is present."[16]

Since the theme of liberation from all kinds of oppression has been and continues to be a dominant note in the W.C.C., a brief explanation of liberation theology is in order.

LIBERATION THEOLOGY

Liberation theology is one of the fastest growing and perhaps one of the most influential modern ideas having to do with the relation between Christianity and society. The context from which the idea of liberation emerged may be first located in the Bandung Conference of 1955, which promoted the concept of the "Third World." Since then the term has come to mean those areas and people that are associated with neither the capitalist nor the communist system—the countries commonly known as "underdeveloped." The Bandung Conference called the world to attend to these people and countries and to aid them in their self-development.

In response to this appeal, many developed countries as well as many church denominations and organizations became heavily involved in the Third World. Technical aid and personnel were made available, and a noble attempt was made to help struggling countries get on their feet.

Disillusionment soon set in, however, because the

expected social and economic changes did not occur. The poor nations were becoming poorer. The conditions of human life, far from being bettered, were gradually becoming worse.

In this context arose what one commentator describes as "a cry that what was needed was the *liberation of persons and peoples to be the subject of their own history* rather than the objects of someone else's history, whether benignly or selfishly conceived."[17] Dependence on other nations and their technical expertise was not what was needed. The answer lay instead in liberation.

At this point, at least, the church was seen to stand on the side of the oppressor. The native church, it seemed, stood on the side of the oppressive regimes; and the foreign churches came hand in hand with the imperialistic policies of their home nations.

In the meantime the clergy, particularly those who worked with the poor, became more and more critical of the church and supportive of the demands being made for change. This pressure prompted five conferences in 1970, all of which (both Catholic and Protestant) produced a number of significant papers and statements calling the church to an active position in the struggle for justice and economic opportunity among the poor. Gradually the concept of liberation became more clear in the context of theological and practical analysis and articulation.

A Definition of Liberation Theology

Liberation theology is rooted in the concern for salvation. Salvation is seen as something intended not merely or exclusively for the "soul" but for the whole person, the whole created order. Liberation theologians want to see Christ's redemptive work applied to the whole person, liberating people from all those forces—personal, social, moral, political, economic, and otherwise—that deny them the experience of being free to enjoy the benefits of salvation in every aspect of life.

Consequently, liberation theology is a confrontational theology. In confronts evil in all its expressions—personal and social—and demands *release* from the power of evil. But it does not confront evil from the outside. It is not as though it were a matter of church versus society, for there is only one history, and what is done to bring about release must be done within the framework of that history. Thus, liberation theology identifies the continuing act of salvation with the very process of history, which is the context of both oppression and liberation. The liberation theologian Gustavo Gutierrez puts it this way:

> Liberation emphasizes that man transforms himself by conquering his liberty throughout his existence and his history. The Bible presents liberation-salvation-in-Christ as the total gift, which by taking on the levels we indicate, gives the whole process of liberation its deepest meaning and its complete and unforeseeable fulfillment. Liberation can thus be approached as a single salvific process. This viewpoint, therefore, permits us to consider the *unity*, *without confusion*, of man's various dimensions, that is, his relationships with other men and with the Lord.[18]

To try to understand this definition more fully and to relate liberation theology to the problem of the church in the world, we will examine four issues that liberation theology poses: (1) the nature of salvation, (2) the historical dimension of salvation, (3) the political dimension of salvation, and (4) the church in the world.

The Nature of Salvation

Liberation theology rejects the notion of the "saved" and the "unsaved." That the church represents the "saved" and that the mission of the church in the world is to "save the pagans" is replaced by the idea of the universality of God's will to save. God has, through Christ, saved and redeemed the world. The redemption of Christ is so far-reaching that we can regard the whole cosmic order as saved. Salvation is therefore not something that is "otherworldly"; it has to do with this life now and may be defined as "the communion of men with God and the communion of men among themselves."[19] The emphasis is not so much on "God did something that you must believe" or "because of Christ God has changed His attitude toward you." Rather, the emphasis falls on the cosmic redemption that took place in history and has immediate implications now.[20]

Biblically, this understanding of salvation is already set forth in the Exodus event. The Exodus, properly understood, is a re-creation of God's world. That is, the Exodus brings creation and redemption together. It emphasizes that God reveals Himself in history and that His salvation takes place through historical events. Creation is the beginning of God's salvation because it initiates history, the context in which God's saving work actually takes place. The source for this vision is the liberation of the children of Israel from their bondage in Egypt.

The liberation of Israel was not only historical but also political. Not only were they called *away from* a situation of bondage, misery, and injustice, but they were also called *to* the task of constructing a just society. They were thus breaking with an old order and creating a new one. "The Exodus is the long march towards the promised land in which Israel can establish a society free from misery and alienation."[21] In this sense, the Exodus is a re-creation. It is a new beginning.

Like the Exodus, the redemptive work of Jesus Christ is a new beginning and is presented in the context of Creation. Paul affirms that "by him all things were created" and that "God was pleased to have all his fullness to dwell in him, and through him to reconcile to himself all things, whether things on earth or things in heaven, by making peace through his blood, shed on the cross" (Col. 1:16, 19–20). The work of Christ is also a liberation from sin and all its consequences. As the Exodus inaugurated a new people, so too the Cross marks a new beginning. It calls into existence a new people who are called to continue the work of creation and redemption through their labor and involvement in life. Gustavo Gutierrez summarizes this notion well:

> Consequently, when we assert that man fulfills himself by continuing the work of creation by means of his labor, we are saying that he places himself, by this very fact, within an all-embracing salvific process. To work, to transform this world, is to become a man and to build the human community; it is also to save. Likewise, to struggle against misery and exploitation and to build a just society is already to be part of the saving action, which is moving towards its complete fulfillment. All this means that building the temporal city is not simply a stage of 'humanization' or 'pre-evangelization' as was held in theology up until a few years ago. Rather it is to become part of a saving process which embraces the whole of man

and all human history. On theological reflection, human work and social praxis ought to be rooted in this fundamental affirmation.[22]

Salvation is therefore not only that which looks back to Creation and re-creates in the present but also that which looks beyond the present into the future. Biblical religion is a religion of promise. Salvation has to do with the progressive unfolding of that promise within history. It is already partially fulfilled in historical events, but is not completely fulfilled. Therefore it is constantly projecting itself into the future as a historical reality that is in the process of being fulfilled. This process is happening now as humankind struggles for a just society.

The Historical Dimension of Salvation

To begin with, liberation theology strongly emphasizes the historical nature of the Christian faith. Not only did God create the world, and by that initiate human history, but He also entered into human history as a man. Therefore it is in human history that we encounter God.[23]

In the Bible, the entrance of God into history is expressed in a twofold process. First, the presence of God is "universalized" and second, His presence is "internalized." Let us see what liberation theologians mean by these two terms.

Scripture reveals a gradual universalization of the presence of God. To begin with, God reveals His presence within history on the mountain. At Sinai, as He entered into a covenant with the people of Israel, He was somewhat distant from them. Gradually, however, He entered more and more into the life of the people. His presence was made known in the tent, then in the ark of the covenant, and finally in the temple. While the tent and the ark were mobile, the temple was localized. To counteract the idea that God could be contained, the prophets emphasized the theme that God's dwelling place was in the heavens. In this way they opposed those who wished to externalize and localize the presence of God.

In the New Testament, God's presence became a reality in the person of Jesus Christ—"the Word became flesh." In the Incarnation, God irreversibly committed Himself to human history. The historical nature of God's presence in the world does not stop there, however, for the Christian community, called by Christ, is His body in the world. Each Christian, as Paul taught, is a temple of the Holy Spirit; the presence of God is within every Christian. That is not all, however, according to Gutierrez: "Not only is the Christian a temple of God; every man is."[24] The presence of God has then gradually extended from "the mountain" to "every man." God's presence is universalized in history in every person.

Secondly, the presence of God has gradually undergone an internalization. A glance at biblical history suggests that God's initial relationship with people was somewhat external. He came to them in the mountain, then in the tent, later in the ark, then in the temple, and finally in a man. The constant problem in the Old Testament was the tendency to externalize the worship of God and obedience to Him. The prophets recognized this failure and insisted that the day would come when a mere external relationship to God would be replaced by an internal commitment to Him. "I will give you a new heart and put a new spirit in you; I will remove from you your heart of stone and give you a heart of flesh" (Ezek. 36:26). With the coming of God into human history and the establishment of the new covenant, the presence of God is transferred from external signs and integrated within the human heart. God is now within people.

This dual process of making God's presence real in history and within people is accomplished in Jesus Christ. He is the focal point for this reality. For this reason, spirituality can no longer be separated from the material reality of human history. Spirituality is expressed within the concrete events of life and through people. This material nature of spirituality is pointed up by certain biblical themes. Two in particular are the emphasis on doing justice and the teaching that Christ is to be found in one's neighbor.

The emphasis on doing justice is central to the preaching of the prophets. It is clear from their teaching that to exploit the weak and poor is to commit an offense against God (Prov. 17:5), while to act with fairness and justice toward the poor and oppressed is to love God (Jer. 22:13–16). The same point is made by Jesus in the parable of the Good Samaritan (Luke 10:30ff.). The point, though, is not solely that one *does* justice but that concern for others grows out of charity. Paul teaches in 1 Corinthians 13 that all actions that do not grow out of charity are empty. God's presence in a person is not a mere objective rule that creates a sense of obligation; rather, the presence of God's love within motivates a person to be charitable.[25]

Charity, moreover, is not a mere wishful desire for the well-being of others. Rather, it is a love like that of Jesus, which manifests itself within the structures of society. As Gutierrez explains it,

> Charity is today a "political charity," according to the phrase of Pius XII. Indeed to offer food or drink in our day is a political action; it means the transformation of a society structured to benefit a few who appropriate to themselves the value of the work of others. This transformation ought to be directed toward a radical change in the foundation of society, that is, the private ownership of the means of production.[26]

This statement leads us from the historical dimension of salvation to its necessary correlative, the political dimension.

The Political Dimension of Salvation

The notion of liberation is complex, and we must differentiate three levels of meaning. The first is political and refers to a real and effective political action; the second is utopian and refers to the ideal projection of history; and the third is on the level of faith and refers to the re-creation of the world effected by the work of Christ. Although these levels may be treated as distinct, they are profoundly linked together by salvation, which both destroys the old order and establishes the new. Political action, then, within the context of salvation is the path that human beings cut out of history toward their own future. It runs between the old order and the new.

The political dimension of salvation presupposes sin. Sin, "a break of friendship with God and others,"[27] is a reality within the structures of society. Consequently, as Paul suggests in Romans 8, the whole cosmos suffers as a result of sin. All violence, greed, hate, injustice, suppression, and oppression that occur in society are results of sin. And the creation is struggling to escape this sin, to become liberated into the new order.

Although Christ has freed people and the creation from the bondage of sin, it is now the responsibility of persons who serve Him as Lord of creation, and who are His co-participants in the historical process of redemption, to work toward the realization of salvation. This process begins with a rejection: Humanity is called to reject sin in all its forms. This rejection takes place within the creation as people affirm their own destiny and confront sin, the ultimate root of all injustice and exploitation. Faith, because it looks to the future, recognizes that the confrontation with sin is not vain, for God calls humans to it and assures them of ultimate victory. In this confrontation, history becomes "a thrust into the future." And within this forward movement of history human beings are committed to the creation of a just society and finally to a new humanity.[28]

The gospel is therefore not a merely private faith; it makes a deep social impact on culture. The political nature of the gospel is not a mere appendage but resides at the very heart of its message. Because the gospel proclaims a "new creation," it takes on Israel's hope and gives it its deepest meaning. It reveals the hope of a just society and calls society to follow unexplored paths and open itself to an era of brotherhood and justice, where communion with God and humanity can become a reality. In this way the political dimension of salvation is made a reality through the work of the church in the world.

The Church in the World

The meaning of the church is clear only when it is set within the plan of salvation. Since the work of salvation is a reality that occurs within history, and since the church is an entity within history, an expression of that salvation is to be found within the church.

The church, then, may be defined as the visible sign of God's saving work. It is not something that exists for itself; rather, it exists for others. Its identity, because it is rooted in the work of Christ, is found outside itself in relation to the reality of the kingdom that it announces.

The church therefore has the responsibility to signify in its own internal structure the salvation it announces. It is in that sense a place of liberation. In the church the break with an unjust order occurs; for the church is the people of God who live in a history oriented toward the future promised by Christ. The church's faithfulness to the gospel leaves it no alternative except, as a visible sign of the presence of the Lord, to aspire to liberation in the struggle for a more humane and just society.

The church signifies this liberation in two ways: in the communion celebration and in the creation of brotherhood.

The first task of the church is to celebrate the death and resurrection of Jesus, which accomplished God's saving action in the world. Communion in its original form is celebrated against the background of the Jewish Passover and all that this means in regard to the Israelites' liberation from Egypt. It signifies the passing over from death to life. It points to the liberation from sin and the ultimate communion with God. In this way communion goes to the heart of liberation, for it points to the destruction of sin and beyond to the ultimate communion with God.

This eucharistic celebration is closely linked to the creation of brotherhood. For one thing, communion is celebrated within the context of a meal, a common sign of brotherhood. Therefore, communion points to and is basic to the experience of brotherhood. Brotherhood, as Gutierrez points out, means three things: First, it has to do with the common ownership of goods (Acts 2:44, 4:32); second, it points to the union that Christians experience with Christ through communion (1 Cor. 10:16); and third, it ultimately speaks to the union that Christians have with the Father (1 John 1:6). Consequently, "the basis for brotherhood is full communion with the persons of the Trinity. The bond which unites God and man is celebrated—that is, effectively recalled and proclaimed—in the Eucharist."[29]

Second, the church signifies liberation outside itself in its functions of denunciation and annunciation.

In its denunciation the church must make clear its position toward social injustice. It must undertake, as Gutierrez explains it, "a prophetic *denunciation* of every dehumanizing situation, which is contrary to brotherhood, justice, and liberty. At the same time it must criticize every sacralization of oppressive structures to which the church itself might have contributed."[30] The best way for the church to achieve this is to cast its lot with the oppressed and the exploited in their struggle for a just society, even if this means being critical of itself and of its own economic security—which may contribute to the problem.

The *annunciation* of the gospel consists not so much in words as in living. The church must live what it proclaims. Says Gutierrez, "The annunciation of the gospel thus has a conscienticizing function, or in other words, a politicizing function. But this is made real and meaningful only by living and announcing the gospel from within a commitment to liberation, only in concrete, effective solidarity with people and exploited social classes."[31]

A most significant way in which the church can live its proclamation is in its involvement with the class struggle. Humanity is divided into oppressors and the oppressed. Oppressed people's struggle to be free takes place in the context of the economic, social, political, and cultural realm. The church cannot be neutral to this struggle. Neither can it ignore the class struggle; otherwise it perpetuates the division of society. In the midst of this struggle the church's calling is to lead society toward the eschatological vision of the kingdom. In this way, society will become transformed as the future becomes a present reality.

EVALUATION

The World Council of Churches has shifted away from a liberal social conscience, based on love, to a church-and-world view founded on biblical language and concepts. The influence of Third World liberation theology has pushed the W.C.C. back to the biblical vision of salvation. Clearly, the victory of Christ over the powers of evil, His exalted state as Lord over the powers, and the church as the institution called to actualize Christ's victory in history in anticipation of the eschaton is the image out of which the current W.C.C. paradigm of church and world is constructed.

Although liberation theology is peculiar to Catholic theologies, especially in Latin America, its language and ideas have crossed over into Protestant theology and find expression in the W.C.C. Liberation theology can range all the way from conservative biblical thought to radical thought that uses biblical terminology without a commitment to the orthodox theology that originally stood behind it. In this extreme form, liberation theology must be criticized for at least three reasons.

First, extreme liberation theology tends to place priority on the situation rather than the gospel. This may arise, at least in part, from a Bultmannian hermeneutic. According to Bultmann, early Christian communities were not concerned with the historical event of Jesus which awakened faith, but in the current existential situation of faith itself.

Consequently, extreme liberation theology uses biblical terms mythologically. These liberation theologians regard as a myth the idea of a God with an existence independent from the creation who becomes incarnate and actually lives among men, dies to conquer evil, is raised as a demonstration of God's power over evil, and will return again at the end of history to create a new heaven and a new earth. Although liberation thinkers are willing to use this mythological language with reference to God and Christ, the notion of an ontological Jesus is denied. They believe Jesus' significance is that He shows us the way to God. By His life and actions on behalf of the poor, they say, Jesus reveals how one becomes a son of God. According to this view, His incarnation is not an enfleshment of God, but the total immersion of Jesus in the historical situation of a poor and impoverished people. His death is not a unique victory over the powers of evil, but an actualization of the suffering experienced by God through this identification with the oppressed. In Christ, we are assured that God has entered human history. As we identify with Jesus by giving ourselves to the liberation of the poor and oppressed, God also enters into the process of history and liberation through us.

Orthodox theology differs from this mythical view in that it has always insisted on a theology based, not in a current situation, but in the actual Christ event of the first century. The truth revealed by that event must be applied to current situations of oppressions and exploitation.

Second, the biblical language about salvation is employed in a socioeconomic and political way. Sin is described in terms of inhumanity; and salvation is viewed as the historical process of humanizing inhumanity. Salvation is described as the process of liberating human persons from the structures of existence which cause their inhuman conditions of poverty and oppression. Radical liberation thinkers believe the Bible provides models for the process of salvation in both the Exodus event and the Christ event. They say the struggle for liberation from oppressive socioeconomic and political forces constitute the church's spiritual struggle today, as the church reaches out to embrace the struggle of the world, to take it into its own process, and to bring it to its own redemption. As the church takes the world into itself, the world is evangelized and converted.

Orthodox Christianity is critical of a gospel that is overtly political. Biblical Christianity is political, in the sense that it is rooted in the victory of Christ over the powers of evil. But Christ's victory, rather than being privatized or nationalized, must be applied to all oppressive situations. Extreme liberation thinkers look upon the historic event of Jesus as mythological, and then interpret the present battle with evil as an incarnation of God's struggle to humanize his creation. In this way, they replace biblical truth with the new content of a humanized, politicized gospel.

This process of salvation is identified with the class struggle as defined by Karl Marx. Christians are not meant to explain the world but, as Marx said, "to change it." Thus, liberation theologians categorize each person as the "oppressor" or the "oppressed." However, unlike Marx (who saw all religion as belonging to the oppressors), liberationists see the Christian religion in particular as a mighty sociological force that can resolve the conflict of the oppressed and oppressor. They believe true Christianity, which is modeled on Jesus, chooses to side with the oppressed; it participates in the class struggle, seeking in the name of Jesus to release the poor and the oppressed so as to humanize man's situation and move toward peace and brotherhood. Orthodox theology is critical of the liberationist's orientation to a particular political ideology, because it attempts to put God and the church on that political side. This does not allow the church to be free to be prophetically critical of the political position it supports.

Third, extreme liberation theology writes a new gospel. It is a gospel of orthopraxis, not orthodoxy. Its concern is to practice a Christian faith that releases people from political and economic systems that are destructive of human personhood. But by divorcing itself from orthodoxy, rooted in the historical action of God in Christ, and by attaching itself to the praxis of a Marxist agenda, liberation theology denies connection with the Christian past as well as the Christian view of the future. It uses Christian ideas and terminology to justify righteous action (orthopraxis), without being rooted in historic Christian teaching (orthodoxy).

These criticisms, as I have indicated, cannot be applied equally to all liberationists. Some have a socioeconomic understanding of salvation. Others are quite orthodox in theology and simply employ the language and images of liberation theology.

Regardless of where one stands on the spectrum of liberation thought, it is clear that liberationists are aware of the new demons, especially the socioeconomic and political structures that oppress, dehumanize, and impoverish human people. Rejecting a privatistic faith, they seek to apply the Christian faith as they understand it to these oppressive structures. And this is done using christological concepts and language.[32]

14

THE CATHOLIC RESPONSE

The Protestant image of the Roman Catholic church as an institution intending to rule the world emerged once again in the 1960 election of John F. Kennedy, America's only Roman Catholic president. Residual elements of antagonism toward the medieval Catholic concept of Christendom have died a slow death and are not, as Kennedy's campaign illustrated, buried.

However, in spite of the persistent caricature of Roman world dominance, the documents of the modern Catholic church—including the statements of Vatican II, local synods, and papal writings—demonstrate that the Catholic church has reconsidered its view of church and world. Gone is the quest for Catholic Christendom. In its place is a view of church and world that is significantly in line with the biblical vision of a conquering, reigning, and coming Christ.

In this chapter we will survey some of the most important Catholic writings of recent decades in order to understand the Catholic view of church and world today. We will look first at the "Pastoral Constitution of the Church in the Modern World," the major church-and-society document of Vatican II; then a brief inquiry will be made of church and world thought since Vatican II, followed by a brief examination of *Redemptor Hominis* by Pope John Paul II; and finally we will conclude with an American example of current Roman Catholic thought, the "Pastoral Letter on War and Peace."

PASTORAL CONSTITUTION ON THE CHURCH IN THE MODERN WORLD

The purpose of the "Pastoral Constitution on the Church in the Modern World" is "to set forth the way it understands the presence and function of the church in the world today."[1] The writers define the world as "the whole human family" and the "theatre of human history."[2] They call us to understand the world in the context of the whole Christian vision of reality. This vision, which sweeps from creation to redemption, emphasizes Christ as crucified and risen again "in order to break the stranglehold of the evil one" and to remake man and the world "anew according to God's design."[3]

The special concern of the writers of the "Pastoral Constitution" is to understand the role of the church in the *modern world*. Consequently, the situation of today's world is addressed. They describe our world as characterized by vast social changes, by a "broad upheaval" introducing new "advances in biology, psychology, and the social sciences" which lead persons into "the technical means of molding the lives of whole people."[4] Thus, "the destiny of the human race is viewed as a complete whole, no longer, as it were, in the particular histories of various peoples: Now it merges into a complete whole."[5]

Some of these worldwide changes taking place in the social order are as follows: Traditional structures of local communities have been drastically altered; industrialization has raised some nations to affluence; urbanization has brought more people to the cities; mass media has raised the level of knowledge; and new social relationships have been created by emigration and socialization.[6] Changes have also occurred in attitudes, morals, and religion: Many are falling away from religion; a new kind of humanism is emerging; and in education new world views are being propagated. Furthermore, there are new imbalances in today's world between those who see the world in the old way and those who see it in the new way; new kinds of family tensions are arising out of economic and social changes; and the gap between the rich and the poor has increased.[7] Meanwhile "there is a growing conviction of mankind's ability and duty to strengthen its mastery over nature and of the need to establish a political, social, and economic order at the service of man to assert and develop the dignity proper to individuals and to societies."[8]

In view of these social questions, the Vatican II conferees addressed the issue of church and world in the twentieth century. What does the church have to offer the world of the twentieth century? The council answered this question by addressing four issues: the dignity of the human person; the community of mankind; man's activity in the universe; and finally, the role of the church in the modern world.

First, what does the council say about the dignity of the human person? Human dignity is understood within the traditional categories of creation, fall, and redemption. Man, created in the image of God, was given a responsible rulership over all creation under God. However, because of sin, through which man "lifted himself up against God, and sought to attain his goal apart from," man upset the proper relationship ordered by God. Consequently, man "is divided in himself. As a result, the whole life of men, born individual and social, shows itself to be a struggle, and a dramatic one, between good and evil, between light and darkness."[9]

However, Christ the new man, who is the "image of the invisible God" (Col. 1:15) has restored the image of God in man which had been disfigured by sin. In His work, Christ has freed us "from the bondage of the devil and of sin."[10] He has "risen again, destroying death by his death, and has given life abundantly to us."[11] Consequently, the Christian is bound "by need and by duty to struggle with evil, through many afflictions and to suffer death; but, as one who has been made a partner in the paschal mystery, and as one who has been configured to the death of Christ, he will go forward, strengthened by hope, to the resurrection."[12] Human dignity, then, derives from creation; and, although marred by sin (which accounts for the human condition), human dignity has been restored by the redeeming work of God in Christ.

Second, what does the council teach about the community of mankind? Here the council deals with God's design for society. It is God's desire "that all men should form one family and deal with each other in a spirit of brotherhood."

However, because of sin the social order is often in upheaval. At its deepest level, economic, political, and social tensions "come from selfishness and pride, two things which contaminate the atmosphere of society." Consequently, man "is often turned away from the good and urged to evil by the social environment in which he lives."[13]

However, what God desires for society "is the sum total of social conditions which allow people, either as groups or as individuals, to reach their fulfillment more fully and more easily." For this reason, the social order "must be founded in truth, built on justice, and enlivened by love: it should grow in freedom towards a more humane equilibrium."[14]

This vision of society demands that all people are called to have respect for the human person, respect and love for enemies, and seek for the essential equality of all men through social justice. "Excessive economic and social disparity between individuals and peoples of the one human race is a source of scandal and militates against social justice, equity, human dignity, as well as social and international peace."[15] Consequently, the bishops call people to transcend an individualistic morality and to act as responsible citizens, participating in the local, national, and world communities. This vision of a world society of interdependent people living in mutual support is rooted in the work of Jesus Christ. In His life He sanctified human life in society, and by His death and resurrection He brought forth a "new brotherly communion . . . in which everyone as members one of the other would render mutual service in the measure of the different gifts bestowed on each."[16] This community is called to be a sign to society of the future community of humankind, a sign by which the world ought to live now.

Next, the council addressed man's activity in the universe. Here the bishops acknowledge the difficulty of fulfilling God's vision for the universe because all human activity is infected by sin. Consequently, values are disordered, evil is present in all things, and people are selfishly concerned only for their own things. But how are we as Christians to function within this distortion of society, this negation of God's vision? The council declares, "The whole of man's history has been the story of our combat with the powers of evil." Consequently, the bishops call Christians to obey the injunction of Paul, "Do not be conformed to this world" (Rom. 12:2 RSV). "World," the bishops state, "means a spirit of vanity and malice whereby human activity from being ordered to the service of God and man is distorted to an instrument of sin."[17]

However, the Christian does not stand against the "world" alone. For the Word of God "entered world history taking that history into himself and recapitulating it."[18] Therefore, the Christian who sees the world through the Christ event is inspired by the vision of a transformed world. The Christian knows that "the effort to establish a universal brotherhood will not be in vain"[19] because God is now preparing "a new earth in which righteousness dwells."[20] This hope in no way diminishes our concern to develop the earth but spurs us on "for it is here that the body of a new family grows, foreshadowing in some way the age which is to come . . . here on earth the kingdom is mysteriously present; when the Lord comes, it will enter into its perfection."[21]

Finally, against this background of human dignity, the community of all peoples, and human activity in the world, the bishops addressed the crucial question of the role of the church in the modern world. The church, which finds its origins in the work of Christ, "has a saving and eschatological purpose which can be fully attained only in the next life."[22] However, since it travels the same journey through history with all other peoples, its relationship to the world and history demands our attention as these words show:

> That the earthly and the heavenly city penetrate one another is a fact open only to the eyes of faith; moreover, it will remain the mystery of human history, which will be harassed by sin until the perfect revelation of the splendor of the sons of God. In pursuing its own salvific purpose, not only does the Church communicate divine life to men but in a certain sense it casts the reflected light of that divine life over all the earth, notably in the way it heals and elevates the dignity of the human person, in the way it consolidates society, and endows the daily activity of men with a deeper sense and meaning. The Church, then, believes it can contribute much to humanizing the family of man and its history through each of its members and its community as a whole.[23]

Specifically, the role of the church is directed toward the individual, toward society, and toward human activity.

What it does for the individual is this: It opens up the

mystery of God and thus brings people to the meaning of existence; it raises the dignity and freedom of the human person because the gospel rejects all bondage resulting from sin; and it proclaims the rights of man.[24]

What the church does for society is equally significant. The church does not seek control over "the political, economic, or social order." Rather, it provides the "source of commitment, direction, and vigor to establish and consolidate the community of men according to the law of God." It therefore fosters the good acts as a sign of unity and promotes "effective living of faith and love." Further, since the church is "not committed to any one culture or to any political, economic or social system" it can call upon all people to put away conflict between nations and races.[25]

The church also makes a significant contribution to human activity through its various members. It exhorts its members to "perform their duties faithfully in the spirit of the gospel."[26] Further, it is their "task to cultivate a properly informed conscience and to impress the divine law on the affairs of the earthly city."[27]

In all this the church is "a sign of salvation in the world"[28] for it has but one sole purpose—"that the kingdom of God may come and the salvation of the human race may be accomplished."[29]

In this document one can observe the predominance of a christological approach to the church-and-world issue. Central to the Roman Catholic vision is the work of Christ through which sin and the Devil have been conquered. And now the church carries on the work of Christ in the world as it lives toward the eschaton. The application of this vision to the various structures of existence is made more clear in the documents after Vatican II.

CHURCH-AND-WORLD THOUGHT
SINCE VATICAN II

The theme of Catholic thinking on the church and the world since Vatican II is captured by Father James S. Rausch, the general secretary of the U.S. Catholic Conference, in his forward to *The Gospel of Peace and Justice: Catholic Social Teaching Since Pope John.* He writes of "a new awareness that it is an essential part of the Christian mission to humanize and thereby Christianize political, social, economic, cultural, and technological life. The 'church' and the 'world' are not identical, but neither are they in irrevocable opposition. For while the 'church' transcends the 'world,' it also exists in the world. Existing there, it has a duty to seek to transform the world according to the mind and message of Christ."[30]

An example of the church's seeking to transform the world through the mind and message of Christ is found in the address of Pope Paul VI to the United Nations in October of 1965. In this speech, Paul VI appealed for a cessation of military build-up by the nations and called upon the nations of the world to adopt the principle of disarmament. The real danger for the future of world history, he pressed, is not in progress nor science but in "man himself, wielding even more powerful instruments, which can be employed equally well for destruction or for the loftiest conquests."[31] His appeal acknowledges that science and technology may be used toward either good or evil ends.

However, it was at the Second General Conference of Latin American Bishops in the summer of 1968 in Bogotá and Medellín, Colombia, where the theological principles for church and world as set forth in the documents of Vatican II were most clearly applied. This conference, which brought the Third World to the attention of the Roman Catholic church, addressed the subjects of justice, peace, family and demography, and the poverty of the church.

The document on "Justice" has as its beginning a section entitled "Doctrinal Bases." This introductory section declares that social justice is rooted, not in natural law, but in the work of Christ. The same God who created "sends His son in the flesh, so that He might come to liberate all men from the slavery to which sin has subjected them: hunger, misery, oppression and ignorance, in a word, that injustice and hatred which have their origin in human selfishness."[32]

The starting point for structural change which will achieve justice is not change in itself but personal conversion. The central message of the Christian gospel "does not so much consist in the affirmation of the necessity for structural change, as it does in the insistence on the conversion of men which will in turn bring about this change." The new person is "created in Christ Jesus," fashioned in Him as a "new creature." This is a profound transformation which compels the newly converted person "to seek out a new, more profound relationship with God, his fellow man, and created things."[33] The motivating factor of this new life is love, which is the key not only to human perfection but to the transformation of the world.

The church plays a central role in the transformation of the structures that perpetuate injustice, for the church is the context in which this new human family is growing. In the past the church separated the sacred and the profane; but now the church seeks to contribute "to the better ordering of human society," which in itself is "of vital concern to the Kingdom of God." In this way the church serves the purposes of God in history. It is like a light in society which "elevates the dignity of the human person," "consolidates the unity of society," and "gives a more profound reason and meaning to all human activity."[34]

It is generally recognized that the Medellín documents represent a Catholic liberation perspective. Again, it should be acknowledged that this liberation language may be understood either in a christological and conservative manner or in a mythological way that is linked with the Marxist critique of society. The extreme element of liberation theology expressed by the Medellín Conference has come under severe attack in the Roman church. The most extreme exponents of liberation theology use it to link the Catholic teaching on Christian charity with the dictators of the Marxist class struggle. In making this union between Christianity and Marxism, the gospel and the church are politicized, for they are put into the service of political revolution. For example, some charge the Roman Catholic church in Nicaragua with complicity with Marxism in the overthrow of dictator Anastasio Somoza Debayle and the establishment of the Sandinista government in 1979.

This fusion of the church with political revolution has prompted Pope John Paul II to call upon priests around the world to withdraw from political involvement. His argument is that the church must be free of political ideologies in order to do its prophetic work which points to a kingdom of a higher order. Nevertheless, Pope John Paul II is the most socially minded Pope of this century, calling constantly for the church to serve the poor. The source of his vision is not Marxism connected with Jesus as a religious symbol, but Jesus Christ as the literal conqueror of sin and the dominion of the Devil, and the church as the present agent of that message in today's world.

Pope John Paul II

Since there are several different interpretations of Vatican II within the Catholic church, it is (as we have seen) difficult to set forth a single view of Catholic thought. Nevertheless, we may point with confidence to papal teaching as representing a main, if not the main current of thought among Catholics. One of the best examples of the thought of Pope John Paul II on the relationship between church and world is found in his work *Redemptor Hominis*, written in 1979.

In this work, the pope affirms the Christian vision of a redeemed cosmos. For him, salvation extends beyond the individual to include the whole of the created order. In "Jesus Christ," he argues, "the visible world which God created for man—the world that, when sin entered, 'was subjected to futility'—recovers again its original link with the divine source of wisdom and love."[35]

The foci from which this cosmic redemption is understood is the mystery of the incarnation, death, and resurrection of Jesus Christ. Christ became one with us in order to redeem us. As Pope John Paul II says, "by his incarnation, he, the Son of God, *in a certain way united himself with each man.*"[36] In this union with man, Christ revealed the "tremendous mystery of love in which the self-giving act of Jesus is found renewed."[37] Here in the self-giving act of Jesus is found that love which is the fullness of justice. In an encounter with this love, man perceives what it means to be man and, by entering into the Incarnation and redemption, man is restored to his original purpose. This is the mystery of faith which "vivifies every aspect of authentic humanism."[38] In this event there is a definitive restoration of the dignity of man and a recovery of the meaning of his life in the world.[39]

The relationship of the church to the world is rooted, therefore, in the Christ event and in the rediscovery through that event of man's place in the world. The church begins its task in the world "by enabling that union to be brought about and renewed continually. The church wishes to serve this single end: that each person may be able to find Christ, in order that Christ may walk with each person the path of life, with the power of the truth about man and the world that is contained in the mystery of the Incarnation and the Redemption and with the power of the love that is radiated by that truth."[40] However, since this union with Christ in the church does not take place in isolation from the cultural situation of the world, it must relate to the historical process, to the "spheres of various systems, ideological concepts of the world and regimes,"[41] and must, in that particular context make life "more human." Nevertheless, the pope insists that the process by which the church humanizes the structures of existence "must avoid collusion with the ideologies of the world." He quotes from the council's "Pastoral Constitution," reminding his readers that the church "must in no way be confused with the political community, nor bound to any political system."[42]

Pope John Paul II does not see the church living in isolation from the world, but in redemptive relationship. For the church, which carries on the mission of Christ in the world, does so in a salvific way, making "human life ever more human."[43] This work of the church is accomplished negatively as the church is "aware of all that is opposed to that process,"[44] seeking at the same time to establish the vision of the future in the present. This is why "the church of our time—a time particularly hungry for the spirit, because it is hungry for justice, peace, love, goodness, fortitude, responsibility, and human dignity—must concentrate and gather around that mystery, finding in it the light and the strength that are indispensable for their mission."[45] But this concern for the world which finds its rootage in the Christ event also looks forward to the consummation, for it is aware of man's "destination to grace and glory."[46] Consequently, the church understands its present mission in the world from both the past and the future. Thus God's people, the church, serve the salvation of the world through their vocational callings in which they exercise the kingly work of Jesus through servanthood in the world.[47]

An Example: A Pastoral Letter on War and Peace

A good example of the application of Catholic teaching on church and world is found in the 1983 "Pastoral Letter on War and Peace," drafted by the American bishops. My concern in evaluating this document is not with its specific teaching regarding nuclear war and disarmament, but rather to probe the theological framework in which the teaching is set.

The bishops place their teaching regarding peace within the universally accepted biblical world view. Early in the document the writers state "the biblical vision of the world, created and sustained by God, scarred by sin, redeemed in Christ and destined for the kingdom, is at the heart of our religious heritage."[48] This overarching concept of redemption is cosmic, extending beyond individual persons to include the redemption of the whole world.

The focal point of this vision is christological, rooted not only in the person and work of Christ but also in His lordship over the creation. The document states, "Jesus Christ, then, is our peace, and in his death-resurrection he gives God's peace to our world. In him God has indeed reconciled the world, made it one, and has manifested definitively that his will is this reconciliation."[49] The resurrection of Jesus is "the sign to the world that God indeed does reign."[50] Consequently, his speech flows from his reign which is "the reconciliation of the world and God (Rom. 5:1–2; Col 1:20); the restoration of the unity and harmony of all creation."[51] This power of God through the reign of Christ was experienced by the early Christians, who looked forward with "unshakeable confidence to the time when the fullness of God's reign would make itself known in the world."[52]

The ecclesiology evident in this document also stands in the tradition of the thought expressed in Vatican II. The church is seen as an extension of Christ's presence in the world. It is "in a unique way, the instrument of the Kingdom of God in history."[53] In the church one sees both the divine and human side of reality, for God works through the church to accomplish His purposes in history, yet the work of the church is carried out by God's people. And this work, at least in part, is the mission of making the peace of the kingdom more visible.[54]

The role of the church in making the kingdom visible has eschatological meaning. It points to "God's promise of a final salvation involving all peoples and all creation and of an ultimate reign of peace."[55] The immediate implication of this eschatological hope has to do with history. History is an "advance toward maturity,"[56] a movement toward the eschatological hope of the church, the sure and total reign of Christ over His entire creation. The fullness of this eschatological hope for peace lies before us, yet we already have the gift of God's peace within us through the reconciliation provided by Jesus Christ.[57] Consequently, the "Christian understanding of history is hopeful and confident but also sober and realistic."[58] Any dream of a society that is totally peaceful is an unattainable utopia because of the presence of sin and human weakness that cannot be eradicated until the consummation.[59]

The presence of sin which thwarts the efforts of the church to fulfill God's peace on earth now drives the bishops to acknowledge that Christians are now "called to live in the tension between the vision of the reign of God and its concrete realization in history." The bishops add, "We already live in the grace of the kingdom, but it is not yet the completed kingdom."[60]

EVALUATION

It is most significant that the Roman Catholic social thought as expressed in these documents appears to be shifting from its former basis in natural law to an understanding of church and world in a more christological framework.[61] The dignity of the human person, the value of work, the social order, and the human community are frequently referred to and understood within this Christ-centered doctrine of both church and world. Central to this christological vision is the victory of Christ over the powers, the church as the instrument of the kingdom, and the eschatological hope that looks for the ultimate destruction of the powers of evil and to the restoration of the entire created order. It is certain that some interpret this christological vision in terms of a radical liberation theology while others try to ally it with the politics of the left. Nevertheless, in the opinion of this author, the central Catholic view is the christological vision as enunciated by the pope.

Contemporary Catholic teaching on church and world, as evidenced in the documents evaluated above, rejects the privatism of faith which the process of secularization has imposed upon the Christian religion. It calls for a faith that addresses the whole spectrum of human and world issues, it wrestles with the "new demons," and it seeks to apply the christological vision of church and world to the turbulent issues of our modern world.

15

THE RELIGIOUS RIGHT

The process of secularization has brought Western society from the church-dominated culture of medieval Europe to the pluralistic conditions of the twentieth century. And now a humanistic and materialistic concept of the universe prevails, not only in atheistic communism but also in many nominally Christian democratic nations.

Atheistic humanism, the plague of the West, has been expressed in the *Humanist Manifesto* of 1933, but more recently in *A Secular Humanist Declaration* of 1980. The fundamental premise of these documents is that the universe exists in isolation, changing in accordance with the theory of materialistic evolution. Consequently, humanists argue that the nature of the universe makes unacceptable any supernatural or cosmic basis for human values.[1] This viewpoint finds contemporary expression in the decline of moral absolutes and the emergence of moral relativity.

An alarm against the decline of human values in the West was set off by Aleksandr Solzhenitsyn in the now famous speech at the Harvard University commencement of 1978. Solzhenitsyn spoke of a "tilt of freedom toward evil" which stems from "a humanistic and benevolent concept according to which man—the master of this world—does not bear any evil within himself, and all the defeats of life are caused by misguided social systems, which must therefore be corrected."[2] Consequently, Solzhenitsyn said, this humanistic way of thinking has resulted in "a total emancipation . . . from the moral heritage of Christian centuries."[3]

Since 1978 a number of fundamentalists and converted liberals have taken up the gauntlet against this modern humanistic spirit and the demise of religious values in the West. The purpose of this section is to summarize this response. To do so, we will look at the teachings of select religious leaders who have opposed secularism. Then we will comment on civil religion, an approach to church and state which is also being used to offer resistance to secularism.

JERRY FALWELL AND THE MORAL MAJORITY

In 1979 Jerry Falwell, pastor of the influential Thomas Road Baptist Church of Lynchburg, Virginia, and director of the popular television program "The Old Time Gospel Hour," expanded his ministry by founding an organization called The Moral Majority. The purpose of this organization as stated in its early literature was to confront secularism, restore moral sanity to America, and save the United States. In an early letter announcing the formation of the Moral Majority, the following question is asked: "Is our grand old flag going down the drain?" The answer given is that "you may wake up some morning and discover that Old Glory is no longer waving freely." Falwell announced that he was called to "go into the halls of Congress and fight for laws that will protect the grand old flag." These laws, as outlined in the letter, pertained to "abortion, pornography, homosexuality, school prayers and military strength."[4]

Falwell's agenda was more completely set forth in the 1980 publication of *Listen America*, a book which blended old-fashioned Americanism and the old-time religion to build a new coalition against the breakdown of both religion and country.

First, in *Listen America* Falwell expressed concern over the demise of moral values. Various chapters address the breakdown of the family, children's rights, the feminist movement, abortion and the right to life movement, violence and immorality on television, the availability of pornography, the demise of educational standards, the low moral tone of contemporary music, and the prevalence of drugs and alcohol. Regarding these conditions, Falwell proclaimed:

> It is time that we faced reality. We are in trouble as a nation. We are very quickly moving toward an amoral society where nothing is either absolutely right or absolutely wrong. Our absolutes are disappearing, and with this disappearance we must face the sad fact that our society is crumbling. . . .
>
> I cannot keep silent about the sins that are destroying the moral fiber of our nation.[5]

Second, in *Listen America* Falwell expressed an equal concern over the decline of American prestige and military might. Addressing these issues throughout the book, he frequently cited the communist ideology as a danger and threat to the American way of life. For example, he claimed that "The United States is for the first time, in my lifetime, and probably in the lifetime of my parents and grandparents, no longer the military might of the world."[6] Later in the book he argued that

> the Soviets have always had only one goal, and that is to destroy capitalistic society. They are a nation committed to communism and to destroying the American way of life. Because of the overwhelming conventional and nuclear strength of the Soviet Union, it is now possible that the Soviet Government could demand our capitulation. Our unwillingness to pay the price of a nuclear conflict could well force our leadership into lowering our flag and surrendering the American people to the will of the Communist Party in Moscow. There has never been a time in our history when such a condition existed.[7]

Finally, these two themes of morality and the demise of American prestige were knit together in a seamless robe of religious patriotism, as this quote demonstrates:

> I do not believe that America will be turned around solely by working in the areas of politics, economics, and defense, as important as these may be. These are crucial issues that face us in the 1980's, but America can only be turned around as her people make godly, moral choices. When history records these ten years, I think it will be fair to project that this will have probably been, since the days

of the American Revolution, the most important decade this nation has known. This is a grave statement because I believe that the outcome of how we stand as a free people at the end of this decade will depend upon the moral decisions we as a people make in the very near future.[8]

Falwell poses an answer to the twin problems of the decline of morality and the decline of America in his chapter, "A Biblical Plan of Action." He suggests change will come when God's people learn to be humble: "We must acknowledge that we are not deserving of God's favor. We must realize that we are totally inadequate to deal with the sins of our own lives, let alone those of an entire nation. We must acknowledge that we are utterly dependent upon God and his grace to deliver us."[9] Further change is dependent upon prayers. "We must lay aside our pious and structured prayers in order to beseech the God of heaven to have mercy on us."[10] Third, Falwell says we must learn to seek the face of God. Principally, this step consists of a willingness "to give up ourselves as the measure of all things, and acknowledge that He alone is the measure of truth."[11] And finally, Falwell says that if we want to see a true revolution in morality and a national restoration, God's people must turn from their wicked ways and confess not only their own sins but also the sins of the nation. America was "founded upon Christian principles," and "we have enjoyed a unique relationship toward God because of that foundation."[12] Thus, Falwell is convinced that we need to experience a true biblical confession of sin and not some superficial acknowledgment of wrongdoing. These biblical steps will then lead Christian people into a groundswell of moral leadership in their private lives, in their homes, in their local areas, and ultimately in the nation. In this way, the secularization of human values will be addressed and the nation will simultaneously be made stronger.

This blend of Americanism and conservative religion is a fundamental theme of the religious right and is found in their best-selling literature. For example, Tim LaHaye in *The Battle for the Mind* wrote:

> Admittedly, many considered America a Christian nation, until the humanists took over the major spheres of influence forty years ago and began to change all of our time-honored moral values. . . . The last six command-

ments of the Decalogue, dealing with man's treatment of his fellowman, and the civil laws of the Old Testament formed the basis for our laws and our Constitution. . . . Our unique check-and-balance system of government would never have been conceived by humanism. It is borrowed directly from Scripture.

Today the humanists ridicule the Puritan work ethic, free enterprise, private ownership of land, and capitalism—even though these concepts, which emanated from biblical teaching, have produced the greatest good for the largest number of people in history. We discard them at our national peril, for a free and healthy economy thrives best on a moral foundation that engenders trust and faith in one's fellowman. Because of the biblical base of most Americans' thinking, this faith was common as our laws were formulated.[13]

The same theme is set forth by Francis Schaeffer who, in the decade of the late seventies and early eighties, increasingly voiced the opinion of the religious right. In *A Christian Manifesto*, he argued that "this linkage of Christian thinking and the concepts of government were not incidental but fundamental."[14] Quoting William Penn, "If we are not governed by God, then we will be ruled by tyrants," Schaeffer comments:

This consensus was as natural as breathing in the United States at that time. We must not forget that many of those who came to America from Europe came for religious purposes. As they arrived, most of them established their own individual civil governments based upon the Bible. It is, therefore, totally foreign to the basic nature of America at the time of the writing of the Constitution to argue a separation doctrine that implies a secular state.[15]

Others in the movement present the relationship between America and religion in terms of "manifest destiny," assuming that God actually brought America into existence as part of His redemptive purpose. For example, Peter Marshall and David Manuel in *The Light and the Glory* compare America to Israel and ask:

What if, in addition to the intimate relationship with the individual through Jesus Christ the Saviour, God continued to deal with nations corporately, as He had throughout Old Testament history? What if, in particular,

He had a plan for those He would bring to America, a plan which saw this continent as the stage for a new act in the drama of mankind's redemption? Could it be that we Americans, as a people, were meant to be a "light to lighten the Gentiles" (Luke 2:32)—a demonstration to the world of how God intended His children to live together under the Lordship of Christ? Was our vast divergence from this blueprint, after such a promising beginning, the reason why we now seem to be heading into a new dark age?[16]

EVALUATION

In previous chapters the evaluation of the movement being considered has appeared at the end. However, since two different movements from the religious right are being considered in this section, and since the evaluation of each is different, the pattern will be broken and an evaluation of the Moral Majority will be given now. First, a theological evaluation.

The most penetrating theological analysis of the pros and cons of the Moral Majority is set forth by Gabriel Fackre in his book, *The Religious Right and Christian Faith*. His concern is to analyze their doctrinal views on "the nature of God, the state of human nature, the meaning of incarnation and atonement, the purpose of the church, and strong convictions about personal salvation in the world and the world to come."[17] His argument is that the biblical vision of reality is in fact the underlying presupposition of the Moral Majority, but that this vision has been so acculturated by secular humanism that it has been greatly modified. Several examples will suffice to illustrate this thesis.

The classical teaching on creation has been in the context of the purposes and plan of God to bring His creation together in communion with Him. The effort on the part of the religious right to turn the biblical account of creation into a doctrine of "how and when" is "to fuse secular cosmology . . . with fundamental affirmations of the Christian faith."[18] Consequently, "an 'ism'—creationism—is substituted for the classical Christian doctrine of creation."[19]

Biblical realism about the Fall, as it affects every human being, is denied. This may be seen for example in the quest for Christian politicians to run the government or the emergence of the "mighty men" in business and education, men in whom confidence can be placed because of moral uprightness. Fackre suggests that "to all intents and purposes the doctrine of universal sin is abandoned. The dividing line which the religious right draws in its explicit theology between all sinners in their fallen state and God the righteous judge is moved: It becomes the line between the morally upright and the immorally fallen. The human problem is no longer the controversy God has with the rebellious race as a whole, but the controversy the Moral Majority has with the immoral majority."[20]

Fackre faults the Moral Majority for placing too much emphasis on America as a covenantal community. It is true, he would argue, that the United States "shares with all peoples the universal covenants of Adam and Noah, and a status and role in the order of preservation." But it is a great departure from Christian doctrine to transfer the "status of special covenant from the elect of God in the particular history of Israel to another people. . . . Here the human constructs of a right-wing political philosophy are substituted for sound doctrine."[21]

In terms of the atonement the Moral Majority stands in line with the classical Western emphasis on the need to satisfy the holiness of God. However, since God satisfied His own holiness because of His love, the motif of compassion is equally as strong as that of holiness in the classical tradition. Consequently, any application of the gospel to political and economic issues must express God's compassion as well as demand holiness. The compassion of God brings into question the world's view of power and emphasizes the power of powerlessness. In this light, the "machismo philosophy of the religious right is a worldly point of view, expressing a secular humanism which sets itself against 'the weakness of God [which] is stronger than men' (1 Cor. 1:25)."[22]

With regard to the doctrine of the church, Fackre criticizes the way in which the religious right politicizes the church toward the political right. (However, it should be noted that the church on the left is guilty of politicizing the church toward the political left). A matter of deep concern is the control exercised by the fundamentalist pastor and leaders of the church over the political life of its members. The political piety of the religious right "entails loyalty to the church and/or pastor's views on 'Christian issues.' "[23]

Unfortunately, salvation is often also politicized. The language of salvation is rightly broadened beyond the individual; but instead of referring to the salvation of the entire cosmos, it is particularized into a national salvation. All too often "the goal of the Religious Right is to save the United States—or, more exactly, to pray and work for God so that he might save it—from internal decadence and the external threat of Communism."[24]

Finally, the consummation of time, rather than an experienced hope in the midst of history, is turned into a timetable of current historical events which are somewhat predictable and always imminent.[25]

What is being argued here is that Christian truths are essential to the ideology of the religious right. But these truths—creation, sin, redemption, church, and consummation—have been interpreted in a way that lends support to the special role of America in fighting communism and strengthening freedom, democracy, and morality. This amalgamation of Christian and political themes has resulted in a message that both politicizes the gospel and Christianizes America.

Second, the Moral Majority may be criticized from a more practical standpoint. It has as its underlying thesis the proposition that America was founded as a Christian nation with a special destiny. This special destiny is not unlike that articulated by John Winthrop and others who came to this country in the early part of the seventeenth century. They were convinced that God had sent them on an errand, that they were to become a "city set on a hill," that the eyes of the world would be upon them. According to the religious right, America has failed to attain its religious destiny and thus has made a mockery of God. They believe it is necessary to recover America's religious calling by summoning the nation to repentance, restoring national morality, and making America strong again. What lies beneath this vision for America is the biblical framework of creation, fall, and redemption: God called America into being (creation); America has fallen away from God (fall); and America must be restored (redemption).

This fundamentalist thesis results in six questionable perspectives:

First, it ascribes to the nation of America what Scripture ascribes to the church. The apostle Paul sets forth in the Book of Ephesians the thesis that the church has been called of God to speak to the powers of evil: "His intent was that now, through the church, the manifold wisdom of God should be made known to the rulers and authorities . . . " (Eph. 3:10). The New Testament theology of the church is that it is a continuation of Israel, that it (and not America or another particular nation) is the focus of God's activity in the world.

Second, the thesis that America is God's chosen nation weds the conservative branch of the church to the political right. Throughout American history, political movements have sought religious sanction. In the 1930s the political policies of Franklin Delano Roosevelt sought the sanction of the liberal religious community. Liberal politics and the social gospel supported one another because their goals were nearly the same. The demise of liberal politics in the late 1970s also brought about the demise of liberal theology. Meanwhile the rising political powers on the right sought and obtained sanction for their policies from the religious right. The consequence of the church's alignment with either the political left or the political right is the same: It is rendered ineffective as a prophetic voice to the political system to which it is attached.

Third, the thesis of a religious America baptizes Americanism and politicizes the church. It gives America a religious veneer and the church a political character. America is thought to be the center of God's activity in the world and the church is supposed to become a political power base, a special agent of capitalist economics, a champion of Western liberty, and a defender of messianic Americanism. Thus the church and the gospel are made the servants of a particular ideology.

The view that America is a religious country baptizes the American economic system of free enterprise. The religious right argues that the free enterprise system is clearly outlined in the Book of Proverbs; that Christ made the capitalist work ethic part of His plan for mankind; that ambitious business management is also part of a Christian's calling in this world. In this way, the message of the gospel is secularized and turned into an agenda for wealth and prosperity.

Fifth, to view America in religious terms lends itself to the support of militarization. The argument is made that, since this is God's country, the base from which God's work is conducted in the world, we must do all we can to maintain its freedom and strength. To let America collapse is to open the doors to the worldwide powers of evil represented by communism.

Finally, the religious American thesis lends itself to the assumption that the church must act as a political lobby to legislate Christian morality in the public sector. The logic follows: God's country must act as God's country. Its laws and way of life must reflect its favored position with God. Consequently, the legislation of prayer in the schools, the teaching of divine creation in the public schools, and legislation against abortion are laws which, if enacted, would strengthen America's religious stance and bring God's approval.

These assertions ignore several basic facts of Western civilization. First, while they acknowledge the secularization of the Western world, the members of the religious right still hold as their ideal the Constantinian model of church-state relationships. Their political action is therefore based on the supposition that it is the responsibility of the state to Christianize the world. This is in sharp contradiction to the religious freedom that has always been a "given" of American life.

Second, the idea of a Christian America ignores the pluralism of the United States and the entire Western world. But both of these facts—secularism and pluralism—need to be seen in the larger context of history and theology. Historically, our times are more akin to the first three centuries of the Christian era than to the Constantinian era. And the christological model of church-state relationships affirms that Christ is already Lord of the universe, and thus of all structures of existence. The work of the church is not to rule over the world, but to proclaim Christ's lordship and witness to it through the prophetic and priestly ministry of the church.

In brief, the criticism that may be leveled against the religious right is that it fails to have a vision of church and world that is truly biblical. Nevertheless, the Christian commitment and the concern for America which arises out of a sincere and zealous heart cannot be faulted.

RICHARD NEUHAUS AND
VARIOUS ORGANIZATIONS

Richard John Neuhaus is an ordained minister in the Lutheran Church, past editor of *Worldview*, and currently the director of The Center on Religion and Society in New York. Through his writing and speaking, his influence has grown significantly since the early 1970s. Recently, with the publication of his book, *The Naked Public Square*,[26] he has emerged as a major spokesman for an intellectually sophisticated concept of the relationship between the Christian faith and America's role in world leadership. Other organizations such as The Ethics and Public Policy Center and The Institute on Religion and Democracy, both headquartered in Washington, D.C., are deeply influenced by his ideas. While these groups do not have the media visibility of the Moral Majority, they are nevertheless highly influential in government circles and among Christian leaders. Their point of view deserves careful attention.

Richard Neuhaus and his colleagues must be distinguished from the Moral Majority. These people do not represent a sophisticated Moral-Majority-like view, as some may want to argue. Nevertheless, they do share some of the concerns articulated by the Moral Majority and, for this reason, are sometimes confused with them. The first order of their argument is found in the conviction that we live in an age of secularism. "It cannot be denied," claims Neuhaus, "that the variant called *secular* humanism has had a pervasive and debilitating effect upon our public life. Without ever having to put them to a vote, without even subjecting them to democratic debate, some of the key arguments of what is properly called secular*ism* have prevailed."[27] Since it is acknowledged that secular*ism* pushes religion into the state of privatism and disallows its presence in public matters, Neuhaus (like the members of the Moral Majority) argues for the return of religion in public life. He does so with a recognition that liberal Protestantism has always argued for the presence of religious conviction in public issues and now ought not to change its mind, simply because it is not sympathetic to the particular public issues addressed by the Moral Majority:

By asserting the public nature of its truth claims, however, fundamentalism serves notice that it is not content to confine itself to the privatized sphere of religion. Those of us in the ecumenical churches who have traditionally railed against the bifurcation of the sacred from the secular and who have insisted that religion cannot remain captive to the personal or private sphere should not now reverse field and charge that fundamentalism's public assertiveness is an assault upon democratic pluralism. Such a reversal would put us in subordinated alliance with secularist proponents of the very privatization of religion that we have rightly criticized.[28]

The current assumption that America is a secular society and that religion has no place in the determination of public policy, public values, and public morality is the attitude that creates what Neuhaus appropriately terms the "naked public square." The presupposition that stands behind this naked public square is the "exclusion of particularist religious and moral belief from public discourse."[29] Unfortunately, the naked public square does not remain naked, for "when the value-bearing institutions of religion and culture are excluded, the value-laden concerns of human life flow back into the square under the banner of politics."[30] Since politics has to fill the void left by the absence of religious values, the result is that society moves "toward the state-as-church, toward totalitarianism. And again, the available form of totalitarianism—an aggressively available form, so to speak—is Marxist-Leninism."[31] Consequently, claims Neuhaus, "we have a deep stake in reconstructing a politics that was not begun by and cannot be sustained by the myth of secular America."[32]

The clue to Neuhaus's answer to secular humanism in America (and the West in general) is to recover the religious basis for the American vision which lies in the Judeo-Christian heritage. "The intention," he claims, "is to restore the role of religion in helping to give moral definition and direction to American public life and policy."[33] This direction derives from the religious leadership—not a partisan leadership of the left or right, but one that is dedicated to reconstructing a "sacred canopy" for the American experiment.[34] It is similar to the leadership of the past, that religious leadership which gave America a sense of its religious destiny. So Neuhaus writes:

Historically, mainline Protestantism in America provided that kind of vision of an experimental and exemplary America. However it was expressed, the confidence was that America had a meaning within the larger purposes of God in world-historical change. One way of expressing it was to say that America has been 'elected' by God. Abraham Lincoln, who has rightly been celebrated as the foremost theologian of the American experiment, talked about America as an 'almost chosen' people. Today most of us eschew the notion of chosenness or election altogether. Such language is condemned as reflecting an unseemly and dangerous hubris—an overweening historical pride that, if acted upon, invites certain destruction. The 'lessons of history' have presumably taught us that there is nothing all that special about America. Sometimes this insight is pressed and twisted into what might be called a reverse election. That is, it is argued that America is indeed singular, but singular in the sense of being the prime source of the world's sundry miseries.[35]

Neuhaus wants a religion at the heart of the state and society that will bring "moral earnestness and theological authority to the task of redefining America and its role in God's purposes."[36] He does not ask that this commitment supplant or change Christian commitment to the vision of God's kingdom, but that because we are also committed to humankind in general, we exercise through America that commitment which has the good of the world in mind. This commitment would include "a devotion to liberal democracy, a near obsession with civil liberties, a relatively open market economy, the aspiration toward equality of opportunity, a commitment to an institutionalized balancing of powers and countervailing forces, and a readiness to defend this kind of social experiment, if necessary, by military force."[37]

The commitment described above can only derive from the conviction that "on balance and considering the alternatives, the influence of the United States is a force for good in the world."[38] This proposition is a "kind of litmus test,"[39] one which accepts with "moral earnestness our citizenship in America."[40] However, such an agreement will put America "under God" again and provide a "transcendent point of reference," a reference point from which secularism may be addressed and conquered.

While Neuhaus's concern to find a religious base for

America and its future in the world is commendable, one problem must be posed from a strictly Christian perspective. His proposal, brilliant as it is, raises the specter of a civil religion. In Neuhaus's view, the nation of America is not only under the sovereign power of God but appears to be a special product of God's election. For example, he asserts that democracy finds its historical roots in biblical religion,[41] and the American enterprise is derived from biblical faith,[42] as is both private and public morality.[43] Consequently, America has a chosen destiny toward the whole world, acting as a global force for good. Unfortunately, such an assertion tends to supplant the role of the church in the world with the role of America in the world, confusing church and nation, blending them together in one patriotic and religious whole, a kind of civil religion. Nevertheless, one must acknowledge that Neuhaus has addressed a particularly difficult issue—the relationship between one's commitment to a Christian vision of reality and one's commitment as a citizen of America to its vision of democracy and freedom. This is a matter which ought not to be avoided, a matter which both the Moral Majority and Richard Neuhaus raise for our continued discussion and thought.

Since the specter of civil religion is raised both by the Moral Majority and Richard Neuhaus, a brief excursion into civil religion is in order.

CIVIL RELIGION

A central motif of civil religion is that it does not recognize a tension between the church and the world. The church sees the role of the nation in the world as a role ordained by God. Therefore, the church tends to support a "national calling" by seeing the spiritual and temporal goals of the church fulfilled through the national consciousness and activity—through social legislation, political influence, and economic stability, as well as the expansion of the nation's influence around the world. In this way, Christ shines through its culture.

Defining the Term

Historians and theologians find civil religion to be an element in the relation between the church and the world almost from the church's beginnings, but particularly after Constantine. However, an exact definition of *civil religion* has eluded the scholars. There is no general agreement on the meaning of the term.

Russell Richey and Donald Jones, in a collection of essays entitled *American Civil Religion,* have attempted to isolate "five meanings of civil religion."[44] Their analysis can help us get a grasp on the issue. They conclude that within American civil religion one can speak about folk religion, a transcendent universal religion of the nation, a religious nationalism, a democratic faith, and a Protestant civic piety. Of these five categories of civil religion, the first three may be found in practically every civilization. The last two are peculiar to the Anglo-Saxon experience.

Folk religion may be identified as those religious ideas, values, symbols, ceremonies, and loyalties that most of the people of any nation hold in common. These may include such things as belief in the existence of God and a positive attitude toward morality, the Bible, church attendance, and prayers at important public events. The *transcendent universal religion* of the nation is harder to grasp. In the nonpluralistic societies of medieval Europe or Russia before the industrial revolution, the transcendent religion would be Catholicism or Orthodoxy. But in a modern pluralistic society, the transcendent religion is above identification with any particular form of faith. It points rather to such ideas of faith as God's purpose for the nation. *Religious nationalism* has to do with those aspects of religion that support patriotism as a religious virtue and glorify the nation by calling for dedication to it and personal sacrifice for its sake. The last two, *the democratic faith* and *Protestant civic piety,* are peculiarly Western and represent an intermingling of the norms and goals of the church with those of the state.

In addition to these five kinds of civil religion we may acknowledge another, that of religious standards applied to the civil order. In the case of the religious right, this idea of civil religion is most apt. Their concern for America arises out of their Christian convictions of truth and morality. Believing that faith is not a merely private matter, these Christians seek to apply moral standards to the various spheres of human existence. The kind of civil religion advocated by the leaders of the religious right is most often of this sixth category. But, because it is blended with the themes of divine destiny for America, the impression one gets is more in keeping with a civil religion that results in faith in American destiny.

Jean-Jacques Rousseau (1712–78) first used the term *civil religion*. He attempted to resolve the problem of the tension between religion and culture in a pluralistic society by speaking of a "social contract." He recognized that no state could exist without having some kind of religion at its base. But he chided Christianity because he felt that it weakened the state by setting forth a dual allegiance for believers. He sought to solve this problem through the creation of a civil religion, which he identified as "a purely civil profession of faith." This would provide the "social sentiments without which a man cannot be a good citizen or a faithful subject." He insisted that these sentiments should be "few, simple, and exactly worded," and suggested they include "the existence of a mighty, intelligent, and beneficent Divinity, possessed of foresight and providence, the life to come, the happiness of the just, the punishment of the wicked, the sanctity of the social contract and the laws."[45] In other words, he saw religion as the moral glue that held society together. It was the will of the people expressed religiously within the state. Consequently, Rousseau thought, the state would assume a religious character.

Civil Religion in Western History

What Rousseau described was not at all his own invention. He merely gave a name to a phenomenon that had existed for centuries in the Western world.

It is generally accepted that the pagan states of Greece and Rome were modeled on a kind of civil religion. Because the Christian religion could not support Roman civil religion, it suffered persecution. The change that came with Constantine has been interpreted by some as a shift toward a Christian civil religion in the Roman Empire. However, it is usually held that a return to civil religion in terms of a universal, state-oriented faith did not occur until the twelfth and thirteenth centuries.

Although the medieval period may be seen as a contest between papal and monarchical power, it was in fact monarchical power that generally ruled the day. Power rested in a monarchical civil religion. The king was considered the direct agent of God. From Paul's teaching of the mystical body of Christ was derived a view that men were joined together morally and politically under their head, the king, in the same way that men were joined spiritually to Christ. All members of the body politic were to be directed by the head and to serve the head. The king's peace was the peace of the church; his battles became the battles of the church.

In the meantime the church developed a similar consciousness about itself. It saw itself as the supreme ruler over both the public and private realms. The church declared itself to be *corpus mysticum*, the mystical body of Christ on earth. All things and all people, including kings, were to be under its jurisdiction, for through the church Christ ruled in the world.

When king and pope clashed over ultimate power, the subjects were forced to choose the one to whom they would be loyal. With the emergence of nationalism and the corruption of the late medieval church, the people of France, Germany, and England chose king over pope. It was not a choice, however, between a secular state and a religious state. The state was already understood to be a religious entity and the king was considered God's instrument, through which His will would be implemented across the land. In this way the state achieved a religious status, and people began to think of their citizenship in religious and moral terms. Gradually, the state and the church became independent bodies. But the state continued to promulgate moral and ethical values that were shaped by its relationship to the church.[46]

The Reformation and the Renaissance of the sixteenth century mark the transitional period from the medieval world to the modern world. During this period, the church and the state became two distinct entities and the idea of a pluralistic society was born. This revolutionary change introduced new complexities into the problem of civil religion. For example, both nationalism and secularism substituted earthly goals and ends for what was once a transcendent goal. In this way the soil was prepared for the religious character of secular ideologies such as communism. More important for our purposes, however, is the way in which the religious notion of the state was carried over into what we call American civil religion.

American Civil Religion

The roots of American civil religion go back to England and its self-concept as a "chosen nation." This idea was popularized by John Foxe in his widely read *Book of Martyrs.* Foxe set forth the story of the suffering Protestants in such a way as to make England appear to be especially called by God to retain and spread the truth. England was God's chosen nation, and through it the divine plan of God would be fulfilled.

The Puritans brought this idea of an elect nation with them to America. The hope of a new people of God is clearly seen in the famous words of John Winthrop:

> Wee shall finde that the God of Israel is among us, when tenn of us shall be able to resist a thousand of our enemies, when hee shall make us a prayse and glory, that men shall say of succeeding plantacions; the Lord make it like that of New England: for wee must consider that wee shall be as a citty upon a Hill, the eies of all people are upon us. . . . [47]

During the eighteenth-century Great Awakening, the idea that America was a chosen nation was further strengthened by the preaching and influence of Jonathan Edwards. He encouraged people to gather and pray for the coming of God's kingdom. In the early days of his ministry it was his conviction that the Millennium, the thousand-year reign of Christ on earth, might come to America. By the mid-1740s he saw the coming of the kingdom as a function of the church universal. But other revivalists picked up this theme, and through them a sense of special destiny was instilled in the American soul.

This sense was heightened through the American Revolution. Politicians and preachers alike compared the American situation to Israel and the Exodus. The British were the Egyptians in hot pursuit of America, the New Israel. But God was on the American side as He was on Israel's—and He would see America through its Red Sea and then through the wilderness to the Promised Land.

In the nineteenth century, most evangelical preachers and leaders thought the Millennium would come as a result of the Christianization of the world. The great revivalists, such as Lyman Beecher and Charles G. Finney, were convinced that God had chosen America to lead the way in the moral and political emancipation of the world. It was America's destiny to prepare the world for the coming of Christ.

Gradually, Protestants began to see the nation as the means through which God was working in history. The concept of a chosen people became that of a chosen nation. Against this background, the role of Christians in the spread of American imperialism is understandable. Spreading Americanism was equal to spreading Christianity, for it was in the American character that one could most clearly see the character of God. Consequently, an American messianic consciousness emerged; it was believed that America would be the savior of the world.[48]

Although the wars and depressions of the twentieth century, as well as the rapid spread of secularism, have eroded the American messianic consciousness, a number of people still find biblical Christianity and the American destiny in agreement. Richard Pierard in *The Unequal Yoke* describes the current phenomenon and questions its validity. In particular he argues that evangelical Christianity is yoked to an unhealthful political conservatism.[49]

Pierard cites, as one of the causes of this unequal yoke, "the capture of the evangelical churches by business interests." This came about through the business connections of D. L. Moody and Billy Sunday, who were supported by magnates like John Wanamaker, Cyrus McCormick, Cornelius Vanderbilt II, and J. P. Morgan. One result of this alignment was the growth of "successful Christianity," the idea that if you give your life to Jesus, He will bless you and make you rich, popular, and powerful. Says Pierard, "The tendency to emphasize results for results' sake, and to justify whatever tended to produce them, subtly but definitely diluted the good news of the gospel. In time, new elements crept into the evangelistic message such as the middle-class success myth, American chauvinism, opposition to actions of organized labor, and of course prohibition."[50]

Northern fundamentalism, which gathered around the cities, became identified with the status quo and with the preservation of the culture that big business had created, one that political conservatism tended to perpetuate in America and around the world. Gradually, an unfortunate marriage occurred between evangelical Christianity and the political right. This attitude began to break down in the early seventies with the emergence of a more critical viewpoint among younger leaders. However, in the late seventies, with the establishment of the Moral Majority and the religious right, a revival of civil religion occurred once again. Its emphasis is on maintaining individualism, the free enterprise system, keeping America free, cleaning up American morality, and advancing America as the one nation in the world that has the adequate resources and know-how to bring the gospel to the world. The sense that America is a chosen nation with a religious destiny remains strong among those who have wed politics and religion.

While the blending of religion with the political right and Americanism may strengthen the moral fiber of a country, it contains some highly dubious alignments. It tends, for example, to put God on the side of Americanism, the free enterprise system, and more specifically the religious right. In this way the gospel and the church are politicized. By making the gospel and the church servants of the state, the true nature of the church is twisted and left vulnerable to the political powers that will use it for their own ends.

In each case—the liberation theology of the Left and the civil religion of the Right—the character of the gospel and the church is altered. It loses its prophetic edge and becomes a tool of one of the powers. In order for the church to freely critique the world, it must remain free from real or implied support of a particular political or economic ideology.[51]

EVALUATION

The positive features of the religious right ought to be acknowledged first. The religious right is decidedly against a privative faith, a faith that has nothing to do with the world or with the issues of science, politics, and behavior. On the contrary, the religious right calls for a faith that recognizes the lordship of Christ over all of life, private and public, personal and national.

Second, the religious right (like other religious groups in the modern world) is earnestly attempting to wrestle with the "new demons." It is particularly concerned over the demise of moral absolutes, expressed especially in the widespread use of abortion on demand, in the breakdown of the family, in the availability of pornography, in the rise of crime, and in personal sexual permissiveness.

Another positive aspect of the religious right is its opposition to secularism, which seeks to keep religious values out of the public sector. Furthermore, the deeper one probes the theology of the religious right, the more clear it becomes that members of this group will affirm the major components of a christological view of reality: They affirm a supernatural Jesus who, by His death and resurrection, has destroyed the powers of evil. They affirm the lordship of Christ over the entire creation. They affirm a supernatural view of the church and a providential view of history, with the hope that a new heavens and a new earth await us at the end of history.

However, their writings do not evidence a great deal of thought about these issues. The christological view of church and world remains somewhat underdeveloped. Furthermore, the way in which they blend Christian themes with Americanism raises a barrier against a more clear biblical and christological concept of church and world. For a more clearly worked out christological vision of church and world, we must turn to the writings of Evangelicalism and to the documents of the World Evangelical Fellowship.

16

THE WORLD EVANGELICAL
FELLOWSHIP

Although the World Evangelical Fellowship is not as well known as the World Council of Churches or the religious right in America, it commands an ever-increasing membership and sphere of influence.

In many ways the organizational structure and method of operation of W.E.F. is similar to the W.C.C., having an active Theological Commission as well as a Mission Commission. Because of its worldwide national memberships and its active voice in social issues since 1974, many regard it as the evangelical counterpoint to the more liberal W.C.C. organization. Consequently, its perspective on church and world is of vital importance to an evaluation of the current church-and-world attitude.

World Evangelical Fellowship, which was founded in 1951, owes its existence to J. Elwin Wright, the Executive Secretary of the National Association of Evangelicals, and Clyde Taylor, the Executive Secretary of the Evangelical Foreign Missions Association, both of whom were concerned to bring evangelicals from around the world into unified fellowship and action. In 1950 they made a trip to various parts of the world including Japan, Hong Kong, India, and England to confer with evangelical organizations and leaders about organizing a world voice for Evangelicalism. Consequently, delegates from these and other countries came together in Holland in 1951 to form the World Evangelical Fellowship.

Although this conference marked the beginnings of W.E.F., the idea of a world organization goes back to a parent organization, the World Evangelical Alliance, which was founded in England in 1846. During the nineteenth and early twentieth centuries, the W.E.A. became an international organization through the promotion of national evangelical organizations in more than fifty countries. However, since the end of World War I the international character and function of these various organizations had been lost, membership had gone into decline, and the W.E.A. was quite inactive. Thus, the founding of W.E.F. was in part a restoration of the idea of the World Evangelical Alliance with a new name and strong leadership from the American National Association of Evangelicals.

In order to understand the social conscience of W.E.F., our main concern in this chapter, we must first understand the rise of an evangelical social conscience in the early seventies, a movement which directly influenced the W.E.F. First, we will discuss the emergence of social concern among American Evangelicals to 1974, then proceed to the emphasis on social action in W.E.F. from 1974 to the present.

THE RISE OF AN EVANGELICAL SOCIAL CONSCIENCE IN AMERICA, 1956–74

During the first half of the twentieth century, Evangelicals were interested mainly in evangelism, mission, and education. However, after World War II increasing attention was paid to social concerns. We can discern two stages in the development of a social conscience: the first from 1956 to 1970 and the second from 1970 to 1974.

Prior to 1970, the dominant note in evangelical social concern was that of an individualistic social ethic. According to Dennis P. Hollinger, professor of church and society at the Alliance Theological Seminary in Nyack, New York, and author of *Individualism and Social Ethics*, Evangelicals of this era "accentuate personal responsibility but largely omit public policy and structural considerations."[1] He quotes a statement of Billy Graham written in 1967 in response to the National Council of Churches' Conference on Church and Society:

The government may try to legislate Christian behavior, but it soon finds that man remains unchanged. The
changing of men's hearts is the primary mission of the
church. The only way to change men is to get them
converted to Jesus Christ. Then they will have the
capacity to live up to the Christian command to 'love thy
neighbor.'[2]

Hollinger calls this rejection of the socio-political involvement of the church a *regenerational perspective*. It is based
on four basic principles: (1) The Bible does not mandate
socio-political involvement. (2) Socio-political involvement
moves the church away from the gospel. (3) It destroys
church unity. And (4) the church lacks the competence to
deal with socio-political issues.[3] Nevertheless, Hollinger
recognizes a growing concern for a social conscience among
Evangelicals during the early sixties as expressed by J.
Howard Pew, a major financial backer of *Christianity Today*:

No one would seriously deny that the individual
Christian must relate his Christian convictions to the
society of which he is a part in the economic, social and
political life about him. He must live out his Christianity
in every phase of life, showing that he is salt and light in
an unbelieving world.[4]

In the late sixties and early seventies, there was a
discernable shift among Evangelicals toward a social ethic
that went beyond individualism and took account of the
powers of evil working through the structures of society. The
emergence of magazines such as *The Other Side* and the
Sojourners gave evidence of the growing concern to change
the structures which cause social, economic, and political
evils. However, a more important influence toward a social
conscience grew out of two congresses which brought
together a number of Evangelicals. The first of these was an
American conference held in Chicago, whereas the second,
the Lausanne Congress of 1974, brought together Evangelicals from around the world.

Ron Sider, the convener of the Chicago meeting,
describes in his book *The Chicago Declaration* the changing
cultural situation and the new patterns of evangelical
thought which set the stage for the conference. He cites the
disruptive events of Vietnam and Watergate as external
influences "freeing Evangelicals from an automatic accept-

ance of traditional socio-political presuppositions."[5] And he regards the work of Paul Rees, David O. Moberg, Tom Skinner, and Leighton Ford—as well as the pleas for biblical social action at the Minneapolis Congress on Evangelism (1969) and Carl Henry's book, *Call for Evangelical Demonstration* (1971)—as signs of the new wind for social change. "Evangelicals," he claims, "are beginning to transcend the unholy dichotomy of evangelism or social concern."[6]

That structural evil, not merely personal moral evil, is the concern of this new Evangelicalism is readily acknowledged by Sider. Referring to the Watergate scandal, he speaks of "the extent of political corruption in high places" that "horrifies and shocks many people who genuinely believed that justice, equality, and freedom were the goals, and honesty and due process the norms in Washington."[7] He predicts that Evangelicals will either withdraw into the "pygmy world of personal piety" or be freed to take a "new, far more critical look at all aspects of American society" and "raise fundamental questions about the justice of the socio-economic status quo."[8] More than fifty evangelical leaders, including a number from the older generation of Evangelicals,[9] signed the following statement drafted at the Chicago meeting:

> As evangelical Christians committed to the Lord Jesus Christ and the full authority of the Word of God, we affirm that God lays total claim upon the lives of his people. We cannot, therefore, separate our lives in Christ from the situation in which God has placed us in the United States and the world.
>
> We confess that we have not acknowledged the complete claims of God on our lives.
>
> We acknowledge that God requires love. But we have not demonstrated the love of God to those suffering social abuses.
>
> We acknowledge that God requires justice. But we have not proclaimed or demonstrated his justice to an unjust American society. Although the Lord calls us to defend the social and economic rights of the poor and the oppressed, we have mostly remained silent. We deplore the historic involvement of the church in America with racism and the conspicuous responsibility of the evangelical community for perpetuating the personal attitudes and

institutional structures that have divided the body of Christ along color lines. Further, we have failed to condemn the exploitation of racism at home and abroad by our economic system.

We affirm that God abounds in mercy and that He forgives all who repent and turn from their sins. So we call our fellow evangelical Christians to demonstrate repentance in a Christian discipleship that confronts the social and political injustice of our nation.

We must attack the materialism of our culture and the maldistribution of the nation's wealth and services. We recognize that as a nation we play a crucial role in the imbalance and injustice of international trade and development. Before God and a billion hungry neighbors, we must rethink our values regarding our present standard of living and promote more just acquisition and distribution of the world's resources.

We acknowledge our Christian responsibilities of citizenship. Therefore, we must challenge the misplaced trust of the nation in economic and military might—a proud trust that promotes a national pathology of war and violence which victimizes our neighbors at home and abroad. We must resist the temptation to make the nation and its institutions objects of near-religious loyalty.

We acknowledge that we have encouraged men to prideful domination and women to irresponsible passivity. So we call both men and women to mutual submission and active discipleship.

We proclaim no new gospel, but the Gospel of our Lord Jesus Christ who, through the power of the Holy Spirit, frees people from sin so that they might praise God through works of righteousness.

By this declaration, we endorse no political ideology or party, but call our nation's leaders and people to that righteousness which exalts a nation.

We make this declaration in the Biblical hope that Christ is coming to consummate the Kingdom, and we accept His claim on our total discipleship till He comes.[10]

While the American Evangelicals who drafted *The Chicago Declaration* were questioning the pietistic individualism of the immediate past, other Evangelicals from around the world were gearing toward a more corporate social ethic as evidenced in the International Congress on World Evangelization held in Lausanne, Switzerland, in 1974. The most enduring written result of the Lausanne Congress is *The Lausanne Covenant*, hammered out under the leadership of Anglican John Stott, an advocate of the union between Evangelicalism and social action. This covenant, which marks a turning point in worldwide evangelical social concern, was signed by a majority of the participants. The following excerpt from the council expressed the new evangelical consensus:

> We affirm that God is both the Creator and the Judge of all men. We therefore should share His concern for justice and reconciliation throughout human society and for the liberation of men from every kind of oppression. Because mankind is made in the image of God, every person, regardless of race, religion, color, culture, class, sex or age, has an intrinsic dignity because of which he should be respected and served, not exploited. Here too we express penitence both for our neglect and for having sometimes regarded evangelism and social concern as mutually exclusive. Although reconciliation with man is not reconciliation with God, nor is social action evangelism, nor is political liberation salvation, nevertheless we affirm that evangelism and socio-political involvement are both part of our Christian duty. For both are necessary expressions of our doctrines of God and man, our love for our neighbor and our obedience to Jesus Christ. The message of salvation implies also a message of judgment upon every form of alienation, oppression and discrimination, and we should not be afraid to denounce evil and injustice wherever they exist. When people receive Christ they are born again into His kingdom and must seek not only to exhibit but also to spread its righteousness in the midst of an unrighteous world. The salvation we claim should be transforming us in the totality of our personal and social responsibilities. Faith without works is dead.[11]

While neither *The Chicago Declaration* nor *The Lausanne Covenant* were products of the World Evangelical Fellowship, they nevertheless expressed the perspective that was to dominate the social stance of the W.E.F. after 1974. Another tie between W.E.F. and these two congresses was their mutual leadership; the leading voices in *The Chicago Declaration* and *The Lausanne Covenant* were also active participants in W.E.F., shaping its social concern in ways already articulate in the previous documents.

RISE OF A WORLD EVANGELICAL
SOCIAL CONSCIENCE, 1974–

One of the leading voices in the Lausanne Covenant was Waldron Scott, who in 1974 was appointed the first full-time executive secretary for the World Evangelical Fellowship. And the leading voice in *The Chicago Declaration*, Ron Sider, was not only an active participant in *The Lausanne Covenant* but the person appointed by W.E.F. to head its consultation on society and ethics. The leadership and writings of these two men in particular, as well as the W.E.F. congresses since 1974, provide sources from which we may gain an insight into the contemporary evangelical understanding of the relationship between church and world.

Our procedure will be to look first at the meetings of the Mission Commission of W.E.F., where Waldron Scott played a dominant role. Then we will examine the statements of the Theological Commission and its subcommittee on ethics and society, where Ron Sider has exercised his influence.

The Missions Commission Conference

The Missions Commission of the World Evangelical Fellowship met in Bad Liebenzel, Germany, in January 1979. Twenty-seven participants from six continents gathered under the theme, "World Mission—Building Bridges or Barriers?"[12] The keynote address, which was given by Waldron Scott, shows the influence of a Third World presence and the shaping of a church-and-world consciousness around Third World problems. For example, in the opening section of his talk, Scott states, "The greatest single issue in today's world is global injustice. Violence— personal and structural—permeate all human relations, creates untold misery for millions (indeed, billions) of people, and poisons any prospect for genuine peace."[13] Consequently, Scott calls evangelical Christians to a "sense of outrage," suggesting that "the zeal of the Lord no longer consumes us in the face of the money-changers of our time. There are more oppressed people on earth today than at any time in history."[14]

During this conference two presentations dealt in more detail with the global injustice singled out by Scott. In "Aids and Development in Mission," Siegfried Wiesinger from Germany refers to the opposition between Evangelicalism and the social gospel as a thing of the past. He combines the two and calls for "Christian Development Service,"[15] which he regards as the "preached Word visible and credible."[16] Henceforth Evangelicals must be concerned for word and deed:

> Thus in the Christian Development Service the crucial points of preaching and *diakonia* stand in a dynamic relationship to each other. Our medical, social and educational ministry cannot free men from the causes that led to their distress, without the witness and the power of the Gospel. On the other hand, preaching of the Word without the practical service of love would not bring the recipient to complete salvation. As truly as we have to give bread to the hungry, medicine to the sick, protection and guidance to the handicapped, just as well we owe all of them the Gospel, the message of salvation through Jesus Christ. As long as the giving of help is not used as a bait or as a means to oppress people with regard to faith, our wish that others may learn to love Christ, to become Christians, is no misuse of Christian service, because this wish only corresponds to the will to help in a most complete and comprehensive sense.[17]

Next, Orlando Costas from Puerto Rico spoke on "A Strategy for Third World Missions." While space does not permit a full evaluation of the strategy suggested, let it be sufficient to quote Costas's statement regarding the "ends" of mission. Here one finds an evangelical relationship between church and world. Costas points out that the work of the church on earth is directly related to its eschatological goal, as it brings kingdom principles to bear on the socioeconomic and political realities of life:

> The ultimate goal of Third World missions should be the final revelation of the kingdom, understood as the total transformation of history by Jesus Christ and the power of His Spirit. This will involve the redemption of creation, the definitive abrogation of evil, chaos, and corruption, and the birth of a world of love, peace and justice. Third World missions, as any Christian mission, should see themselves, fundamentally, as witnesses to the coming Kingdom.

The kingdom of God, however, is not just a future, transcendent reality. It is also a present and imminent order of life, characterized by the forgiveness of sins, the formation of a new community and commitment to a new ethic. This order of life is centered on the person and work of Jesus Christ. Hence to witness to the kingdom is to declare the name of Jesus Christ as the Lord and Saviour of humankind. This in turn implies that the announcement of Jesus Christ in the world has personal communal and socio-political dimensions. Personal, in the sense that it is accompanied by the call to faith and repentance and the concomitant experience of forgiveness of sin. Communal, in that it implies incorporation into the church, understood as a community or fellowship of faith and commitment. And socio-political, in the sense that it involves a new lifestyle based on love, whose practical expression is justice and ultimate hope is peace (or well-being) for all.

To lead others to Christ implies not only guiding them to a new experience, but to a new commitment and a new way of life. This means that Third World missions, if they are to be faithful to God's kingdom, will have a threefold orientation: (1) the communication of the gospel, (2) the growth and development of the church and (3) social justice and world peace. This triple orientation will have its fulcrum on Jesus Christ. It represents rallying points for the organization of the missionary endeavor. In the process of organization, however, it should avoid atomization and compartmentalization. For if these penultimate ends are to be intermediate goals between the future of the kingdom and its present manifestation, they must be kept together. In fact, each should be able to point to and presuppose the other, otherwise mission will lose its wholeness and the gospel will end up being truncated.[18]

In sum, the Missions Commission provides evidence for the strong influence of the Third World socioeconomic and political plight on the development of current evangelical church and world thought. This influence is not unlike that exercised by the Third World on the thought of the World Council of Churches.[19]

The Theological Commission

The Theological Commission of W.E.F. consists of fifty-four scholars from every continent. These scholars work in six subgroups to study and evaluate topics of importance to the church. We will look at selective church and world comments from each of the major statements since Lausanne in 1974 as a means of understanding the current consensus of evangelical scholars.

Church and Nationhood Conference of 1976

Evangelicals representing a variety of ecclesiastical traditions from all parts of the world gathered at St. Chrischona near Basel, Switzerland, in 1976 to hammer out a statement on the church and nationalism. While a number of papers were presented representing the thought from America, Africa, Asia, Europe, and Latin America, the most helpful report of the conference for our purposes is "The Basel Letter," a unified statement intended to provide leadership for the whole evangelical world. The letter begins with a summary of the Christian world view and gospel as "God's message for our generation"; then it moves to the "situations Christians face today," enumerating secular powers, social systems that are unjust, racist, and oppressive; hostility and exploitation of governments; and the oppression of multinational corporations. While these references are a matter of interest because they point to an evangelical awareness of evil in the structures of existence, what follows is even more striking. In the section entitled "Power Belongs to God Alone," these writers betray a belief in the power of the demonic working through structures of existence:

> Scripture reveals that fallen man is prey to spiritual powers in the invisible world (Col. 2:8). These evil 'principalities and powers' are active not only in the lives of individuals but also in cultural, national and political life. Under demonic influence sinful human leaders enslave men rather than serve them. Like all human beings, political leaders have a capacity for injustice and demonically energized activity. This becomes apparent when the State absolutizes its claims and values, seeks its own glorification, and transgresses divinely appointed bounds of good order.

Thus we understand why patriotism can degenerate into self-assertive, idolatrous nationalism . . . how slogans of 'national security' can render even Christians insensitive to repressive acts of governments . . . how racism and unjust economic structures are institutionalized and protected by the State.[20]

Next, the letter addresses "serious matters that must be faced" and gives the following specific instructions on how the church should relate to the world:

We should resist pressure on churches to make them mere religious tools of the State (Acts 5:29).

We should not permit our churches to enlist the State as their political tool (John 18:36).

We should not tolerate an intermingling of the Gospel with any political, economic, cultural or nationalistic ideology in such a way as to compromise the Gospel (Matt. 6:24; Mic. 3:11).

We should never yield to the temptation of making our people or nation or our nation's institutions the object of near-religious loyalty (Deut. 5:7; Isa. 2:8).

We should oppose every attempt, civil or religious, to control arbitrarily the thoughts and consciences of men and all serious infringements of Christian conscience (1 Cor. 4:5; Acts 4:18–21).

We should take advantage of all possibilities to remedy injustice in State legislation, administrative and judicial affairs (Acts 25:10f.).

We should summon our civil authorities to their God-appointed task to promote justice in society. However, it needs to be emphasized that such a prophetic witness may require the participatory suffering of those who make it, e.g., John the Baptist (Mark 6:17f.).

We should resist the demands which the powerful make to obtain benefits and privileges for themselves, and call upon the State to promote equal justice for all, especially the poor, the orphan and the widow (Jer. 22:1–3; Amos 2:6–7; Matt. 23:23).

Our loyalty to the one worldwide Body of Christ, which is also 'a chosen race and a holy nation' (1 Peter 2:9), should be higher than that which we extend to our tribe, class, race or nation (Gal. 3:28; 6:10; Luke 13:29).

Our Christian concern for the community of mankind, created by God in His likeness, should enable us to stand firmly against all forms of legislated discrimination based on race or color (Acts 17:26; 11:1ff.).

We hold that the will of God for His Church embraces suffering for Jesus' sake and being faithful unto death rather than seeking at any cost the survival of traditional patterns of church life (Mark 8:34–38; Rev. 2:10).

We should enlarge the concept of religious liberty to include the right to provide religious instruction for our children, publish and distribute the Scriptures, share the Gospel with our neighbors, and promote personal righteousness and social justice (Deut. 6:6–9; Matt. 28:19f.; Eph. 6:4; Col. 1:28).

We should recognize that the Church, as well as the State, is prone to anxiety, covetousness, injustice and corruption, and needs constant reformation according to the Scriptures (1 Peter 4:17; Rom. 12:2).[21]

The final portion of the letter entitled "The Call to Servanthood" urges evangelical Christians "to recognize that our highest duty and greatest privilege is to embrace the role the Son embraced. Our Lord Jesus became the servant of men (Mark 10:45). This led Him ultimately to the cross. And to this calling He directs us."[22]

The International Consultation on Simple Lifestyle, 1980

The theme of servanthood set forth in the 1976 "Basel Letter" is expanded and particularized in the next Consultation held at Huddeson, England, in March of 1980. Here Dr. Ron Sider, the convener of the 1973 Chicago Declaration and a participant in the Lausanne Conference, acted as chairman, thus linking W.E.F. with previous developments on the evangelical social conscience. Sider, the author of the best-selling and widely acclaimed book *Rich Christians in an Age of Hunger*,[23] led the delegates into a consideration of an evangelical response to the imbalance of wealth. Their response was published in a statement entitled "An Evangelical Commitment to Simple Lifestyle."[24]

Eighty-five Evangelicals from twenty-seven countries forged this simple lifestyle statement. In the preamble they described themselves as "disturbed by the injustice of the world, concerned for its victims and moved to repentance for our complicity in it."[25] They commit themselves to a simple lifestyle and support of the poor and the oppressed. But most important in understanding the changing attitude of Evangelicals toward the world is their commitment issued under section 7, "Justice and Politics." Here they set forth a clear vision of structural evil and call God's people to oppose the structures that create these evils:

> We are also convinced that the present situation of social injustice is so abhorrent to God that a large measure of change is necessary. Not that we believe in an earthly utopia. But neither are we pessimists. Change can come, although not through commitment to simple lifestyle or human development projects alone.
>
> Poverty and excessive wealth, militarism and the arms industry, and the unjust distribution of capital, land and resources are issues of power and powerlessness. Without a shift of power through structural change these problems cannot be solved.
>
> The Christian church, along with the rest of society, is inevitably involved in politics which is "the art of living in community." Servants of Christ must express his lordship in their political, social and economic commitments and their love for their neighbors by taking part in the political process. How, then, can we contribute to change?
>
> First, we will pray for peace and justice, as God commands. Second, we will seek to educate Christian people in the moral and political issues involved, and so clarify their vision and raise their expectations. Third, we will take action. Some Christians are called to special tasks in government, economics or development. All Christians must participate in the active struggle to create a just and responsible society. In some situations obedience to God demands resistance to an unjust established order. Fourth, we must be ready to suffer. As followers of Jesus, the Suffering Servant, we know that service always involves suffering.
>
> While personal commitment to change our lifestyle without political action to change systems of injustice lacks effectiveness, political action without personal commitment lacks integrity.

The Grand Rapids Report on Evangelism and Social Responsibility, 1982

Evangelical theology can hardly be construed as a move away from Evangelicalism toward a liberal social gospel. Nevertheless when Christians shift toward a candid appraisal of social and structural evil, they must ever be on their guard to maintain the unity between personal evangelism and corporate structural change as an effect of kingdom preaching. In June of 1982, a joint consultation sponsored by the Lausanne Committee for World Evangelization and the World Evangelical Fellowship met in Grand Rapids, Michigan. This meeting produced a declaration that, according to Ron Sider, was the most important evangelical statement to date on church and world.[26] This statement was published in a booklet entitled *Evangelism and Social Responsibility: An Evangelical Commitment.* [27] The unique feature of this book is that it goes beyond a declaration of wrong and sets forth in systematic fashion a theology for social action. A brief summary of that theology will provide us with insight into the current justification for evangelical social action.

The main premise of the book is that evangelism and social action are two sides of the same coin. They are both rooted in the work of Christ, which extends not only to personal salvation but also to the ultimate restoration of the created order. There are, claim the authors, three dimensions of salvation. They are the *new life*, or the new birth; the creation of the *new community*, the church which is the collective expression of individuals who constitute a new society; and the *new world* which is the future "renovation of the entire created order, which will be liberated from decay, pain and death."[28] The authors refer to seven signs of the presence of the kingdom (Christ Himself, preaching of the gospel, exorcism, healing and nature miracles, conversion, the church, and suffering).[29] Of special interest is the comment on exorcism as a sign of kingdom presence:

> We refuse to demythologize the teaching of Jesus and his apostles about demons. Although the "principalities and powers" may have a reference to demonic ideologies and structures, we believe that they certainly are evil, personal intelligences under the command of the devil. Demon possession is a real and terrible condition. Deliverance is possible only in a power encounter in which the name of Jesus is invoked and prevails.[30]

This power of Jesus to confront evil and dispel it as a sign of kingdom presence is rooted in the overpowering of the wicked one:

> Since "the reason the Son of God appeared was to destroy the devil's work" (1 John 3:8), he inevitably came into collision with the prince of darkness. The signs of the Kingdom were evidences that the devil was retreating before the advance of the King. As Jesus put it, once the strong man has been overpowered by the Stronger One, his possessions can be taken from him (Matt. 12:29; Luke 11:22).[31]

In spite of the fact that Christ is the victor of the kingdom of evil, we must distinguish between Christ's kingship *de facto* and *de jure* in the here and now:

> It is important to maintain the tension between what Christ rules *de facto* and *de jure*. For if we assume that all authority has in fact been given to him, we shall not take seriously the evil powers which have not yet capitulated. If, on the other hand, our horizon is bounded by the community in which the King is consciously confessed, we may be tempted to dismiss the rest of the world as beyond redemption. From these extremes of naive optimism and dark pessimism we return to the radical realism of the Bible, which recognizes both the defeat of evil and its refusal to concede defeat. This double conviction will persuade us to work hard in evangelism and in the quest for justice, while at the same time putting our whole trust and confidence in God.[32]

And in the present the church's mission is the proclamation not only of personal salvation but of the kingdom rule of Christ, which will one day extend over all His works of creation:

> Christians have often debated the relationship between the church and the Kingdom. We must not identify them, but neither must we separate them. The church is the community in which God's kingly rule is revealed, which therefore witnesses to the divine rule, and is the firstfruits of the redeemed humanity (James 1:18). It lives by new values and standards, and its relationships have been transformed by love. Yet it continues to fail. For it lives in an uneasy tension between the "already" and the "not yet," between the present reality and the future expectation of the Kingdom.[33]

During this interim period between Christ's conquest of evil and the establishment of His kingdom, the church is called to a twofold task. On the one hand, it must challenge the old fallen society and the powers which work evil through the structures of existence; and second, as it lives alongside the world, it must infuse into the new world the values of the kingdom which it anticipates.[34]

What then is the relationship between the eschatological vision and present evangelism and social responsibility? Since the eschatological vision is a "revelation of what God Himself is going to do in the end,"[35] it is an incentive to participate in that goal. For example, both redemption of persons and righteousness and peace are characteristics of the eternal kingdom. Consequently, the future reality calls us to the pursuit of evangelism and righteousness in the present world.

Having set forth the theological roots of social responsibility in the biblical vision of Christ the Creator who conquers sin and establishes His kingdom, the authors of the Grand Rapids statement proceed to make a distinction between social service and social action. *Social service* is relieving human need, philanthropic activity, a ministry to individuals and families, and works of mercy. However, *social action* goes to the root cause, to the structures of existence:

> The other kind of social responsibility is the quest for justice. It looks beyond persons to structures, beyond the rehabilitation of prison inmates to the reform of the prison system, beyond improving factory conditions to securing a more participatory role for the workers, beyond caring for the poor to improving—and when necessary transforming—the economic system (whatever it may be) and the political system (again, whatever it may be), until it facilitates their liberation from poverty and oppression. Such social changes often necessitate political action (for politics is about power), and some Evangelicals fear it because they imagine it will entail civil strife and even revolution. But this is not what we mean by "sociopolitical involvement." We are thinking rather of political processes which are consistent with biblical principles— such as the rights of the individual and of minorities, respect for civil authority, the welfare of the whole community, and justice for the oppressed.

The Bible lays great emphasis on both justice (or righteousness) and peace. For God is the author of both, and both are essential characteristics of his Kingdom. We, therefore, who claim to be members of his Kingdom, must not only seek justice for others but must "do justice" ourselves (Mic. 6:8), in relation to our family, our fellow workers, and any servants or employees we may have. In the same way, it is not enough to "seek peace and pursue it"; we must also ourselves, so far as it depends on us, "live peaceably with all" (1 Peter 3:11; Rom. 12:18). This applies to churches as well as individual Christians. If discrimination and disunity are tolerated in the church, how can we denounce them in the nation? Conversely, it is churches which visibly demonstrate the righteousness and peace of the Kingdom which will make the greatest evangelistic and social impact on the world. The salt must retain its saltness, Jesus said; otherwise, it is good for nothing (Matt. 5:13).[36]

This cross section of Evangelicals—which includes a range of people from John Stott and Ron Sider to Harold Lindsell[37] and Arthur P. Johnston [38]—have affirmed in this report their recognition of structural evil.

The Wheaton Statement, 1983

The view of structural evil expressed in previous statements and dealt with theologically in the Grand Rapids report is once again affirmed in one of the Wheaton statements of 1983. The statement was put together by representatives from thirty countries and titled "Social Transformation: The Church in Response to Human Need." This statement is not a theological groundbreaker; it stands in continuity with what has already been laid out theoretically. A brief excerpt from section V on "Social Justice and Mercy" will demonstrate the continued concern to attack structures of existence which, by their malfunction due to evil, cause human need:

Our time together enabled us to see that poverty is not a necessary evil but often the result of social, economic, political and religious systems marked by injustice, exploitation and oppression. Approximately eight hundred million people in the world are destitute, and their plight is often maintained by the rich and the powerful. Evil is not only in the human heart but also in the social structures. Because God is just and merciful, hating evil and loving righteousness, there is an urgent need for Christians in the present circumstances to commit ourselves to acting in mercy and seeking for justice. The mission of the church includes both the proclamation of the Gospel and its demonstration. We must therefore evangelize, respond to immediate human needs and press for social transformation. The means we use, however, must be consistent with the end we desire.

As we thought of the task before us, we considered Jesus' attitude toward the power structures of His time. He was neither a Zealot nor a passive spectator of the oppression of His people. Rather, moved by compassion, He identified Himself with the poor, whom He saw as 'harassed and helpless, like sheep without a shepherd' (Matt. 9:36). Through His acts of mercy, teaching and lifestyle, He exposed the injustices in society and condemned the self-righteousness of its leaders (Matt. 23:25; Luke 6:37–42). His was a prophetic compassion and it resulted in the formation of a community which accepted the values of the Kingdom of God and stood in contrast to the Roman and Jewish establishment. We were challenged to follow Jesus' footsteps, remembering that His compassion led Him to death (John 13:12–17; Phil. 2:6–8; 1 John 3:11–18).[39]

EVALUATION

This brief overview of the World Evangelical Fellowship sufficiently demonstrates that contemporary Evangelicals have moved away from a privative, personal faith toward a faith that seeks to express the lordship of Christ over every area of life. They have been forced to confront and deal with the new demons, the contours of contemporary structures of existence through which the powers of evil work to dehumanize life.

It is also clear that the church-and-world theology of the World Evangelical Fellowship is deeply rooted in the biblical vision of reality and stands in the current tradition of biblical interpretation. It affirms the goodness of creation, the power of evil expressed through the structures of existence, the victory of Christ over evil, the church as witness to the powers, and the eschatological vision of the kingdom. It differs from the theology of the World Council of Churches in that it is less likely to promote liberationism, a politicized form of the gospel; it differs from the view of the religious right in that it backs away from civil religion, another way of politicizing the gospel; it differs from the Roman Catholic view in that it places less emphasis on the role of natural law. Yet, as will be developed in the next chapter, the new evangelical outlook typified by the W.E.F. has strong affinities with the underlying biblical presupposition of the relationship between church and world, as explicated in both the World Council of Churches documents and in "The Pastoral Constitution on the Church in the Modern World" of Vatican II.

IV

FACING THE FUTURE

17

CONVERGENCE OF THOUGHT

A study of church history suggests, as we have seen, that a variety of church-and-world models have taken shape over the centuries. However, it appears that in the twentieth century with its global village a new unanimity between the various church-and-world traditions is being formed.

By recognizing this convergence of thought, I do not mean to suggest that the classical models of antithesis, paradox, and transformation are no longer being taught or lived out. Such an argument would ignore the presence of the Amish, the Dutch Calvinists, or the Swedish Lutherans. Furthermore, it would be naive to argue that there is no difference between a liberation theology which presupposes a mythical Jesus or a liberation theology based on a literal cosmic salvation in Jesus. It would be equally incorrect to assume there are no surviving proponents of civil religion, as we have already noted the presence of moralists who call for reform on the basis of humanitarian principles or the teaching of Jesus.

My argument is that in the face of all these existing differences there seems to be a convergence of opinion toward generally agreed principles regarding church and world. It seems that a center has developed, a cluster of theological ideas around which Roman Catholics, Protestants, and Evangelicals are gathering.

My purpose in this chapter is to clarify the contours of this agreement and thus to suggest the future shape of church and world thought that is now being embraced by a variety of Christian traditions. I find this convergence occurring in three respects: First, the fixed nature of past church-and-world models is being questioned; second, there is a growing unanimity with regard to the theological components of church-and-world thought; and third, a consensus regarding theological method seems to be appearing. An examination of each of these motifs is in order.

THE INADEQUACY OF PAST
CHURCH-AND-WORLD MODELS

The best summary of past models of church and world is found in the classic work of H. Richard Niebuhr, *Christ and Culture.* Although his five classifications of church and world have been immensely important as a means of understanding the various approaches taken by different denominations to the world, they are now valuable mainly as models of the past rather than models of the present or future. The current situation of a secularized world, together with the emergence of global problems, appear to demand a response based on an ecumenical understanding of the church and world. Church leaders are becoming less satisfied with church-and-world views that bear the peculiarities of a particular denominational theology. Nor are church leaders interested in addressing issues of local importance alone. There seems to be a new demand for the whole church to be united in its global strategy of evangelical and social witness. One evidence of this emergence of an ecumenical approach is found in the growing conviction that the categories of Christ and culture set forth by Niebuhr are not adequate for an understanding of the relationship between church and world today. This shift in thought can be illustrated by quotes from three modern representatives of the classic Reformed, Lutheran, and Anabaptist approaches to church and world.

In an article entitled "Reforming Cultural Calvinism," Richard Mouw claims, "The Niebuhrian Christ and Culture categories have misled us in important ways—or they have, at least, provided us with the opportunity to mislead ourselves."[1] Mouw argues that these categories tend to block our understanding of the way another group (or ourselves for that matter) functions. Is it true that the Anabaptists are always in antithesis? Not so, says Mouw. "The Amish have been more vigorous in their attempts to 'transform' farming than the Calvinists have been." Further, Mouw takes a swipe at his own denomination, acknowledging that "white Reformed politics in South Africa is a paradigm case of 'the Christ of Culture.' "[2]

Ulrich Duchrow raises a similar question when he asks, "I wonder whether it is possible and advisable to choose one model of H. R. Niebuhr's to spell out the interaction between the Christian faith and culture, namely the model of 'Christ Transforming Culture' so that, in principle, e.g., the other model of 'Christ Against Culture' is excluded."[3]

Duchrow finds much within the "Christ Against Culture" model to commend itself to Lutherans. In regard to economic questions in particular, he states, "I want to raise the question whether the situation is not developing into a stage where Christians will have to say a clear 'NO!' "[4] What he has in mind is the church's response to the multinational corporations who "oppress and destroy all the poor ones like a shark does with a smaller fish—just as if they could be Lord of God's creatures and not bound by the laws of faith and love."[5] He is not asking Christians to opt out of the money market. He does suggest, however, that "we try out economic disobedience." In the case of apartheid in South Africa, he quotes with approval the proposal of the Lutheran Church in America to "withdraw church money from companies and banks cooperating with South African economy under white rule."[6] For him, transformation of the economic system is the goal, and the way to accomplish that is through the model of antithesis.

Anabaptist John Howard Yoder has also raised severe questions about the Niebuhrian categories in an unpublished article.[7] He expresses concern with the way Niebuhr has slanted his argument toward the transformationalist approach. He also questions Niebuhr's insistence on consistency. He rejects the idea that each position must be regarded as either all paradox, all transformation, or all antithesis. He also expresses concern over Niebuhr's failure to take into consideration the diversity of cultures, the variety of issues, and the various responses needed from the church. A similar concern is voiced by Richard Mouw, who states, "We do not relate as Christians to culture as such. We stand in a relationship to one or another historically embodied culture—to North American culture, South African culture, Scottish culture, Chilean culture."[8] Consequently, culture is not a single bloc, demanding a single uniform response by the church.

These three critics of the classical models of Christ and culture point to the need for modern Christians to rethink and reformulate traditional understandings of the relationship between church and world toward a view that is in keeping with the global changes that have taken place in the twentieth century. For example, Mouw questions the relevance of an unchanged classical model by raising the issue that "the Reformed and Presbyterian confessional documents were all written in a Constantinian setting."[9] He asks his readers to interpret the biblical teaching on church and world with an eye toward the contemporary situation. He calls his fellow Reformed Christians to "painful self-examination, as well as an openness to the accounts of other perspectives."[10] Further, he claims, "We have received nothing from our past, even from our recent past, which has prepared us to respond adequately for contemporary cultural change."[11] He does not deny guidance from the past, but recognizes the past provides us with "hints and suggestions." Consequently, it is not enough to simply apply past formulations to the present, but to "reformulate—reform—on the level of theory."[12] This reformulation on the level of theory has occurred in two ways—the search for a new theological consensus and a christological method.

TOWARD A NEW THEOLOGICAL CONSENSUS

The reformulation of church-and-world understanding which Mouw invites is found in the new consensus of Protestant and Catholic scholars in the biblical and theological construct from which the church thinks about its role in the world. Specifically, it includes five theological ideas:
1. The orders of creation are under God.
2. Evil powers work through the structures of existence.
3. Christ is victorious over these evil powers.
4. The church is Christ's witness to the powers of evil.
5. The church lives in eschatological hope of Christ's return.

Since each of these points have been developed in the material of the previous sections, I will illustrate the current agreement among Christians by drawing on Catholic, Lutheran, Reformed, and Anabaptist sources only. These examples, together with the material already developed, sufficiently illustrate the prevailing consensus among theologians from a variety of Christian traditions.

The Structures of Existence Are Under God

It is now generally recognized that the structures of existence are to be seen under God and not autonomous. For example, the Roman Catholic "Pastoral Constitution on the Church in the Modern World" acknowledges the right of the human person to scientifically investigate the creation and to pursue discovery and knowledge. But any notion "that material being does not depend on God and that man can use it as if it had no relation to its creator"[13] is repudiated as false. It is false to give an autonomous status to the creation, to the structures of existence, and to treat them as though they are not accountable to God.

Ulrich Duchrow's criticism of the autonomy granted to the structures of existence between the seventeenth and early twentieth centuries also illustrates the trend found among Catholics and Protestants today. He charges that "the separation between the spheres of life had already begun at the end of the middle ages,"[14] that modern Christians "instead of locating dualism in the proper place (namely in the struggle against the power of evil in every sphere of life) . . . introduced (a dualism) on the level of God's twofold governance."[15] This perversion of the Reformers' teaching that all of life is under God's justice and love "established the theoretical justification of the notorious concept that the spheres of life are autonomous."[16] Consequently, "the essential meaning of religion and of the church could find expression only in the realm of the private life, and even then only in personal relationships and within the family. The economic, scientific, and public spheres of life were to be accepted and sanctioned automatically."[17] Duchrow's answer to this perversion of God's superintendency over the entirety of His creation is to affirm once again that God rules not only in the church but also in the world. His laws of love and justice are to be fulfilled in the church as well as in the world. While Christian traditions differ as to how the ideal of God's reign over all things is to find expression, there is a new unity of conviction that God rules over every corner of His creation.

Evil and the Structures of Existence

Another common conviction of today's church is that evil powers work through the structures of existence. If God rules over the entire creation, and if Satan who is the "prince of this world" seeks under God's sovereignty to turn creatures and their cultural activity against God, it follows that Satan does his diabolical work not merely through the attitudes and motivation of humans, but through the results of their cultural functioning in the structures of existence. The struggle between good and evil is not only a matter of the heart but of the human cultural activity in history.

The documents of Vatican II speak of this reality in clear terms: "The hierarchy of values has been disordered, good and evil intermingle, and every man and every group is interested in its own affairs . . . the whole of man's history has been the story of our combat with the powers of evil . . . finding himself in the midst of a battlefield, man has to struggle to do what is right."[18] Quoting Romans 12:2, "Do not be conformed to this world," the writers of the document say that *world* here means "a spirit of vanity and malice whereby human activity from being ordered to the service of God and man is distorted to an instrument of sin."[19]

John Howard Yoder comments on the change from individualism in ethics to the more corporate understanding of the power of evil. "Under the shadow of Protestant individualism it was assumed that the Apostle [Paul] did not deal with structural problems . . . driven by the events that shook Europe between 1930 and 1950, Protestant theology sought a more adequate theological understanding of the power of evil which had been breaking through the crust of the most civilized of societies."[20] Yoder argues that it is in the rediscovery of the Pauline concept of the powers working through the structures of existence that we find "a very refined analysis of the problems of society and history, far more refined than the other ways in which theologians have sought to describe the same realities."[21] These words echo the assessment of the W.C.C., the W.E.F., the religious right, and the Catholics.

Restoration of the *Christus Victor* Theme

A third common concern is to restore the *Christus Victor* interpretation of Christ's work as a victory over sin, death, and the dominion of the Devil. This theme proclaims the power of Christ to restore and renew His entire created order. The ancient concept of recapitulation found in Paul and developed in the second century theology of Irenaeus (which affirms the renewal of the entire creation by the incarnation, death, and resurrection of Jesus) is a central motif of contemporary Catholic understanding of church and world. "He entered world history, taking that history into himself and recapitulating it."[22] But the purpose of that recapitulation is to point toward "the transformation of the world."[23] The future transformation of the world, the vision of the prophets and of John in Revelation 21–22 is made possible only because Jesus Christ has conquered sin and death by overcoming Satan, the source of world disturbance. Yoder describes the victory of Christ over the powers as the "eschatological foundation of Christian involvement in politics."[24] He says, "This is not a statement concerning the benevolent disposition of certain men to listen or of certain powers to be submissive. It is a declaration about the nature of the cosmos and the significance of history, within which both our conscientious participation and our conscientious objection find their authority and their promise."[25] Richard Mouw, arguing from the same perspective, writes, "The promise of political transformation must be embodied in a specific ruler . . . in the New Testament this ensign appears when God assumes human flesh and dies on the cross to liberate his creation."[26] The cosmic persuasion of Paul in Colossians 1:13–23 is that Christ is not only the Creator, the one in whom all things exist, but the one through whom all things will be redeemed. Surely no Christan can pretend to understand the world—its meaning, purpose, and history—without careful inquiry into the radical and far-reaching consequences of the ruination of the power of evil through Christ's death and resurrection.

A consequence of the *Christus Victor* theme is the rediscovered emphasis of the lordship of Christ, of His reign over the powers, over the whole of creation, and over history. This reign, which is the rule of His kingdom, is now expressed in the church, which—through its proclamation of the lordship of Christ—continually witnesses to the defeat of the powers and to the ultimate victory of Christ over all evil.

Church as Witness to the Powers of Evil

Breaking away from its overemphasis on the church as institution, contemporary Christians now emphasize the church as the community in which the mystical presence of the risen Christ is made real in and to the world. According to the documents of Vatican II, the church "travels the same journey as all mankind and shares the same earthly lot with the world: it is to be leaven and, as it were, the soul of human society in its renewal by Christ and transformation into the family of God."[27] For Yoder "the church is under orders to make known to the Powers, as no other proclaimer can do, the fulfillment of the mysterious purposes of God (Eph. 3:10) by means of that Man in whom their rebellion has been broken and the pretensions they had raised been demolished."[28] While Reformed theologians will disagree with the Anabaptist Yoder on *how* the church is to address the powers that exercise their influence through the spheres, the recognition that the church is the primary focus of this work is acknowledged. Consequently, Mouw can describe the church in terms of its past, future, and present functions. In terms of the past it is rooted in God's "creative purposes which had become thwarted by sin"; with regard to the future it "manifests the first fruits of a kingdom that is yet to come." In its present function it is to be a "model and agent of healing."[29] Contemporary theologians have rediscovered the purpose and significance of the church. In its mission it is to carry on the work of Christ by applying the redemption that Christ brought to the created order through the ministry of servanthood and healing.

The Eschatological Hope

Finally, contemporary church-and-world thought has put all these matters in eschatological perspective. Eschatology has shifted from a theological object of study to the dynamic expectation of the new heavens and new earth, an expectation which reaches all the way back to the origin of creation and permeates all aspects of Christian thought. Eschatology as a branch of Christian theology which debates pre-, post-, or amillennialism has become less important as the church regains the eschatological consciousness of primitive Christianity, defined as hope in the future outcome of history. The documents of Vatican II speak of the significance of this eschatological consciousness for the reform of the world: "Far from diminishing our concern to develop this earth, the expectancy of a new earth should spur us on, for it is here that the body of a new human family grows, foreshadowing in some way the age that is to come . . ."[30] Yoder, evidencing the same eschatological hope, echoes a statement of Johann Christoph Blumhardt, the German theologian who rediscovered the eschatological foundations of Christian involvement in politics: "*Dass Jesus siegt ist ewig ausgemacht. Sein ist die ganze welt!*" "That Jesus is conqueror is eternally settled: the universe is his!"[31] Likewise, Richard Mouw concludes, "Jesus has already begun to transform the patterns of human authority. He calls us to cast our lot with lowly ones, to identify with the poor and the oppressed of the earth. To live in this manner is to anticipate the coming political vindication, when 'the least one shall become a clan, and the smallest one a mighty nation.' " (Isa. 60:22)[32] Later, Mouw states, "We can act politically in the full assurance that our political deeds will count toward the day of reckoning that will occur in the transformed city."[33]

These five areas of theological consensus are related to the christological method of thinking about the relationship of the church to the world, a matter to which we now turn.

A CHRISTOLOGICAL METHODOLOGY

One of the most striking shifts in current church-and-world thought is the move toward a christological method.[34] This method differs strikingly from the natural-law approach of medieval and later Catholic thought, from the two-kingdom theory of the Reformation era, and the love motif of Protestant liberalism. It constructs its view of the world, the church, and the work of the church directly out of a christology rooted in the cosmic nature of the Christ event.

The starting point for all theological reflection about the world—creation, structures of existence, the powers, the church, history, and the eschaton—is through the lens of the Christ event. It is the overarching Christ of Colossians—the Creator, the One in whom all things consist, the Redeemer of all things (Col. 1:15–20)—who is the key for understanding the role of the church in the world. The motif that Christ has overcome the powers of evil by His death and resurrection and now reigns over the world till all enemies have been put under His feet is the focal event. Here, in this event, is found the distinct and unique perception of the Christian view of reality.

Specifically, two aspects of the Christ event provide the theological thrust for Christian social action. These are the incarnation and the lordship of Christ.

First, the incarnation, which sets forth the model of the divine-human relationship, may be seen as analogous to the relationship of the church with the structures of existence. The model of the Christian's relationship to the world is found in Jesus Christ, God incarnate. In Jesus, God entered human history and life; through His person and work He modeled the relationship that His body, the church, is to express to the world. He identified with the world, yet He was separate from the ideologies that rule it; and by His death, resurrection, and second coming He assures its transformation.

Christ Identified With the World

In the first place, Christ identified with the natural order. He was, as the New Testament teaches and the creeds confess, "fully man." He assumed our nature and became flesh and blood. The early church's insistence that He was "born of a virgin, suffered under Pontius Pilate, was dead and buried, and on the third day rose again" was directed against all Gnostic denials of the full humanity of Christ. The church has always taught that He was one of us. He endured hunger, loneliness, pain, temptation, and all other human emotions. The writer of Hebrews affirms that "we have not a high priest who is unable to sympathize with our weaknesses, but one who in every respect has been tempted as we are, yet without sinning" (4:15).

Christ also identified with the social order. He was a particular person in a particular culture. He was part of the Jewish culture of His time and freely moved within it. His customs of life were not different from the norm. His dress, mannerisms, and habits of life such as eating, drinking, traveling, and worshiping were all in keeping with the acceptable norms of the day (except when He wished to make a point against the Pharisees). He made friends with all classes of people: Nicodemus the wealthy man, Levi the hated tax collector, Luke the physician, and Peter the fisherman. He was involved in the religious life of His culture. He attended the synagogue, participated in the Passover, and prayed in the temple. He was involved in the social life of society, such as the wedding in Cana. Because of His involvement in life, the Pharisees accused Him of being "a glutton and a drunkard, a friend of tax collectors and 'sinners'" (Matt. 11:19). Furthermore, it appears that He supported the government. When He was asked, "Is it right to pay taxes . . . ?" He answered, "Give to Caesar what is Caesar's, and to God what is God's" (Matt. 22:17, 21).

Christ does not identify with the world as someone who is "above" the world, nor merely "running alongside" the world. Rather, He is present in the world. The kingdom of God is "in the midst of you" (Luke 17:21).

By implication, the Christian church (which is His body) must be present to the world in the way in which Christ Himself identified with society. We are the instruments of His kingdom and witnesses to it. For this reason, we must not withdraw our presence from any legitimate structure of society. All dimensions of life—including the social, political, economic, educational, and recreational—are to be affirmed by Christians. Society belongs to God by virtue of Creation and has been sanctified by the presence of Christ within it. Our willingness to identify with the world as image-bearers of God dare not be less than that which Christ, the true and complete imprint of God, exemplified.

Christ Was Separate From the Ideologies That Rule the World.

The notion of separation may have physical implications as it did for John the Baptist and the monastics; they went into the desert and from that stance assumed a prophetic role toward society. In the life of Jesus, however, separation is more clearly defined as spiritual separation from the powers and ideologies that rule the world. He did not identify with what Paul calls "the ways of this world . . . the ruler of the kingdom of the air, the spirit who is now at work in those who are disobedient" (Eph. 2:2).

A casual reading of the New Testament is enough to convince the reader that Christ was continually confronted with the "powers." These "powers" are not so much the strengths of men and organizations, but forces that transcend the earthly. They are the powers of evil.

An example of this may be found in Christ's repudiation of the power of material possessions. The structure of economics is simply a reality of life. In order to live, man must meet his basic needs for food, shelter, and clothing. Christ affirms there is nothing wrong with meeting these needs, and the structure of creation makes such material goods available. But because of the radical nature of human fallenness, the structure of economics have been altered to the extent that money may become no longer the servant but master. A person may become controlled by the power of money. He or she may make its acquisition the goal of life. Money and material possessions become a thing of ultimate value. The whole course of a person's life may be ordered in the service of money.

Jesus confronted the power that money and material possessions hold over people. In the synoptic Gospels, an average of one out of ten verses deals with the problem of the rich and the poor. Jesus demanded that His followers make a radical break with the service of money. He insisted that one "cannot serve both God and Money" (Matt. 6:24), and His own life was an example of this teaching.

Although a radical break with money is a major concern of Jesus, it is only *one* of a number of concerns. Money is one of five prominent issues that recur in the demand Christ makes on His followers. The others include a break with reputation, violence, family, and "religion."

At its root, the issue involved in Christ's stance against the powers is the problem of idolatry. Jesus was truly free because He served the Father; and although He lived in the midst of the structures and in constant relationship to the powers, He never lived in the service of the powers. By His life and teaching, He witnessed against the powers and the hold they have when they become man's god.

In today's world, Christians and the church live under the constant temptation to idolize the structures of life. We make them our saviors. We worship them by serving them. The Devil's desire is to pervert our lives in such a way that we will express our commitment to selfishness, greed, injustice, and the like—all of which come from the power and influence of evil. Against this, Christ advocates *separation*; we are to separate ourselves not only from a commitment to evil but from the support of evil in all areas of life. Evil finds its way into all the structures of existence, even the church. Christians must take a prophetic stance toward the presence of evil in all its forms, both personal and corporate. The powers of materialism, sensualism, greed, war, hate, oppression, and injustice are not to rule the Christian; wherever they express themselves, they are to be fought.

By the Death, Resurrection, and Second Coming of Christ, the Transformation of the World Is Assured.

The Incarnation of God in Christ was a prelude to His death. Any discussion of the Incarnation that fails to recognize its relationship to the death, resurrection, and second coming of Christ is inadequate; it is all of a single piece and must be treated that way.

In the first place, it must be recognized that the death and resurrection of Christ destroys the sovereignty that the powers hold over man. The apostle Paul specifically teaches this in reference to the power of death in 1 Corinthians 15. More specifically, Paul refers to the blow that Christ's death rendered to the powers in the complementary verbs in Colossians 2:15: "He *disarmed* the principalities and the powers and *made a public example* of them, *triumphing* over them in him" (RSV, italics mine).

In the second place, Christian eschatology recognizes that the completion of Christ's work against the powers will not occur until the Second Coming. John provides in the Book of Revelation a description of the final judgment of Satan and the powers. After death and hades are thrown into the lake of fire, the new heavens and the new earth will become visible. In this New Jerusalem, this restoration of paradise, all things will be new. The Devil will "deceive the nations no more" (Rev. 20:3 RSV).

Because Christ has broken the power of sin over man, man is free not to be a slave to the powers. The biblical allusions to new life in Christ affirm this principle throughout the New Testament. In Romans, Paul reminds Christians that "you have been set free from sin and have become slaves to righteousness" (6:18). In Galatians, he describes this new relationship as an effort to "live by the spirit" (5:16, 25) as opposed to a life that grows out of the "desires of the sinful natures" (v. 16). The Christians in Colossae are reminded that they have "put to death" their "earthly nature" (3:5) and "put on the new self" (v. 10). Christians have been set free so that they can choose not to serve the powers. But what about the rest of creation? Is the creation still in bondage to the fallen state of the powers? Paul answers this question in Romans 8. The creation has not yet been set free. It "waits in eager expectation . . . in hope that the creation itself will be liberated from its bondage to decay and brought into the glorious freedom of the children of God" (vv. 19–21). In the meantime both man and creation live in the hope of ultimate redemption, and it is in this hope that we are saved (v. 24).

Today the church lives in the recognition that the powers have been disarmed and that Christ will ultimately destroy all evil. Christ's power over evil is both a present reality and a future hope. Thus, we are called to a social involvement that seeks to transform the present culture, moving it toward a greater approximation of the ideal. We ought not to expect a utopia to result; rather, we should believe that change is possible and that working for this change is a way of witnessing to the ultimate reality of God's kingdom. The Christian hope that sin will be destroyed and peace will reign is more than a dream. It is a goal toward which we work, even though we know it will be universally realized only by the consummation of Christ's work in His second coming.

Contemporary thinkers seem to agree that the Incarnation is an integral facet of christological doctrine which reflects helpfully on the role of the Christian and the church in the world. As a revelation of the Father, Christ was *identified* with the natural and social order. He was *separate* from the powers of evil that rule the course of the world. And He began the *transformation* of the world in His death and resurrection—a transformation that will be completed in His second coming. *This three-sided view of reality points to the relationship that exists between the Christian and the world, as well as between the church and the world.*

The second aspect of christology giving shape to church-and-world thought today is the lordship of Christ. Christ exerts His lordship in His present reign over the principalities and powers, a reign that He obtained by virtue of His victory over them in the Cross and resurrection. The earliest New Testament christologies emphasize the lordship of Christ in His exaltation over the whole cosmos. Evidence of His cosmic lordship is found in the New Testament's frequent use of Psalm 110:1: "The LORD says to my LORD: Sit at my right hand until I make your enemies a footstool for your feet" (see Mark 14:62; Acts 2:34–35; 1 Cor. 15:20–27; Eph. 1:20, 22; Heb. 1:13). His cosmic lordship is also stressed in the great christological hymn of Philippians 2:6–11. This hymn declares that the power of evil has been broken, resulting in the exaltation of Christ, a position acknowledged "in heaven and on earth and under the earth." Other liturgical passages such as Colossians 1:15–20 and Ephesians 1:20–22 proclaim Christ's position of lordship over the entire cosmos. They are not descriptions of how we see things empirically, for the battle with evil still rages; rather, they are doxological expressions of faith, proclaimed in the assurance that "the kingdom of the world has become the kingdom of our Lord and of his Christ, and he will reign for ever and ever" (Rev. 11:15). This confession that "Jesus is Lord" (Rom. 10:9) relates to our understanding of church and world in three ways: the lordship of Christ over the church, over the structures of existence, and over history.

The Lordship of Christ Over the Church

The relationship of the risen and conquering Lord to the church finds expression in the enthronement scene at the end of Matthew. Jesus said to His disciples, "All authority in heaven and on earth has been given to me" (Matt. 28:18). This authority is then invoked by Jesus as He declares the mission of the church: ". . . Go and make disciples of all nations, baptizing them in the name of the Father and of the Son and of the Holy Spirit, and teaching them to obey everything I have commanded you. And surely I am with you always, to the very end of the age" (Matt. 28:19–20). The church's mission is not to establish His lordship over the world; rather, it proceeds on the basis of a lordship already gained and announced by Jesus. The work of the church is to witness to His lordship. But how?

In a primary sense, the church itself is a sign of the lordship of Christ over the world. Its very existence is a sign that the powers of evil have been defeated, that Jesus is Lord. Thus it is God's intent that through the church—and not through America or some other country or organization—that "the manifold wisdom of God should be made known to the rulers and authorities in the heavenly realms" (Eph. 3:10). This witness of the church occurs in worship, evangelism, and social action.

The worshiping church witnesses to the lordship of Christ in prayer (1 Tim. 2:1–4), which points to the ultimacy of Christ in all matters; in baptism, which is a sign of the renunciation of evil (Rom. 6:1–7); and in the celebration of communion, which proclaims our rejection of the demonic (1 Cor. 10:21) and affirms the new community relationships established on justice (1 Cor 11:17–21).

In evangelism, the convert is snatched away from the power of the evil one and brought into an entirely new realm of life (Eph. 2:1–10). In this new realm the convert is actually "seated . . . with him in the heavenly places" (Eph. 2:6 NASB). Thus, the source and power for living comes from the lordship of Christ under whose command the Christian now lives.

In social action, the church functions by principles of justice which derive from the kingdom of light, the kingdom over which Christ rules (Eph. 5).

The Lordship of Christ, the Church, and the Structures of Existence

The lordship of Christ over the structures of existence is a paradigm of the relationship of the Christian and of the church to the structures. Since Christ has conquered and now reigns over the powers of evil that work through the structures to pervert human life and history, the Christian's relationship toward these structures is through the lordship of Christ. This means that the Christian is no longer under the powers, at least in principle.

The new believer is called to enter into Christ and turn away from a commitment to the distorting powers, to repudiate the hold that evil exerts upon life, and to turn toward the qualities of love, peace, and justice as a new walk of life. This repentance (Gk., *metanoia*) calls for a radical break with the powers of evil, a break that affects one's relationship to the perversions of God's intention for the structures.

Second, the evangelized one is called into a new community, the church, a community covenanted to the risen Lord, a community in which individuals relate to each other out of a new vision of reality established by the relationship Christ holds to the structures by virtue of His lordship over them.

This new vision operates on two levels. One has to do with personal relationships within the church, as noted above. The other has to do with the relationship of the church to the structures which, though still fallen, are under the promise of redemption (Rom. 16:20). God's people are called to relate to the structures of existence in the confidence of Christ's victory over them, and in the assurance of His ultimate and final defeat of their continuing presence in the world. In this sense, the church acts as a witness to the reign of Christ over the structures through which the powers of evil continue to work. So the task of the church is not to defeat evil, but to witness to the defeat that has already taken place and will be consummated in the eschaton. For this reason, the church must be careful in making political commitments lest by its commitment to a particular economic policy or political structure it becomes subservient to that structure and the evil it may represent. Furthermore, the church must guard against an imposition of its own institutional life on the world, lest through its attempt to "Christianize the world" it becomes a power itself. The church is called to witness through servanthood to the lordship of Christ (1 Peter 3:8–22), not to reign in the world.

The Lordship of Christ, the Church, and History

The eschatological hope of the church, which is the conviction that all sin will ultimately be put away forever, is not only the hope of the church, but the hope of the world— the world which was "subjected to frustration" now "waits in eager expectation" for the day when it "will be liberated from its bondage to decay and brought into the glorious freedom of the children of God" (Rom. 8:19–21). The church knows how "the whole creation has been groaning as in the pains of childbirth right up to the present time" (Rom. 8:22), for the church also lives in anticipation of that time when the lordship of Christ will be exercised over the entire creation in an empirical way (Rev. 20–22). Yet, the church's view of history is optimistic. It knows the final outcome. And it now witnesses to the lordship of Christ in the history that is moving toward the eradication of all evil in every sphere of existence. In this hope it is saved (Rom. 8:24).

CONCLUSION

In this book I have attempted to show the meaning of the gospel for the life of the church in the world. It seems abundantly clear that the life, death, resurrection, and exaltation of Jesus Christ, who has defeated the powers of evil which rage in the world, ought to be central to our construct of the church in the world. Perhaps it is a sign of spiritual vitality that the church universal is being driven back to a world view that begins with Christ. For it is Christ and Christ alone who has defeated the powers of evil. As we learn how to rest and work in God's action, our witness to the potential this world has in Christ will become more effective by our proclamation and example.

APPENDIX A :
KOSMOS (WORLD)

Generally, the word kosmos[1] is used to refer to the material earth (Matt. 24:21); the world of people (Matt. 4:8; John 3:16, 12:19, 18:20); the mission of Jesus which is related to the world (John 1:29, 6:33; 1 Tim. 3:15); a materialistic approach to life (Luke 12:30); and Christian witness, as for example the disciples who are to be lights to the world (Matt. 5:14; cf. Matt. 28:19; Mark 16:15). Kosmos also refers to the sphere of human life in passages such as 1 Tim. 6:7, "For we brought nothing into the world, and we can take nothing out of it." A similar usage is found in the reference to "languages in the world" (1 Cor. 14:10). Paul also refers to sin that "entered the world" (Rom. 5:12) and to his own conduct "in the world" (2 Cor. 1:12). The writer of Hebrews makes the claim that the "world was not worthy" of the heroes of faith (Heb. 11:38). More specifically, John uses the word to refer to the order of existence into which people are born (6:14, 9:39, 18:37). Hence Jesus can refer to His human life as being in the world (John 9:5) and to His death as departing from the world (John 13:1). In some cases, the word may refer to the physical environment, as in the statements, "We have been made a spectacle to the whole universe" (1 Cor. 4:9) and "Abraham . . . would be heir of the world" (Rom. 4:13). In all of these instances, there is no hint that the world is evil; nor is there any teaching that Christians are to forsake the world. Rather, the world is seen as God's creation, a place to live, to affirm, and to be part of.

The World of Adverse Spiritual Agencies

In the New Testament, evil is personified in a single being, Satan.[2] He is seen as the supreme agent of evil; he claims a dominating influence over the world; he is the tempter and is frequently seen in conflict with another person, Jesus. According to John, Satan is the "prince (ruler) of the world" (John 12:31, 14:30, 16:11), the father of lies and a murderer (John 8:44).

In the New Testament world view, Satan also has an

army of evil agents who carry out his work, the demons.[3] In the Synoptics, demon possession is seen as specific examples of satanic activity. For example, a man in Capernaum was "possessed by an evil spirit" (Mark 1:23, cf. Matt. 12:45). These demonic spirits create evil effects such as the blind and dumb demoniac (Matt. 12:22), the dumb spirit (Mark 9:17), and uncontrollable violence (Mark 5:1ff.). Paul is also highly conscious of the activity of evil agencies. He says that Satan tempts Christians to forfeit self-control (1 Cor. 7:5), harasses God's people (2 Cor. 12:7), transforms himself into an angel of light (2 Cor. 11:14), and blinds the eyes of people so that they cannot see the light of the gospel (2 Cor. 4:4). According to Paul, the presence of the demonic is highly powerful (1 Cor. 10:19ff). Demonic power is so strong that conversion to Christ may be regarded as a liberation from the power of the demonic (Eph. 2:2). Yet the demons continue to try the Christian, seducing the believer into error (1 Tim. 4:1) and captivating them under the elemental spirits (Col. 2:8, 20). Indeed, they are the adverse spiritual agencies that are behind the world rulers and world system, seeking constantly to create havoc and evil in God's creation (Rom. 8:38–39).

According to the author of Hebrews, Satan holds the "power of death" (Heb. 2:14). Peter states that the demonic is the source of evil desires which create corruption in the world (2 Peter 1:4, 2:20). John emphasizes the role of these evil agencies in the Apocalypse. He frequently mentions Satan (Rev. 2:9, 13, 24; 3:9; 12:9; 20:2, 7), the Devil (2:10; 12:9, 12), the Dragon (12:3; 13:2; 20:2), and the Serpent (12:9, 14-15; 20:2). John states that he is the deceiver of the whole world (12:9) and the accuser of Christians (12:10). He has counterfeit angels (12:9); he counterfeits the triune God by exercising authority through a second beast and false prophet (ch. 13); he claims absolute homage and worship (13:4); and he exercises control over people, symbolized by his mark on their foreheads (13:16). And finally, he gathers the evil spirits together to fight the final battle at Armageddon (16:13ff.).

These texts strongly suggest that the New Testament writers saw themselves and their world in terms of spiritual agencies, both good and bad. They appear to be keenly aware of a cosmic struggle taking place between these forces, a dual influence that was exercised upon the world order. This awareness led them to use the word *kosmos* in a negative way, referring to the power of the evil one in and through the order and systems of the world. Consequently, *kosmos* is frequently seen in contrast to God.

John sees the *kosmos* as the sinful world that is in conflict with God. This is the "world that did not recognize him" (John 1:10), a world that Jesus said "hates me because I testify that what it does is evil" (John 7:7). Jesus is "not of this world" (John 8:23) because the world is a system opposed to God (John 16:33).

James bluntly states that "friendship with the world is hatred toward God" (James 4:4), which "pollutes" the believer (James 1:27). Paul also picks up the gauntlet against the world. He says the world is on its own "without hope and without God" (Eph. 2:12). The Spirit of God stands over against the spirit of the world (1 Cor. 2:12). The wisdom of the world is foolishness (1 Cor. 1:20, 3:19); consequently, the world which is accountable to God (Rom. 3:9) stands under the judgment of God (Rom. 3:6; 1 Cor. 6:2, 11:32). Paul speaks of the ways of this world, which are equated to following "the ruler of the kingdom of the air, the spirit who is now at work in those who are disobedient" (Eph. 2:2). Paul believes the world is the arena in which the Christian is in a continual conflict with evil powers (Eph. 6:12).

John also consistently sees the disciples set against the world. He quotes Jesus as saying, "They are not of the world, even as I am not of it" (John 17:16; cf. v. 14). The disciples are distinguished from the world (17:9). However, Jesus does not pray for them to be taken from the world (17:15), but to be sent into the world (17:18) so that the world may believe (17:21, 23).

Nevertheless there is a clear dualism in John and other New Testament writers. John especially accents the antithesis Christians have with the world in his first letter. Christians are not to "love the world or anything in the world. For everything in the world—the cravings of sinful man, the lust of his eyes and the boasting of what he has and does—comes not from the Father but from the world" (1 John 2:15–16). Consequently, the world hates Christians (3:13), receives false prophets (4:1), harbors the spirit of antichrist (4:3), listens to the evil one (4:5), and can be spoken of as "under the control of the evil one" (5:19). For this reason, Paul calls upon Christians to live differently (Col. 2:20), to give no opportunity to the Devil (Eph. 4:27), and to stand "against the devil's schemes" (Eph. 6:11). He warns against falling "under the same judgment as the devil" (1 Tim. 3:6) or into "disgrace and into the devil's trap" (1 Tim. 3:7), since the Devil makes people "captive to do his will" (2 Tim. 2:26). Other New Testament writers, such as the author of Hebrews (11:7) and Peter (1 Peter 5:8), also describe the world over against God, although the strongest sense of dualism comes from Paul and John.

In summary, it must be acknowledged that the phrase, "the world" (*kosmos*) has at least two uses in the New Testament. In the first place, "the world" may be regarded as the created order which, although affected by the Fall, is good and not to be avoided. In the second place, "the world" may refer to evil spiritual agencies that seek to control and dominate the order of creation. These worldly powers have been routed out by the Cross of Christ and eventually, in the consummation of God's plan, they will be utterly destroyed and put away forever.[4] These concepts have undoubtedly given rise to different Christian attitudes toward the world. In the creational sense, Christians know they are to identify with the world; but so far as "the world" refers to adverse spiritual agencies, Christians will either flee them or seek to overcome them in the name of Jesus. These ideas will be expanded later. First we must look at the nature of the church.

APPENDIX B :
EKKLESIA (CHURCH)

The Greek New Testament's word for *church* (*ekklesia*) literally meant "those called out." It was borrowed from the language of the Greek city-state, in which the voting citizens who had the privilege of participating in civic debate were called the *ekklesia*—they were "called out" from the rest of the populace to decide matters affecting them all. Thus, when the New Testament uses the word *ekklesia* in reference to the church, it emphasizes the church's role of spiritual leadership. The people of the church were still "in the world," yet they were called to exercise a spiritual influence quite apart from anything that was typical of the world.

Paul, a Jew yet the missionary to the Gentiles, is deeply concerned with the relationship of the church to Israel. He asks the most difficult question of all: Has God cast away His people Israel? (Rom. 9–11). His conclusion stated in Galations is that the true people of God, whether Jew or Gentile, are "in Christ": "There is neither Jew nor Greek, slave nor free, male nor female, for you are one in Christ Jesus" (Gal. 3:28). Paul realized that a new people have come into being, rooted to be sure in the old nation of Israel, in whom the new people were anticipated, but linked with Christ in His death, resurrection, and exaltation (Gal. 3:14, 16, 29; Rom. 4:11–17). The church is therefore bound up with the mystery of Christ, for "through the gospel the Gentiles are heirs together with Israel, members together of one body, and sharers together in the promise in Christ Jesus" (Eph. 3:6). It is through this church, then, that "the manifold wisdom of God should be made known to the rulers and authorities in the heavenly realms" (Eph. 3:10). Because the church is now the people of God, the expression of God's redemptive power in history, the church is the primary agent through whom the diabolical powers of evil are confronted.

But this special position of the church in the world is inseparably linked to the presence and power of the Holy Spirit in the church.[1] Through the Holy Spirit, the inner connection between the work of Christ on the cross and the work of Christ in the world through the church is estab-

lished. The church is more than an association of believers or
an institution established by Jesus. It is a spiritual reality in
the world that unfolds within the order of existence and
participates in salvation history. Paul characterizes God's
new community as a Spirit-filled community (2 Cor. 3:6–18).
This Spirit who animates and gives life to the church is from
"the last Adam, a life-giving spirit" (1 Cor. 15:45). It is the
crucified, resurrected, and exalted Christ who sends His
Spirit upon the church. Thus the church is "built on the
foundation of the apostles and prophets, with Christ Jesus
Himself as the chief cornerstone" (Eph. 2:20). And through
Him it becomes a "dwelling in which God lives by his Spirit"
(Eph. 2:22). By the Holy Spirit, the work of Christ continues
in the world. Consequently, the church carries on its
struggles against the world not by its own might but through
the Holy Spirit. According to John, it is the Holy Spirit who
will "convict the world of guilt in regard to sin and
righteousness and judgment" (John 16:8). And this is
because "the prince of this world now stands condemned"
(John 16:11).

The presence of Christ in the world through the church
is further clarified and given substance by the Pauline
metaphor which describes the church as the body of Christ.[2]
This metaphor, along with others such as "the people of
God," "the church of God," "the new covenant," "the vine
and the branches," seek to describe the profound relationship that exists between Christ and the church. Of these, the
concept of the "body of Christ" is the most intimate and
perhaps the most profound. In Colossians and Ephesians,
Christ is described as "the head" of His body, the church
(Col. 1:18; Eph. 1:22–23, 4:15, 5:23). In this image, the
heavenly Christ rules His church and causes it to grow up
into His own maturity (Eph. 4:12–16) through love. Therefore, the church becomes "the fullness of him who fills every
thing in every way" (Eph. 1:23). And through this church,
which is His fullness, His rule in the world is expressed, for
"God placed all things under his feet and appointed him to
be head over everything for the church" (Eph. 1:22).

Christ who is the victor over the adverse powers that
hold sway in the world (Col. 2:14–15) allows His body to
share in that victory. His body, which has an earthly
appearance, is the human face of His continued heavenly
operation. In and through His body, the fight with Satan and

the diabolical forces of evil that roam the world take place (Eph. 2:10, 6:10–18). The church strives toward what its head, Christ, has already achieved. This perfection will be realized in the eschaton, when all the powers that have warred against Christ and His church will be put down forever (Rev. 20).

APPENDIX C :
STOICHEIA (PRINCIPALITIES) AND DUNAMIS OR EXOUSIA (POWERS)

The writings of Paul refer to two basic concepts of power.[1] On the one hand, Paul uses the Greek words for *power* to refer to the diabolical and sinister influence of evil. On the other hand, he uses *principalities* or *principles* to refer to what we may call structures of existence.[2]

First, Paul frequently uses the Greek terms *dunamis* or *exousia* to describe demonic influences. For example, he speaks of the final destruction of "all dominion, authority and power [*dunamis*]" (1 Cor. 15:24). These powers are synonymous with the "principalities and powers [*exousia*]" of Ephesians 1:21 over which Christ rules now while seated at the right hand of the Father in heavenly places (Eph. 1:20). His rule over them was demonstrated to the church at the Cross (Col. 2:15). Nevertheless, the Christian continues to wrestle with these principalities and powers (Eph. 6:12) whose ultimate origin and source may be identified with the "god of this age" (2 Cor. 4:4). These powers cause people to follow "the ways of this world and . . . the ruler of the kingdom of the air, the spirit who is now at work in those who are disobedient" (Eph. 2:2). Paul identifies powers as the invisible forces of evil that oppose God, seek to distort the right uses of his creation, and work upon human beings to lead them astray.[3]

There is also a second possible understanding of the term *power* in Paul. These are powers that can be identified as "experienced realities" or "structures of earthly existence."[4] The argument rests especially on Paul's use of the word *stoicheia* ("the basic principles of this world") in Colossians 2:8, 20 and Galatians 4:3, 9, as well as the implications of Romans 8:38 and 1 Corinthians 2:8 and 3:22.

The root meaning of *stoicheia* comes from *stoicheioō*, which literally means "to stand in a row" as, say, the letters of the alphabet.[5] In a figurative sense, it can refer to "first principles," as in Hebrews 5:12, where the author chides his readers, "You need someone to teach you the elementary truths of God's word all over again." In Greek philosophy and in Hellenistic Judaism, the word is used to refer to the basic materials from which the world is put together (see Wisdom of Solomon 7:17, 19:18; 4 Macc. 2:13). Peter uses the word in this sense when, referring to the end of the age, he writes that "the elements will be destroyed by fire" (2 Peter 3:10). Apparently, in keeping with the philosophical usage of the word, Paul and Peter use the word to connote the stuff of which creation is made. These "powers" may be described as the structures of existence that provide the frame of reference in which persons live out their lives. These are not angelic beings or super earthly powers but realities such as the civil state (which Paul calls a "power" in Romans 13:1 KJV) and human regulations such as dietary laws and the like (Gal. 4:1–10).

Paul seems to have the structures of existence in mind in Romans 8:38, when he says, "Neither death nor life, nor angels nor principalities, nor present nor future, nor *powers*, nor height nor depth, nor any other creature (creation) will be able to separate us from the love of God." Here Paul names a number of realities (aspects of existence) which not only define the parameters of life but dominate and condition earthly well-being. In this context, the powers are not demonic forces but orders, structures, and institutions (such as political and economic institutions)—realities that define and order our existence in the world.

A hint to the specific nature of these structures is given in 1 Corinthians 2:8. Here Paul tells his readers that it was the "rulers of this age" (*archōntes*) who actually crucified the Lord of glory.[6] The institutions which correspond to this statement were the Roman state and Jewish religion. These visible realities were concretely active in the crucifixion of Jesus. But behind these realities was the invisible working of a higher power.

Further information about these structures of existence can be garnered from Paul's discussion of "the basic principles (*stoicheiōn*) of this world" in Colossians 2:20. Apparently, the Christians were being drawn into a destructive legalism which held a negative power over their lives. The same emphasis is found in Galatians 4:1–11, where Paul admonishes the Christians of Galatia not to return again to the "weak and miserable principles" (v. 9), becoming subject to days, months, seasons, and years. Here Paul challenged the Galatians to break away from the false security that one can attain from a trusting attachment to structures of existence. The emphasis is similar to that enunciated to the Romans when he admonishes them against worshiping and serving created things rather than the Creator (Rom. 1:25). The importance of these passages is that they provide us with a concrete understanding of specific aspects of life through which invisible evil powers may be at work. To summarize, the biblical references to these powers include:

> Romans 8:38—time (present and future), space (depth and height), death, and life

> 1 Corinthians 2:8—the state, religion

> Colossians 2:6–23; Galatians 4:1–11—manmade religious observances, manmade social regulations.

The biblical record does not provide an inclusive list of the structures of existence. Nevertheless, it seems to set forth the principle that *concrete structures of existence which are created by God may be the context through which adverse spiritual powers work to produce evil in the world.*

As we consider the role of the structures of existence in our understanding of the relationship between church and world, there are three biblical ideas we need to keep in mind: First, these structures have been created by God. Second, their use has been affected by the Fall. And third, they are now channels through which the power of evil works in the world.

In spite of the fact that these structures can be subject to Satan and through him exercise an evil influence over our lives, they are to be seen as under God by virtue of His creative act.

The passage in which Paul connects the powers as structures of existence with creation is found in Colossians: "He is the image of the invisible God, the firstborn over all creation. For by him all things were created: things in heaven and on earth, visible and invisible, whether thrones or *powers* or rulers or authorities; all things were created by him and for him. He is before all things, and in him all things hold together" (Col. 1:15–17, italics added). The phrase, "in him all things hold together," emphasizes the fact that Christ and not the structures of existence are ultimate. The structures of existence—like "all things"—were "created by him and for him." Like everything else in God's creation, the structures of creation are good and not to be viewed as intrinsically evil. For to view the structures as evil would be to set up a false dualism between the Creator and the creation, which this passage will not allow.[7]

Unfortunately, we do not know any of these structures of existence in their pure and unadulterated sense. Because of the Fall the only way we know and experience these orders is as they are bound up with sin. Paul speaks of our relationship to them as one of enslavement; he says they have become "gods" to us.

Paul expounds how a structure of existence may become a god in his discussion of the "law issue" with the Galatians (Gal. 4:8–11). The Galatians had been confused by the Judaizers, who insisted they could not be saved by Christ alone. The Judaizers said they had to put themselves under Jewish law in order to be redeemed. Paul finds this suggestion abhorrent. He says, "Formerly, when you did not know God, you were slaves to those who by nature are not gods" (v. 4). Here Paul affirms that the law is good in and of itself; but the Judaizers were turning the law into a god, making it a source of salvation. By worshiping the law, they became enslaved to the distorted interpretation they had given the law. Consequently, the law became a power over their lives. The nature and function of the law had become twisted so that those who sought salvation through the law were trusting in a lie and had become enslaved by "weak and miserable principles (stoicheia)."

This principle of distortion is applicable to all other aspects of existence. If humans can turn a law into a god, then it is possible for the same thing to occur in science, psychology, economics, politics, and even religion. The distorting effect of the demonic principle can cause humans to absolutize an aspect of the creation, ascribing to it a godlike character so that they become enslaved to its distortion. For example, scientism elevates the physical sciences to a position of ultimacy, insisting that only scientific explanations of things count for anything, that only scientific methods give us knowledge, and that only science can solve our problems. In short, scientism advocates a secular salvation. Such a perversion of science is the result of the influence that Satan exercises over the structure of science. Science is treated as a god having ultimate power over life. Another example can be found in patriotism, which can be turned into a blind and loyal trust in national goals and aspirations, causing one to suppose the nation has a near-messianic role in world affairs. These two examples illustrate how Satan works through structures of existence which are good in and of themselves—such as scientific inquiry or the structure of the state—and imposes upon them a diabolical character by making people think they provide the answer to life or can act to save mankind. These structures of existence are turned into false illusions, leading people astray from the true God of creation and history by causing them to trust science, nationalism, or some other structure of existence for their salvation.

NOTES

CHAPTER 1

[1] See for example R. Bultmann, *Jesus Christ and Mythology* (New York: Scribner, 1958), p. 15: "The whole conception of the world which is presupposed in the preaching of Jesus as in the N.T. generally is mythological; i.e., the conception of the world as being structured in three stories, heaven, earth, and hell; the conception of the intervention of supernatural powers in the inner life of the soul, the conception that men can be tempted and corrupted by the devil and possessed by evil spirits."

[2] Donald Guthrie, *New Testament Theology* (Downers Grove: InterVarsity, 1981), pp. 121–50. My analysis of the use of the word *kosmos* in the N.T. is particularly indebted to Guthrie.

[3] For further discussion of the christological concept of creation, see R. P. Martin, *Colossians and Philemon* (London: Oliphants, 1974), pp. 57ff. See p. 137.

[4] A particularly helpful work on the New Testament idea of the church is Rudolf Schnackenburg, *The Church in the New Testament* (New York: Seabury, 1965). See especially his discussion of "Church and World" and "Church and Kingdom of God," pt. 4, chs. 5 and 6.

[5] Ibid., pp. 171ff.

[6] Ibid., pp. 187ff. See also Guthrie, pp. 702–6.

CHAPTER 2

[1] See for example Hendrik Berkhof, *Christ and the Powers* (Scottdale, Pa.: Herald, 1977); Clinton D. Morrison, *The Powers That Be* (Naperville, Ill.: Allenson, 1960); G. B. Caird, *Principalities and Powers* (London: Oxford University Press, 1956); Heinrich Schlier, *Principalities and Powers in the New Testament* (New York: Herder and Herder, 1961); John Howard Yoder, *The Politics of Jesus* (Grand Rapids: Eerdmans, 1972).

[2] This is a passage in which the three interpretations mentioned above may be readily found. Gene Miller, "*Archonton Tou Aionos Touton*—A New Look at I Corinthians 2:6–8," *Journal of Biblical Literature* 91 (1972): 522–28, argues that only earthly rulers are in mind. Whereas J. Young, "Interpreting the Demonic Powers in Pauline Thought," *Novum Testamentum* 12 (1970): 54–69, argues for an interpretation that accents the role of spiritual powers. My own sympathies lie with G. B. Caird, who states in *Principalities and Powers*, "Paul discerned the existence of angelic rulers who shared with their human agents the responsibility for the crucifixion" (p. 17).

[3] For a discussion of the Old Testament background to the powers of evil in society, see Caird, *Principalities and Powers*, pp. 1–15; Morrison, *The Powers That Be*, pp. 17ff; and Cyril H. Powell, *The Biblical Concept of Power* (London: Epworth, 1963), pp. 5–68.

[4] For a more detailed description, see John Warwick Montgomery, *Principalities and Powers* (Minneapolis: Bethany House, 1973), pp. 177–80 (App. A, "The Early Church's Concept of Demonic Activity").

[5] Berkhof, *Christ and the Powers*, p. 29.

CHAPTER 3

¹Cyrill H. Powell, *The Biblical Concept of Power* (London: Epworth, 1963), pp. 82ff.

²Donald Guthrie, *New Testament Theology* (Downers Grove, Ill.: Inter-Varsity, 1981), pp. 519ff.

³For a brief but helpful discussion of the tension between a present and future eschatology in John, see ibid., pp. 778ff.

⁴Berkhof, *Christ and the Powers*, pp. 30ff.; Powell, *The Biblical Concept of Power*, pp. 117ff.

⁵Charles K. Barrett, *The First Epistle to the Corinthians* (New York: Harper and Row, 1968), pp. 356ff.

⁶For further elaboration of the tension between the "now" and the "not yet," see Oscar Cullmann, *The Early Church* (London: SCM Press, 1956), pp. 141ff, and *Christ and Time* (London: SCM Press, 1951).

⁷Berkhof, *Christ and the Powers*, pp. 47ff. See also Powell, *The Biblical Concept of Power*, pp. 142ff. For example, Powell writes, "The church is thus the agency continuing Christ's ministry, proclaiming His gospel, carrying the fact and the power of His victory to men, and bringing them into the life of salvation" (p. 150).

⁸Justin Martyr, *First Apology* ch. 61.

CHAPTER 4

¹For an elaboration of church-state relations, see Robert M. Grant, *The Sword and the Cross* (New York: Macmillan, 1955).

²Irenaeus, *Against Heresies* IV. 36. Unless otherwise indicated, all references to the early Fathers are taken from *The Ante-Nicene Fathers* (Grand Rapids: Eerdmans, 1971), hereafter cited as *Fathers*.

³Justin Martyr, *First Apology*.

⁴Ibid.

⁵Theophilus, "Letter to Autolycus" III.

⁶Aristides, *Apology*.

⁷Irenaeus, *Against Heresies* 5.

⁸*Didache*.

⁹See Acts 8:27; 10:1; 13:12; 16:27–34; 18:8; Phil. 4:22; Rom. 16:10–11.

¹⁰Burton Scott Easton, ed., *The Apostolic Tradition* (Hamden, Conn.: Archon, 1962), ch. 16.

¹¹Ibid.

¹²Tertullian, *On Idolatry*.

¹³Tertullian, *On Shows*.

¹⁴Athenagoras, *A Plea*.

¹⁵Lucian, *The Passing of Peregrinus*.

¹⁶Justin Martyr, *Apology*.

¹⁷Martin Hengel, *Property and Riches in the Early Church* (Philadelphia: Fortress, 1974), p. 1.

¹⁸Aristides, *Apology*.

¹⁹Ibid.

²⁰*An Epistle to Diognetus* ch. 5, quoted in Cyril C. Richardson, ed., *The Library of Christian Classics*, vol. 1: *Early Christian Fathers* (Philadelphia: Westminster, 1953).

²¹Irenaeus, *Against Heresies* 1. 10.

[22] Tertullian, *On Baptism* ch. 3. Quoted from Coleman J. Barry, *Readings in Church History* (Westminster, Mass.: Newman, 1964), p. 54.

[23] Jeffrey Burton Russell, *Satan: The Early Christian Tradition* (Ithaca: Cornell University Press, 1981).

[24] Irenaeus, *Against Heresies* 5. 24. 3.

[25] Tertullian, *Apology* 82. 4.

[26] Origen, *The Fundamental Doctrines* 1. pref. 5.

[27] Origen, *Commentaries on John*, hom. 12.

[28] *Didache* 10. 5.

[29] Hippolytus, *The Apostolic Tradition*, pars. 7–8

[30] Ibid., 20. 8.

[31] Ibid., 21. 9–10.

[32] Richardson, *Early Christian Fathers*, p. 218.

[33] Ibid.

CHAPTER 5

[1] Charles Norris Cochrane, *Christianity and Classical Culture* (New York: Oxford University Press, 1957), pp. 177–78.

[2] See the most pertinent section of this decree in Henry Bettenson, *Documents of the Christian Church*, 2d ed. (London: Oxford University Press, 1963), pp. 22–23.

[3] Ibid.

[4] Ibid.

[5] For an expansion of these points, see Andrew Alfoldi, *The Conversion of Constantine and Pagan Rome*, trans. Harold Mattingly (Oxford: Clarendon, 1948).

[6] Eusebius, *Oration* 10.

[7] Lactantius, *Divine Institutes* 5. 5.

[8] Lactantius, *Divine Institutes* 5. 7.

[9] Cochrane, *Christianity and Classical Culture*, p. 196.

[10] Bettenson, *Documents*, p. 31.

[11] Alexander Schmemann, *Introduction to Liturgical Theology* (New York: St. Vladimir, 1966), pp. 72–101.

CHAPTER 6

[1] Augustine, *The City of God*, ed. David Knowles (Baltimore: Penguin, 1972), 14. 28. 583.

[2] Ibid., 15. 2. 596.

[3] John Neville Figgis, *The Political Aspects of St. Augustine's "City of God"* (Gloucester: Peter Smith, 1963), p. 51.

[4] Augustine, *The City of God* 4. 3. 138

[5] Ibid., 4. 4. 139.

[6] Ibid., 20. 9. 915.

[7] Ibid., 20. 9. 914.

[8] Ibid., 2. 9. 916.

[9] Figgis, *Political Aspects*, pp. 79–80.

[10] H. Richard Niebuhr, *Christ and Culture* (New York: Harper, 1956), pp. 215–16.

[11] Quoted by Brian Tierney, *The Crisis of Church and State 1050–1300* (Englewood Cliffs, N.J.: Prentice-Hall, 1964), p. 13.

[12]Ibid., p. 132.
[13]Ibid.
[14]Ibid.
[15]Ibid.
[16]Ibid., p. 130.

CHAPTER 7

[1]Franklin Littell, *The Anabaptist View of the Church* (Boston: Starr King, 1958), p. xvii.

[2]For the various types of Anabaptists and for a good review of their history, see George H. Williams, *The Radical Reformation* (Philadelphia: Westminster, 1962), and William R. Estep, *The Anabaptist Story* (Grand Rapids: Eerdmans, 1975).

[3]Littell, *Anabaptist View*, pp. 47ff.

[4]Ibid., pp. 64–72.

[5]For further elaboration of this idea, see Robert Friedmann, *The Theology of Anabaptism* (Scottdale, Pa.: Herald, 1973), pp. 36–48.

[6]For the complete text of this confession, translated by John C. Wenger, see *The Mennonite Quarterly Review* 19 (October 1945): 247–53.

[7]See Friedmann, *The Theology of Anabaptism*, pp. 38–40.

[8]Sect. IV, pt. 70, as quoted in Friedmann, *The Theology of Anabaptism*, pp. 39–40.

[9]Robert Friedmann, "On Mennonite Historiography and on Individualism and Brotherhood," *The Mennonite Quarterly Review* 18 (April 1944): 121.

[10]Robert R. Kreider, "Anabaptists and State," in Guy F. Hershberger, ed., *The Recovery of the Anabaptist Vision* (Scottdale, Pa.: Herald, 1957), p. 189.

[11]Article 6.

[12]Kreider, "Anabaptists and the State," p. 187.

[13]Article 6.

[14]See J. Lawrence Burkholder, "The Anabaptist Vision of Discipleship," in Hershberger, ed., *The Recovery of the Anabaptist Vision*, pp. 135–51.

[15]Peter Klassen, *The Economics of Anabaptism 1525–1560* (London: Nouton, 1964), p. 43.

[16]Harold S. Bender, "The Anabaptist Vision," in Hershberger, ed., *The Recovery of the Anabaptist Vision*, p. 51. See also James M. Stayer, *Anabaptists and the Sword* (Lawrence, Kan.: Coronado, 1972).

[17]Harold S. Bender, "The Pacifism of the Sixteenth Century Anabaptists," *Church History* 24 (1955): 119–31.

[18]Harold S. Bender, *The Anabaptists and Religious Liberty in the 16th Century* (Philadelphia: Fortress, 1970), pp. 2–3.

[19]Menno Simons, "Instruction on Excommunication," *The Complete Writings of Menno Simons* (Scottdale, Pa.: Herald, 1974), p. 994.

[20]Simons, "Reply to Martin Micron," ibid., p. 838.

[21]Simons, "Confession of the Distressed Christians," ibid., pp. 517–21.

[22]Ibid., pp. 508–13.

[23]Simons, "A Kind Admonition on Church Discipline," ibid., pp. 406–418. See also "A Clear Account of Excommunication," pp. 455–85 and "Reply to Gellius Faber," pp. 723–24.

[24]Simons, "A Clear Account of Excommunication," ibid., p. 469.

[25] Simons, "Reply to Gellius Faber," ibid., pp. 734–63.

[26] Simons, "The New Birth," ibid., p. 93.

[27] Simons, "Why I Did Not Cease Teaching and Writing," ibid., p. 300.

[28] John Howard Yoder, *The Politics of Jesus* (Grand Rapids: Eerdmans, 1972). See also Yoder, *The Christian Witness to the State* (Newton, Kan.: Faith and Life, 1964) and "The Biblical Mandate," *Post American* (April 1974). Other contemporary Anabaptist writers have been mentioned in the footnotes above.

[29] Yoder, *Politics of Jesus*, p. 144.

[30] Ibid., p. 147.

[31] Ibid., p. 151.

[32] Ibid., p. 153.

[33] Ibid., pp. 163–250.

[34] Ibid., p. 175.

[35] Ibid.

[36] Ibid., p. 180.

[37] Ibid., p. 183.

[38] This major thesis is developed in Yoder, ch. 9, pp. 163ff.

[39] Ibid., p. 240.

[40] Ibid., p. 242.

[41] Ibid.

[42] Ibid., p. 244.

[43] Ibid., p. 245.

CHAPTER 8

[1] Gerhard Ebeling, *Luther: An Introduction to His Thoughts*, trans. R. A. Wilson (Philadelphia: Fortress, 1970), p. 25.

[2] Martin Luther, "Temporal Authority: To What Extent It Should be Obeyed" (1523), in *Luther's Works* (Philadelphia: Fortress, 1971), 45:85–87. My analysis of Luther's two-kingdom theory is based on this document.

[3] There is a difference between Luther's early views and his later views. I am setting forth only his later, more mature thought on the question. An excellent work documenting Luther's developing thought is F. Edward Cranz, *An Essay on the Development of Luther's Thought on Justice, Law, and Society* (Cambridge: Harvard University Press, 1959).

[4] For an excellent study of Luther's two kingdoms, see Paul Althaus, *The Ethics of Martin Luther* (Philadelphia: Fortress, 1972), ch. 4.

[5] Luther, "Temporal Authority," p. 88.

[6] For Luther's understanding of creation and natural law, see Althaus, *The Ethics of Martin Luther*, ch. 2.

[7] For a brief but helpful analysis of the Christian's struggle with himself, see Althaus, *The Ethics of Martin Luther*, ch. 1.

[8] Luther, "Temporal Authority," p. 91.

[9] For a helpful insight into Luther's understanding of the spiritual and civil use of the law, see his comments on Galatians 3, *Luther's Works* 26:335–51.

[10] Luther, "Temporal Authority," p. 89.

[11] Ibid., p. 92.

[12] Ibid., p. 94.

[13] Luther, *Luther's Works*, 21:3–294.

[14]For a discussion of Luther's teaching on this point, see Ebeling, *Luther: An Introduction to His Thoughts*, ch. 12.

[15]See "A Sermon on the Estate of Marriage" (1519), in *Luther's Works*, 44:7–14 and "On Marriage Matters" (1530) in *Luther's Works*, 46:265–320.

[16]Luther felt that the church's responsibility is to proclaim God's will for marriage. Marriage is an ordained institution of creation, not an institution of the church.

[17]See Luther's interpretation of Psalm 127 and Psalm 128 in D. Martin, ed., *Luther's Werke, Briefwechsel* (Weimar: 1930–1948), pp. 202ff., pp. 278ff.

[18]Luther, *Luther's Works* 21:12ff.

[19]In addition to "Temporal Authority," see Luther's "Commentary on Psalm 82" (1530), *Luther's Works* 13:41–72; his "Commentary on Psalm 101," *Luther's Works* 13:145–224; and his "Commentary on the Song of Solomon," D. Martin, *Luther's Werk, Briefwechsel*, pp. 586–769.

[20]The Christian is also obliged to support the state in any war it may wage for the purpose of defending its subjects against injustice and violence. Waging war against aggressors and others who threaten the peace of the state is a work of love because it ensures justice and preserves the peace. Implicit in Luther's understanding is the assertion that any aggressive war by a state is wrong and should not be supported by Christians. An aggressive war is waged not for the purpose of keeping peace and order but for selfish gain, to the destruction of peace and order.

[21]For a discussion of Luther's view of the church, see Werner Elert, *The Structure of Lutheranism*, trans. Walter A. Hansen (St. Louis: Concordia, 1962), chap. 20.

[22]Luther, *Bondage of the Will* 25:72–74, quoted in Hugh T. Kerr, ed., *A Compend of Luther's Theology* (Philadelphia: Westminster, 1968), p. 90.

[23]Luther, "Commentary on Galatians," ibid., p. 91.

[24]Luther, "On the War Against the Turks," ibid., p. 203.

[25]Luther, "Large Catechism," ibid., p. 205.

[26]Luther, "On War Against the Turks," ibid., p. 202.

[27]Gustaf Aulen, *Christus Victor* (New York: Macmillan, 1979), p. 6.

[28]Luther, "Against Hanswert," quoted by John Tonkin, *The Church and the Secular Order in Reformation Thought* (New York: Columbia University Press, 1971), p. 70.

[29]Luther, "Epistle Sermon, Third Sunday after Easter," quoted in Kerr, *A Compend of Luther's Theology*, p. 119.

[30]Luther, "Treatise on Good Works," ibid., pp. 220–23.

[31]Luther, "An Earnest Exhortation for All Christians, Warning Them against Insurrection and Rebellion," ibid., pp. 228–29.

[32]Luther, "Secular Authority: To What Extent It Should Be Obeyed," ibid., p. 231.

[33]H. Richard Niebuhr, *Christ and Culture* (New York: Harper, 1951), p. 187.

[34]Ulrich Duchrow, ed., *Lutheran Churches—Salt or Mirror of Society* (Geneva: Lutheran World Federation, 1977). See also Karl H. Hertz, ed., *Two Kingdoms and the World* (Minneapolis: Augsburg, 1976). This work contains a considerable amount of the writings of Ulrich Duchrow and other Lutherans who are working on a similar reinterpretation of Luther.

[35]Duchrow, *Lutheran Churches*, pp. 8–9. A similar critique is found in Duchrow's unpublished convocation address, "The Doctrines of the Two Kingdoms as Resource for Our Time: Help or Hindrance?" (Convocation on Luther and the Modern World, Chicago, October 19–24, 1980), pp. 1–3.

36 Duchrow, *Lutheran Churches*, p. 8; "The Doctrines of the Two Kingdoms," p. 3.

37 Duchrow, 'The Doctrines of the Two Kingdoms," p. 5.

38 Duchrow, *Lutheran Churches*, pp. 9–17.

39 Arthur C. Cochrane, *The Church's Confession under Hitler* (Philadelphia: Westminster, 1962).

40 Ibid., p. 297.

41 Ibid., p. 293.

42 Ibid., p. 299.

43 Ibid., p. 295.

44 Ibid.

45 Ibid., p. 291.

46 Ibid., p. 297.

47 Ibid., p. 299.

48 Ibid., pp. 297–98.

49 Duchrow, 'The Doctrines of the Two Kingdoms," p. 14.

50 Ibid.

51 Ibid., p. 15.

52 Ibid., p. 16.

53 Ibid.

54 Ibid., p. 17.

CHAPTER 9

1 A number of other passages also bring creation and redemption together (Pss. 74, 89, 93, 135, 136; Isa. 43:1ff.; 42:5–6; 54:5; Jer. 33:25ff.; 10:16; 27:5; 32:17; Amos 4:12ff.; Mal. 2:10). What is redeemed is not just "souls" but the whole created order.

2 Calvin, *Institutes*, 1. 16. 1.

3 Henry Van Til, *The Calvinistic Concept of Culture* (Philadelphia: Presbyterian and Reformed, 1959), p. 53.

4 John Calvin, *Concerning the Eternal Predestination of God*, trans. J. K. S. Reid (London: James Clarke, 1961), p. 97.

5 John Calvin, *Institutes of the Christian Religion*, ed. John T. McNeill, 2 vols. (Philadelphia: Westminster, 1960), 20:14. 20. 179.

6 Ibid., 1:5. 5. 58.

7 Ibid., 1:14:2. 161–62.

8 Ibid., 1:14:16. 175.

9 Ibid., 1:14:15. 174.

10 Ibid., 1:3. 3. 146.

11 Calvin, *Institutes*, 1:14. 14. 173.

12 Andre Bieler, *The Social Humanism of Calvin* (Richmond: John Knox, 1964), p. 18.

13 John Calvin, *Calvin's New Testament Commentaries*, ed. David W. Torrance and Thomas F. Torrance (Edinburgh: Oliver and Boyd, 1965; reprint, Grand Rapids: Eerdmans, 1960–73), 11:129.

14 Ibid.

15 Calvin, *Calvin's New Testament Commentaries* (Grand Rapids: Eerdmans, 1949), 4:356–58.

16 Calvin, *Calvin's New Testament Commentaries*, 11:129.

17 John Tonkin, *The Church and the Secular Order in Reformation Thought* (New York: Columbia University Press, 1971), pp. 121ff.

[18] Ibid., p. 127.

[19] Bieler, *The Social Humanism of Calvin*, p. 20.

[20] Ibid.

[21] Calvin, *Calvin's New Testament Commentaries*, 12:180.

[22] Calvin, "Sermon," October 25, 1522. See Tonkin, *The Church and the Secular Order*, p. 115.

[23] William Mueller, *Church and State in Luther and Calvin* (Nashville: Broadman, 1954), p. 127.

[24] Calvin, *Institutes*, 4:20. 2.

[25] Ibid., p. 4.

[26] Ibid., p. 9.

[27] Bieler, *Social Humanism*, p. 23.

[28] W. Fred Graham, *The Constructive Revolutionary* (Richmond: John Knox, 1971), pp. 61–63.

[29] Bieler, *Social Humanism*, p. 31.

[30] Graham, *Constructive Revolutionary*, p. 75.

[31] Bieler, *Social Humanism*, p. 51.

[32] Ibid., p. 45.

[33] Graham, *Constructive Revolutionary*, p. 83.

[34] Bieler, *Social Humanism*, p. 51.

[35] Ibid., p. 51.

[36] Calvin, *Institutes* 2:1. 5. 246.

[37] Calvin, *Calvin's New Testament Commentaries*, 8:173.

[38] Ibid., pp. 173–74.

[39] Ibid., 11:218.

[40] Ibid., 11:307.

[41] Ibid., 8:174.

[42] Ibid.

[43] Ibid., 12:365.

[44] Tonkin, *The Church and the Secular Order*, p. 119.

[45] Jerald C. Brauer, *Protestantism in America* (Philadelphia: Westminster, 1953), p. 25.

[46] Richard J. Mouw, *When the Kings Come Marching In* (Grand Rapids: Eerdmans, 1983).

[47] Ibid., p. xiv.

[48] Ibid., p. 17.

[49] Ibid., p. 23.

[50] Ibid., p. 30.

[51] Ibid., p. 30.

[52] Ibid., p. 64.

[53] Ibid., p. 35.

[54] Ibid., p. 63.

[55] Ibid., p. 17.

[56] Ibid., p. 37.

[57] Ibid., p. 52.

[58] Ibid., p. 64.

[59] Ibid., p. 46.

[60] Ibid., p. 46.

[61] Ibid., p. 37.

[62] Ibid., p. 50.

[63] Ibid., p. 53.

[64] Ibid., p. 13.

[65]Ibid., p. 75.

CHAPTER 10

[1]Karl Hall, *The Cultural Significance of the Reformation* (New York: Meridian Books, 1959). For an explication of the spirit of the Renaissance and Reformation, see Ida Walz Blayney, *The Age of Luther* (New York: Vantage, 1957).

[2]Steven E. Ozment, *The Age of the Reformation (1250–1550): An Intellectual and Religious History of Late Medieval and Reformation Europe* (New Haven: Yale University Press, 1980).

[3]Binkerd Frederick Artz, *Renaissance Humanism 1300–1550* (Kent, Ohio: Kent State University Press, 1966).

[4]Robert Henry Murray, *The Political Consequence of the Reformation: Studies in Sixteenth-Century Political Thought.* (New York: Russell and Russell, 1960). See also Lawrence P. Buck and Jonathan W. Zophy, eds., *The Social History of the Reformation* (Columbus, Ohio: Ohio State University Press, 1972).

[5]For an excellent summary of those forces that have shaped the contemporary humanistic perspective, see Crane Brunton, *The Shaping of Modern Thought* (Englewood Cliffs, N.J.: Prentice-Hall, 1964).

[6]Willson Havelock Coates, et al., *The Emergence of Liberal Humanism: An Intellectual History of Western Europe* (New York: McGraw-Hill, 1966).

[7]Robert Mandrov, *From Humanism to Science* (Atlantic Highlands, N.J.: Humanities, 1979).

[8]Wesley Everett Hall, *Modern Science and Human Values: A Study in the History of Ideas* (Princeton, N.J.: VanNostrand, 1956).

[9] Alfred Rupert Hall, *The Scientific Revolution, 1500–1800: The Formation of the Modern Scientific Attitude* (Boston: Beacon, 1956).

[10]Jacques Maritain, *The Twilight of Civilization* (London: Sheed and Ward, 1946).

[11]David J. Hoeveler, *The New Humanism: A Critique of Modern America, 1900–1940* (Charlottesville, Va.: University of Virginia Press, 1977).

[12]Paul Kurtz, *The Humanist Alternative: Some Definitions of Humanism* (Buffalo: Prometheus, 1973); see also the *Humanist Manifestos I and II* (Buffalo: Prometheus, 1973) for a description of the basic world attitude of humanism. While not all people subscribe to the particulars of humanism, the spirit of humanism seems evident in our twentieth-century lifestyle.

[13]For an expansion of this idea, see Ernst Troeltsch, *Protestantism and Progress* (Boston: Beacon, 1958).

[14]For a comparison of Luther and Calvin in matters of church and state, see William A. Mueller, *Church and State in Luther and Calvin* (Nashville: Broadman, 1954).

[15]A. C. McGiffert, *Protestant Thought Before Kant* (New York: Harper and Row, 1961), pp. 186–245.

[16]For an excellent review of the various views of secularization, see John A. Coleman, "The Situation for Modern Faith," *Theological Studies* (1977): 601–32. For a description of secularization from a Christian point of view, see James Hitchcock, *What is Secular Humanism?* (Ann Arbor: Servant, 1982). See also Os Guinness, *The Gravedigger Files: Papers on the Subversion of the Modern Church* (Downers Grove, Ill.: InterVarsity, 1983) and Jacques Ellul, *The New Demons* (New York: Seabury, 1973). For a general study of

secularization, see Bernard E. Meland, *The Secularization of Modern Cultures* (New York: Oxford University Press, 1966) and David Martin, *A General Theory of Secularization* (New York: Harper and Row, 1978).

CHAPTER 11

[1] William Law, *A Serious Call to a Devout and Holy Life* (New York: E. P. Dutton, 1961).

[2] August Francke, *Three Practical Discourses* (London: Joseph Downing, 1716). See Clyde Manschreck, *A History of Christianity* (Englewood Cliffs, N.J.: Prentice-Hall, 1964), p. 277.

[3] Earle E. Cairns, *Saints and Society* (Chicago: Moody, 1960), p. 30.

[4] Manschreck, *A History of Christianity*, p. 420.

[5] Donald Dayton, *Discovering an Evangelical Heritage* (New York: Harper, 1976), p. 4.

[6] Ibid.

[7] Ibid., p. 18.

[8] Ibid., p. 19.

[9] Ibid., p. 28.

[10] The best discussion of fundamentalism and its relation to culture is George M. Marsden's *Fundamentalism and American Culture* (New York: Oxford University Press, 1980).

[11] For a good overview of social gospel origins, see William A. Visser't Hooft, *The Background of the Social Gospel in America* (St. Louis: Bethany, 1928).

[12] Walter Rauschenbusch, *A Theology for the Social Gospel* (New York: Abingdon, 1945). Another classic work of early twentieth-century thought is William Temple, *Christianity and Social Order* (1942; reprint, New York: Seabury, 1977).

[13] Ibid., p. 50.

[14] Ibid., p. 60.

[15] Ibid., p. 72.

[16] Ibid., p. 90.

[17] Ibid., p. 81.

[18] Ibid., p. 87.

[19] Ibid., p. 54.

[20] Ibid., p. 55.

[21] Ibid., p. 135.

[22] Ibid., p. 137.

[23] Ibid., p. 140.

[24] Ibid.

[25] Ibid., p. 141.

[26] Ibid., p. 142.

[27] Ibid., p. 143.

[28] Ibid., p. 145.

CHAPTER 12

[1] Jacques Ellul, *The New Demons* (New York: Seabury, 1975), p. 34.

[2] "The Pastoral Constitution on the Church in the Modern World," in *Documents of Vatican II*, ed. Austin P. Flannery (Grand Rapids: Eerdmans, 1975), p. 905.

[3] *Humanist Manifestos I and II* (Buffalo: Prometheus, 1973), p. 23.

[4] H. Cunliffe-Jones, *Technology, Community and Church* (London: Independent Press, 1961), p. 71.

[5] Dean Wooldridge, *Mechanical Man: The Physical Basis of Intelligent Life* (New York: McGraw-Hill, 1968), p. 3.

[6] Ibid., p. 191.

[7] Cunliffe-Jones, *Technology, Community and Church*, p. 21.

[8] Karl Barth, *The Church and the Political Problem of Our Day* (London: Hodder and Stoughton, 1939), p. 41.

[9] Ibid., p. 39.

[10] David M. Beekmann, *Where Faith and Economics Meet* (Minneapolis: Augsburg, 1981), p. 25.

CHAPTER 13

[1] Quoted in "World Council of Churches," *The New Catholic Encyclopedia* (Washington, D.C.: Catholic University of America Press, 1967) 14:1025.

[2] Paul Bock, *In Search of a Responsible Society* (Philadelphia: Westminster, 1974), p. 33.

[3] Ibid., pp. 41–42.

[4] John W. Turnbull, *Ecumenical Documents on Church and Society, 1925–1953* (Geneva: World Council of Churches, 1954), p. 192.

[5] Bock, *In Search*, pp. 74–75.

[6] *Evanston Speaks: Reports from the Second Assembly of the World Council of Churches, 1954* (Geneva: World Council of Churches, 1955), p. 53.

[7] Bock, *In Search*, p. 44.

[8] *The New Delhi Report: The Third Assembly of the World Council of Churches*, ed. W. A. Visser't Hooft (New York: Association, 1962), pp. 100–101.

[9] Bock, *In Search*, p. 46.

[10] *The Uppsala Report 1968: Official Report of the Fourth Assembly of the World Council of the Churches*, ed. by Norman Goodall (Geneva: World Council of Churches, 1968), p. 45.

[11] *Breaking Barriers: Nairobi 1975, the Official Report of the Fifth Assembly of the World Council of Churches*, ed. David M. Dutton (Grand Rapids: Eerdmans, 1976), pp. 12–13.

[12] Ibid., p. 48.

[13] Ibid., pp. 86–97, par. 2, 11, 28.

[14] Ibid., pp. 100–102.

[15] Ibid., pp. 119–41, par. 37, 38.

[16] James M. Wall, "Worship Powers WCC Assembly," *Christian Century* (August 17–24, 1983): 732.

[17] Monika Hellwig, "Liberation Theology: An Emerging School," *Scottish Journal of Theology* 30:138.

[18] Gustavo Gutierrez, *A Theology of Liberation* (Maryknoll, N.Y.: Orbis, 1973), p. x.

[19] Ibid., p. 151.

[20] Rene Lawrentin, *Liberation, Development and Salvation*, trans. Charles Underhill Quinn (Maryknoll, N.Y.: Orbis, 1972), esp. pp. 63–84.

[21] Gutierrez, *Theology of Liberation*, p. 193.

[22] Ibid., pp. 159–60.

[23] For a discussion of the relation between history and liberation, see Jose Miguez Bonino, *Doing Theology in a Revolutionary Situation* (Philadelphia: Fortress, 1975), pp. 132–52.

[24] Gutierrez, *Theology of Liberation*, p. 193.

[25] For the development of liberation ethics, see Denis Goulet, *A New Moral Order* (Maryknoll, N.Y.: Orbis, 1974).

[26] Gutierrez, *Theology of Liberation*, p. 202.

[27] Ibid., p. 172.

[28] For an expansion of liberation and political theology, see Dorothee Soelle, *Political Theology* (Philadelphia: Fortress, 1974), and J. G. Davies, *Christian Politics and Violent Revolution* (Maryknoll, N.Y.: Orbis, 1976).

[29] Gutierrez, *Theology of Liberation*, p. 265.

[30] Ibid., p. 267.

[31] Ibid., p. 269.

[32] For an expanded critique of liberation theology, see Stanley H. Gundry and Alan F. Johnson, *Tensions in Contemporary Theology* (Chicago: Moody, 1976), chs. 8–9.

CHAPTER 14

[1] "Pastoral Constitution on the Church in the Modern World," Austin P. Flannery, ed., *Documents of Vatican II* (Grand Rapids: Eerdmans, 1975), p. 904.

[2] Ibid.

[3] Ibid.

[4] Ibid., p. 906.

[5] Ibid., pp. 906–7.

[6] Ibid.

[7] Ibid., pp. 908–9.

[8] Ibid., p. 909.

[9] Ibid., p. 914.

[10] Ibid., p. 923.

[11] Ibid., p. 924.

[12] Ibid., pp. 923–24.

[13] Ibid., p. 926.

[14] Ibid., p. 927.

[15] Ibid., p. 930.

[16] Ibid.

[17] Ibid., p. 936.

[18] Ibid., p. 937.

[19] Ibid.

[20] Ibid., p. 938.

[21] Ibid.

[22] Ibid.

[23] Ibid., p. 940.

[24] Ibid.

[25] Ibid., p. 942.

[26] Ibid.

[27] Ibid., p. 944.

[28] Ibid., p. 945.

[29] Ibid., p. 947.

[30]Johesh Gremillion, *The Gospel of Peace and Justice: Catholic Social Teaching Since Pope John* (Maryknoll, N.Y.: Orbis, 1976), p. ix.

[31]Ibid., p. 386.

[32]Ibid., p. 446.

[33]Ibid., p. 447.

[34]Ibid.

[35]Pope John Paul II, "Redemptor Hominis," *The Papal Encyclicals 1958–1981* (New York: McGrath Publishing Company, 1981), p. 250, par. 21.

[36]Ibid., p. 250, par. 22.

[37]Ibid., p. 250, par. 23.

[38]Ibid., p. 252, par. 27.

[39]Ibid.

[40]Ibid., p. 254, par. 37.

[41]Ibid.

[42]Ibid., p. 255, par. 38.

[43]Ibid., p. 256, par. 42.

[44]Ibid.

[45]Ibid., p. 263, par. 71.

[46]Ibid.

[47]Ibid., pp. 267–269, par. 85–88.

[48]"A Pastoral Letter on War and Peace," *The Challenge of Peace: God's Promise and Our Response* (Washington, D.C.: United States Catholic Conference, 1983), p. 6, par. 14.

[49]Ibid., p. 17, par. 54.

[50]Ibid., p. 16, par. 50.

[51]Ibid., p. 16, par. 51.

[52]Ibid., pp. 16–17, par. 53.

[53]Ibid., p. 8, par. 22.

[54]Ibid., p. 8, par. 22–23.

[55]Ibid., p. 12, par. 36.

[56]Ibid., p. i.

[57]Ibid., p. 17, par. 55.

[58]Ibid., p. 18, par. 56.

[59]Ibid., pp. 18–19, par. 57, 59, 60.

[60]Ibid., p. 18, par. 58.

[61]For a defense of natural-law theory in contemporary Catholic teaching, see Roger Charles with Drostan Macharen, *The Social Teaching of Vatican II* (San Francisco: Ignatius, 1982).

CHAPTER 15

[1]*Humanist Manifestos I and II* (Buffalo: Prometheus, 1977), p. 8.

[2]Aleksandr Solzhenitsyn, "A World Split Apart," *Solzhenitsyn at Harvard* (Washington, D.C.: The Ethics and Public Policy Center, 1980), p. 9.

[3]Ibid., p. 17.

[4]This material comes from an undated 1979 letter. The same content is found in the early brochures announcing the Moral Majority.

[5]Jerry Falwell, *Listen America* (New York: Doubleday, 1980), p. 117.

[6]Ibid., p. 9.

[7]Ibid., p. 11.

[8] Ibid., p. 8.

[9] Ibid., p. 250.

[10] Ibid.

[11] Ibid., p. 251.

[12] Ibid., p. 252.

[13] Tim LaHaye, *The Battle for the Mind* (Old Tappan, N.J.: Revell, 1980), pp. 38–39.

[14] Francis Schaeffer, *A Christian Manifesto* (Westchester, Ill.: Crossway, 1981), pp. 31–32.

[15] Ibid., p. 34.

[16] Peter Marshall and David Manuel, *The Light and the Glory* (Old Tappan, N.J.: Revell, 1977), p. 19.

[17] Gabriel Fackre, *The Religious Right and Christian Faith* (Grand Rapids: Eerdmans, 1980), pp. ix–x.

[18] Ibid., p. 41.

[19] Ibid.

[20] Ibid., p. 46.

[21] Ibid., pp. 62–63.

[22] Ibid., p. 70.

[23] Ibid., p. 75.

[24] Ibid., p. 82.

[25] Ibid., pp. 82ff.

[26] Richard Neuhaus, *The Naked Public Square* (Grand Rapids: Eerdmans, 1984).

[27] Ibid., p. 25.

[28] Ibid., p. 19.

[29] Ibid., p. 89.

[30] Ibid., p. 157.

[31] Ibid., p. 89.

[32] Ibid., p. 113.

[33] Ibid., p. 59.

[34] Ibid., p. 60.

[35] Ibid., p. 61.

[36] Ibid., p. 65.

[37] Ibid., p. 69.

[38] Ibid., p. 72.

[39] Ibid., p. 73.

[40] Ibid., p. 65.

[41] Ibid., p. 94.

[42] Ibid., p. 95.

[43] Ibid.

[44] Russell Richey and Donald Jones, *American Civil Religion* (New York: Harper and Row, 1974), pp. 14–18.

[45] Jean-Jacques Rousseau, *The Social Contract and Discourses,* trans. and ed. G. D. H. Cole (New York: Dutton, 1950), p. 139.

[46] For a detailed examination of this transition, see the discussion in Ernst H. Kantorowicz, "*Pro Patria Mori* in Medieval Political Thought," *The American Historical Review* 56 (April 1951): 472–92.

[47] "A Model of Christian Charity," in H. S. Smith, R. T. Handy, and Lefferts A. Loetscher, *American Christianity: An Historical Interpretation with Representative Documents,* 2 vols. (New York: Scribner, 1960–63) 1:102.

⁴⁸For an excellent brief survey of this development, see Robert T. Handy, "The American Messianic Consciousness: The Concept of the Chosen People and Manifest Destiny," *Review and Expositor* (Winter 1976): 47–58.

⁴⁹Richard Pierard, *The Unequal Yoke* (New York: Lippincott, 1970).

⁵⁰Ibid., pp. 32–33.

⁵¹For a critical treatment of civil religion, see Martin E. Marty, *The New Shape of American Religion* (New York: Harper, 1959) and *The Pro and Con Book of Religious America* (Waco, Tex.: Word, 1975). See also Mark A. Noll, Nathan O. Hatch, and George M. Marsden, *The Search for Christian America* (Westchester, Ill.: Crossway, 1983).

CHAPTER 16

¹Dennis P. Hollinger, *Individualism and Social Ethics* (Washington, D.C.: University Press of America, 1983), p. 109.

²Ibid., p. 100.

³Ibid., p. 102.

⁴Ibid., p. 103. See also J. Howard Pew, "The Mission of the Church," *Christianity Today* 14 (July 3, 1964): 11.

⁵*The Chicago Declaration* (Carol Stream, Ill.: Creation House, 1974), p. 12.

⁶Ibid., pp. 13ff.

⁷Ibid., p. 18.

⁸Ibid., p. 19.

⁹Frank Gaebelein, Vernon Grounds, Carl F. H. Henry, Bernard Ramm, and Paul Rees.

¹⁰*The Chicago Declaration*, preface.

¹¹See the full Lausanne Covenant in *Let the Earth Hear His Voice* (Minneapolis: World Wide Publications, 1975), pp. 3–9. The quote is section 5, found on pp. 4–5. The following biblical support is listed with this paragraph: Acts 17:26, 31; Genesis 18:25; Isaiah 1:17; Psalms 45:7; Genesis 1:26–27; James 3:9; Leviticus 19:18; Luke 6:27, 35; James 2:14–26; John 3:3, 5; Matthew 5:20; 6:33; 2 Corinthians 3:18; James 2:20.

¹²Theodore Williams, ed., *Building Bridges or Barriers* (Bangalore, India: Evangelical Literature Service, 1979).

¹³Ibid., p. 5.

¹⁴Ibid., pp. 5–6.

¹⁵Ibid., p. 43.

¹⁶Ibid., p. 45.

¹⁷Ibid.

¹⁸Ibid., p. 36.

¹⁹For an expanded understanding of this influence, see Waldron Scott, *Bring Forth Justice* (Grand Rapids: Eerdmans, 1980). For other mission conferences, see Waldron Scott, *Serving Our Generation* (Colorado Springs: World Evangelical Fellowship, 1980) and Theodore Williams, *Together in Mission* (Bangalore, India: World Evangelical Mission Commission, 1983).

²⁰*Church and Nationhood* (New Delhi: World Evangelical Theological Commission, 1978), pp. 7–8.

²¹Ibid., pp. 9–10.

²²Ibid., p. 10.

[23] Ronald J. Sider, *Rich Christians in an Age of Hunger* (Downers Grove, Ill.: InterVarsity, 1977)

[24] Available through World Evangelical Fellowship, P.O. Box WEF, Wheaton, IL 60187. Also, a book of papers related to the conference has been published: Ronald J. Sider, ed., *Lifestyle in the Eighties: An Evangelical Commitment to Simple Lifestyle* (Philadelphia: Westminster, 1982).

[25] Ibid., n. p.

[26] Phone conversation with Ronald J. Sider, January 30, 1985.

[27] A joint publication of the Lausanne Committee for World Evangelization and the World Evangelical Fellowship. Available through WEF, P.O. Box WEF, Wheaton, IL 60187.

[28] Ibid., p. 30.

[29] Ibid., pp. 31–32.

[30] Ibid., p. 30.

[31] Ibid.

[32] Ibid., pp. 33–34.

[33] Ibid., p. 30.

[34] Ibid., p. 34.

[35] Ibid., p. 39.

[36] Ibid., pp. 45–46.

[37] Harold Lindsell, *The Armageddon Spectre* (Westchester, Ill.: Crossway, 1984).

[38] It is especially surprising that Arthur P. Johnston was on the committee that wrote this statement. See his book, *The Battle for World Evangelism* (Wheaton: Tyndale, 1978).

[39] "Social Transformation: The Church in Response to Human Need," *Transformation* 1:1 (January/March 1984): 23–27.

CHAPTER 17

[1] Richard Mouw, "Reforming Cultural Calvinism," *The Reformed Journal* 31:3 (March 1981): 15.

[2] Ibid.

[3] Ulrich Duchrow, "The Doctrine of the Two Kingdoms as Resources for Our Time: Help or Hindrance?" (Paper presented at the Convocation on Luther and the Modern World, Chicago, October 19–24, 1980), p. 12.

[4] Ibid., p. 13.

[5] Ibid., p. 14.

[6] Ibid.

[7] John H. Yoder, "Christ and Culture: A Critique of H. Richard Niebuhr" (Unpublished paper, 1976). Yoder requests that no quotations be taken from this paper. I will, therefore, allude to his conclusions without direct quote.

[8] Mouw, pp. 15–16.

[9] Ibid., p. 16.

[10] Ibid., p. 15.

[11] Ibid., p. 16.

[12] Ibid.

[13] Austin P. Flannery, ed., *Documents of Vatican II* (Grand Rapids: Eerdmans, 1975) p. 935.

[14] Ulrich Duchrow, ed., *Lutheran Churches: Salt or Mirror of Society?* (Geneva: Lutheran World Federation, 1977), p. 11.

[15] Ibid., p. 12.

[16] Ibid., p. 13.

[17] Ibid., pp. 14–15.

[18] Flannery, *Documents of Vatican II*, p. 936.

[19] Ibid.

[20] John H. Yoder, *The Politics of Jesus* (Grand Rapids: Eerdmans, 1972), p. 141.

[21] Ibid., p. 146.

[22] Flannery, *Documents of Vatican II*, p. 937.

[23] Ibid.

[24] Yoder, *Politics of Jesus*, p. 161.

[25] Ibid.

[26] Richard Mouw, *When Kings Come Marching In* (Grand Rapids: Eerdmans, 1983), p. 37.

[27] Flannery, *Documents of Vatican II*, p. 940.

[28] Yoder, *Politics of Jesus*, p. 160.

[29] Richard Mouw, *Politics and the Biblical Drama* (Grand Rapids: Baker, 1983), p. 56.

[30] Flannery, *Documents of Vatican II*, p. 938.

[31] Yoder, *Politics of Jesus*, p. 161.

[32] Mouw, *Kings*, p. 37.

[33] Ibid.

[34] Thomas E. Clarke, ed., *Above Every Name: The Lordship of Christ and Social Systems* (Ramsey, N.J.: Paulist, 1980).

APPENDIX A

[1] See the discussion on *kosmos* in Gerhard Kittel and Gerhard Friedrich, eds., *Theological Dictionary of the New Testament*, 10 vols. (Grand Rapids: Eerdmans, 1964–76), 3:868ff.

[2] For a discussion of Satan in the New Testament, see James Kallas, *Jesus and the Power of Satan* (Philadelphia: Westminster, 1968) and *The Satan World View: A Study in Pauline Theology* (Philadelphia: Westminster, 1966). For a psychological and mythological view of Satan in the Old Testament, see Rivbah Scharf Kluger, *Satan in the Old Testament* (Evanston: Northwestern University Press, 1967). For a survey of Satan in Christian thought, see Jeffrey Burton Russell, *Satan and the Early Christian Tradition* (Ithaca: Cornell University Press, 1981).

[3] For a discussion of demons in the New Testament, see Edward Langton, *Essentials of Demonology: A Study of Jewish and Christian Doctrine, Its Origin and Development* (London: Epworth, 1949). For an application to modern times, see John Richards, *But Deliver Us From Evil: An Introduction to the Demonic Dimension in Pastoral Care* (New York: Seabury, 1974). For a more historical study, see Henry Ansgar Kelly, *The Devil, Demonology and Witchcraft* (New York: Doubleday, 1968).

[4] For an elaboration of this theme in the New Testament and early church, see Gustav Aulen, *Christus Victor* (New York: Macmillan, 1979).

APPENDIX B

[1] Rudolf Schnackenburg, *The Church in the New Testament* (New York: Seabury, 1965), pp. 160ff.

²Ibid., pp. 165ff.

APPENDIX C

¹It is not the purpose of this writing to discuss the basis for this distinction. This material has been presented in the literature mentioned in note 1 of chapter 2. A concise survey of this discussion is found in the footnotes of Hendrik Berkhof, *Christ and the Powers* (Scottdale, Pa.: Herald, 1977), pp. 72–79.

²Throughout this discussion the phrase, "structures of existence," will be used to refer to those structural realities through which life is experienced. I have in mind categories such as: [1] political structures (the state; nationalism; agencies that have the power to govern, to make and execute laws, to war against another state, to regulate and condition the lives of its citizens); [2] economic structures (ways of regulating economic growth and progress, especially the free enterprise system, capitalism, socialism, communism); [3] educational structures (public and private institutions that have as their goal the dissemination of knowledge and the formation of a person's world view); [4] intellectual structures (world views based on philosophical inquiry, science, reason, or intuition, such as the well-known "isms" and "ologies"—e.g., materialism and scientology); [5] religious structures (attempts to give a religious interpretation of life, such as Buddhism, Islam, Shintoism, and even various interpretations of the Christian faith); [6] moral structures (rules and regulations that determine moral conduct, customs, and various kinds of behavior such as those rooted in each particular culture). This is not an exhaustive list. Nevertheless, the concrete nature of these structures will serve to illustrate the broad and perhaps inexhaustible idea that is being referred to as "structures of existence." I intend to include *everything* that is part of the overall structure of society.

³See G. J. C. MacGregor, "Principalities and Powers: The Cosmic Background of Paul's Thought," *New Testament Studies*, 1954, p. 18. For a summary of the current disputes over the interpretation of the word *power*, see Clinton D. Morrison, *The Powers That Be* (Naperville, Ill.: Alec R. Allenson, 1977), pt. 1.

⁴The argument defending this distinction is ably set forth in Berkhof, *Christ and the Powers*. See especially pp. 18–26. Berkhof identifies the powers as "structures of earthly existence." For a discussion of the complexities of this interpretation, see Richard Mouw, *Politics and the Biblical Drama* (Grand Rapids: Eerdmans, 1976), pp. 85ff.

⁵See *stoicheoō* and related words in Gerhard Kittel and Gerhard Friedrich, eds., *Theological Dictionary of the New Testament*, 10 vols. (Grand Rapids: Eerdmans, 1964–76), 7:666ff.

⁶Three choices of interpretation seem possible with reference to the word *archontes*. First, Paul may have been referring only to earthly rulers; second, only to spiritual powers; and third, a double reference may be intended. Considering the supernatural theology of Paul, the third option seems most appropriate.

⁷See the discussion in Morrison, pp. 118–22.

BIBLIOGRAPHY

I. GENERAL

Adams, James Luther. *Paul Tillich's Philosophy of Culture, Science and Religion.* New York: Schocken, 1970.

Barbour, Ian G. *Myths, Models, and Paradigms: A Comparative Study in Science and Religion.* New York: Harper, 1974.

Berger, Peter. *Facing Up to Modernity.* New York: Basic Books, 1977.

_____. *The Noise of Solemn Assemblies.* New York: Doubleday, 1961.

_____. *The Precarious Vision.* New York: Doubleday, 1967.

_____. *The Sacred Canopy.* New York: Doubleday, 1967.

Bredemeier, Harry; Davis, Kingsley; and Levy, Marion, eds. *Modern Society: Readings of Order and Change.* New York: Rinehart, 1948.

Brock, Paul. *In Search of a Responsible Society: The Social Teachings of the World Council of Churches.* Philadelphia: Westminster, 1974.

Cailliet, Emile. *The Christian Approach to Culture.* Nashville: Abingdon-Cokesbury, 1953.

Calhoun, Wallace. *The Cultural Concept of Christianity.* Grand Rapids: Eerdmans, 1950.

Carman, John B., and Dawe, Donald G. *Christian Faith in a Religiously Plural World.* Maryknoll: Orbis, 1978.

Corry, James A. *The Changing Conditions of Politics.* Toronto: University of Toronto Press, 1963.

Cox, Harvey. *The Church Amid Revolution.* New York: Association, 1967.

Dewey, John. *Individualism, Old and New.* New York: Capricorn, 1924.

Dubos, Rene. *So Human an Animal.* New York: Scribner, 1968.

Durkheim, Emile. *The Elementary Forms of the Religious Life.* New York: Free Press, 1965.

Elder, Fredrick. *Crisis in Eden: A Religious Study of Man and His Environment.* New York: Abingdon, 1970.

Eliot, Thomas Stearns. *Notes Toward the Definition of Culture.* New York: Harcourt, Brace, 1949.

Ellul, Jacques. *The Meaning of the City.* Grand Rapids: Eerdmans, 1970.

_____. *The New Demons.* New York: Seabury, 1975.

_____. *The Presence of the Kingdom.* New York: Seabury, 1948.

Forell, George W. *History of Christian Ethics: From the New Testament to Augustine.* Minneapolis: Augsburg, 1979.

Fowler, James W. *To See the Kingdom: The Theological Vision of H. Richard Niebuhr.* New York: Abingdon, 1974.

Gilkey, Langdon. *How the Church Can Minister to the World without Losing Itself.* New York: Harper and Row, 1964.

Goulet, Denis. *A New Moral Order.* Maryknoll, N.Y.: Orbis, 1974.

Greeley, Andrew M. *Unsecular Man: The Persistence of Religion.* New York: Schocken, 1972.

Heschel, Abraham J. *Between God and Man.* Edited by Fritz A. Rothschild. New York: Harper, 1959.

Hoekstra, Harvey T. *The World Council of Churches and the Demise of Evangelism* Wheaton: Tyndale, 1974.

Honigmann, John Joseph. *Understanding Culture.* New York: Harper, 1963.

Hopkins, C. Howard, and White, Ronald C., Jr., *The Social Gospel*. Philadelphia: Temple University Press, 1978.

Jersild, Paul, and Johnson, Dale A., eds. *Moral Issues and Christian Response*. New York: Holt, Rinehart and Winston, 1983.

Knoeber, Alfred Louis. *The Nature of Culture*. Chicago: University of Chicago Press, 1952.

Lewis, C. S. *Mere Christianity*. New York: Macmillan, 1960.

Lipton, Michael. *Why Poor People Stay Poor*. Cambridge: Harvard University Press, 1977.

Moltmann, Jurgen. *Theology of Hope*, 5th edition. Trans. James W. Leitch. New York: Harper and Row, 1967.

Myrdal, Gunnar. *Asian Drama: An Inquiry into the Poverty of Nations*. Abr. Seth S. King. New York: Vintage, Random House, 1972.

Niebuhr, Reinhold. *The Children of Light and the Children of Darkness*. New York: Scribner, 1944.

_____. *Moral Man and Immoral Society*. New York, 1932. London: Scribner, 1932.

_____. *The Nature and Destiny of Man*. New York: Scribner, 1941.

Niebuhr, Richard H. *Christ and Culture*. New York: Harper, 1951.

Nisbet, Robert. *The Quest for Community*. New York: Oxford University Press, 1953.

Norman, Edward. *Christianity and the World Order*. Oxford: Oxford University Press, 1979.

Pannenberg, Wolfhart. *Theology and the Kingdom*. Philadelphia: Westminster, 1966.

Pincus, John A., ed. *Reshaping the World Economy*. Englewood Cliffs, N.J.: Prentice-Hall, 1968.

Pittenger, Norman. *The Christian Church as Social Process*. Philadelphia: Westminster, 1971.

Reilly, Michael Collins. *Spirituality for Mission: Historical, Theological and Cultural Factors for a Present-Day Spirituality*. Manila: Loyola School of Theology, 1976.

Scherer, James A. *Global Living Here and Now*. New York: Friendship, 1974.

Shinn, Roger L. *Forced Options: Social Decisions for the 21st Century*. New York: Harper and Row, 1982.

Sider, Ronald J., and Taylor, Richard K. *Nuclear Holocaust and Christian Hope*. Downers Grove, Ill.: InterVarsity, 1982.

Vernon, Raymond. *Sovereignty at Bay: The Multinational Spread of U.S. Enterprises*. New York: Basic Books, 1971.

Weber, Hans-Ruedi. *Salty Christians*. New York: Seabury, 1963.

White, Leslie A., *The Concept of Culture*. Minneapolis: Burgess, 1973.

White, R. E. O. *Christian Ethics*. Atlanta: John Knox, 1981.

Wilbur, Charles K., ed. *The Political Economy of Development and Underdevelopment*. New York: Random House, 1973.

Wilkins, Mira *The Emergence of the Multinational Enterprise*. Cambridge: Harvard University Press, 1970.

II. BIBLICAL

Berkhof, Hendrik. *Christ and the Powers*. Scottdale, Pa.: Herald Press, 1977.
Brandon, S. G. F. *Jesus and the Zealots: A Study of the Political Factor in Primitive Christianity*. New York: Scribner, 1967.
Bright, John. *The Kingdom of God*. Nashville: Abingdon, 1953.
Caird, G. B. *Principalities and Powers*. London: Oxford University Press, 1956.
Cullmann, Oscar. *Christ and Time*. Philadelphia: Westminster, 1950.
Grant, Robert M. *Early Christianity and Society*. New York: Harper and Row, 1977.
Green, Michael. *Evangelism in the Early Church*. Grand Rapids: Eerdmans, 1970.
Guthrie, Donald. *New Testament Theology*. Downers Grove, Ill.: InterVarsity, 1981.
Kallas, James. *Jesus and the Power of Satan* Philadelphia: Westminster, 1968.
————. *The Satanward View*. Philadelphia: Westminster, 1966.
Kerans, Patrick. *Sinful Social Structures*. New York: Paulist, 1974.
Ladd, George Eldon. *Crucial Questions Aout the Kingdom*. Grand Rapids: Eerdmans, 1952.
————. *Jesus and the Kingdom*. New York: Harper and Row, 1964.
Laymon, Charles M. *Christ in the New Testament*. New York: Abingdon, 1958.
Ling, Trevor. *The Significance of Satan*. London: SPCK, 1961.
MacGregor, G. H. C. "Principalities and Powers: The Cosmic Background of Paul's Thought." *New Testament Studies* 1 (1954–55): 17–28.
Montgomery, John Warwick. *Principalities and Powers*. Minneapolis: Bethany House, 1973.
Morrison, Clinton D. *The Powers That Be*. Naperville: Allenson, 1960.
Perrin, Norman. *The Kingdom of God in the Teaching of Jesus*. London: SCM, 1963.
Rupp, E. Gordon. *Principalities and Powers: Studies in the Christian Conflict in History*. London, 1952
Schlier, Heinrich. *Principalities & Powers in the New Testament*. New York: Herder & Herder, 1961.
Schnackenburg, Rudolph. *The Church in the New Testament*. New York: Herder and Herder, 1965
————. *God's Rule and Kingdom*. Trans. John Murray. London: Herder and Herder, 1963.
Stewart, James S. "On a Neglected Emphasis in New Testament Theology." *Scottish Journal of Theology* (1951): 292–301.
Stringfellow, William. *An Ethic for Christians and Other Aliens in a Strange Land*. Waco: Word, 1973.
VonRad, Gerhard. *Old Testament Theology*. New York: Harper, 1962.

III. HISTORICAL

Alfoldi, Andrew. *The Conversion of Constantine and Pagan Rome*. Trans. Harold Mattingly. Oxford: Clarendon, 1948.
Barth, Karl. *Community, State, and Church*. Ed. Will Herberg. New York: Doubleday, 1960.
————. *This Christian Cause: A Letter to Great Britain from Switzerland*. Trans. E. L. H. Gordon and George Hill. New York: Macmillan, 1941.

Bronowski, J. and Mazlish, Bruce. *The Western Intellectual Tradition*. New York: Harper, 1960.

Brunner, Emil. *Christianity and Civilization*. 2 vols. New York: Scribner, 1948.

Burckhart, Jacob. *The Civilization of the Renaissance in Italy*. New York: Mentor, 1960.

Buttrick, George. *Christ and History*. New York: Abingdon, 1963.

Childress, James F. and Harned, David B., eds. *Secularization and the Protestant Perspective*. Philadelphia: Westminster, 1970.

Coates, Willson H., and White, H. V. *The Emergence of Liberal Humanism: An Intellectual History of Europe*. New York: McGraw-Hill, 1966.

Cochrane, Arthur C. *The Church's Confession Under Hitler*. Philadelphia: Westminster, 1962.

Cochrane, Charles Norris. *Christianity and Classical Culture*. New York: Oxford University Press, 1957.

Cox, Harvey. *The Secular City*. Rev. ed. New York: Macmillan, 1966.

Dawson, Henry Christopher. *The Historic Reality of Christian Culture*. New York: Harper, 1960.

Dayton, Donald. *Discovering an Evangelical Heritage*. New York: Harper, 1976.

Dennis, James S. *Christian Mission and Social Progress*. 3 vols. New York: Revell, 1897–1906.

Doerries, Hermann. *Constantine and Religious Liberty*. Trans. Roland H. Bainton, New Haven: Yale University Press, 1970.

————. *Constantine the Great*. New York: Harper, 1972.

Dooyeweerd, Herman. *Roots of Western Culture*. Toronto: Wedge, 1979.

Friedman, Milton. *Capitalism and Freedom*. Chicago: University of Chicago Press, 1962.

Grant, Robert M. *Early Christianity and Society*. New York: Harper, 1977.

————. *The Sword and the Cross*. New York: Macmillan, 1955.

Hayek, Friedrich. *Individualism and the Economic Order*. Chicago: University of Chicago Press, 1948.

Luzbetak, Louis J. *The Church and Cultures*. Techny, Ill.: Divine World Publication, 1970.

Maritain, Jacques. *The Twilight of Civilization*. London: Sheed & Ward, 1946.

Martin, David. *A General Theory of Secularization*. New York: Harper and Row, 1978.

————. *The Religious and the Secular*. New York: Schocken, 1969.

Meland, Bernard E. *The Secularization of Modern Cultures*. New York: Oxford University Press, 1966.

Munby, P. C. *The Idea of a Secular Society*. London: Oxford University Press, 1963.

Newsome, David. *The Wilberforces and Henry Manning*. Cambridge: Belknap, 1966.

Pratt, Vernon. *Religion and Secularization*. New York: Macmillan, 1970.

Rauschenbush, Walter. "Christianity and the Social Crisis" in *Classics of Protestantism*. Ed. Vergilius Ferm. New York: Philosophical Library, 1959.

————. *A Theology for the Social Gospel*. New York: Abingdon Press, 1945.

Rousseau, Jean Jacques. *The Social Contract*. New York: Dutton, 1950.

Russell, Jeffrey Burton. *A History of Medieval Christianity, Prophecy and Order*. Arlington Heights, Ill.: Harlan Davidson, 1968.

Santa Ana, Julio de. *Good News to the Poor: the Challenge of the Poor in the History of the Church*. Geneva: World Council of Churches, 1977.

Shiner, Larry. *The Secularizaton of History*. New York: Abingdon, 1966.

Sigmund, Paul E. *Nicholas of Cusa and Medieval Political Thought*. Cambridge: Harvard University Press, 1963.

Smith, Adam. *The Wealth of Nations*. New York: Random, 1937.

Tawney, R. H. *Religion and the Rise of Capitalism* New York: Mentor, 1926.

Temple, William. *Christianity and the Social Order*. New York: Seabury, 1977.

Tierney, Brian. *The Crisis of Church and State 1050–1300*. Englewood Cliffs, N.J.: Prentice-Hall, 1964.

Tocqueville, Alexis. *Democracy in America*. London: Oxford University Press, 1952.

Troeltsch, Ernst. *The Social Teaching of the Christian Churches*. Trans. Olive Wyon. 2 vols. New York: Macmillan, 1931.

Ullman, Walter. *The Individual and Society in the Middle Ages*. Baltimore: Johns Hopkins University Press, 1966.

Vahanian, Gabriel. *The Death of God: The Culture of our Post-Christian Era*. New York: George Braziller, 1957.

Verduin, Leonard. *The Anatomy of a Hybrid*. Grand Rapids: Eerdmans, 1976.

IV. THE ANTITHESIS MODEL

Eller, Vernard. *The Simple Life* Grand Rapids: Eerdmans, 1973.

Epp, Frank H. *Mennonites in Canada, 1786–1920*. Toronto: Macmillan, 1974.

Estep, William, R., ed. *Anabaptist Beginnings (1523–1533). A Source Book*. Nieuwkoop: B. de Graaf, 1976.

————. *The Anabaptist Story*. Grand Rapids: Eerdmans, 1975.

Friedman, Robert. *The Theology of Anabaptism*. Scottdale, Pa.: Herald, 1973.

Friesen, P. M. *The Mennonite Brotherhood in Russia (1789–1910)*. Fresno, Calif.: Board of Christian Literature, General Conference of Mennonite Brethren Churches, 1978.

Gross, Leonard. *The Golden Years of the Hutterites: The Witness and Thought of the Communal Moravian Anabaptists During the Walpot Era. 1565–1578*. Scottdale, Pa.: Herald, 1980.

Hershberger, Guy F. *The Recovery of the Anabaptist Vision*. Scottdale, Pa.: Herald, 1957.

————. *War, Peace, and Nonresistance*. Scottdale, Pa.: Herald, 1969.

Jackson, David and Neta. *Living Together in a World Falling Apart*. Carol Stream, Ill.: Creation, 1974.

Kauffman, J. Howard, and Leland Harder. *Anabaptists Four Centuries Later: A Profile of Five Mennonite and Brethren in Christ Denominations*. Scottdale, Pa.: Herald, 1975.

Kraus, Norman C., ed. *Evangelicalism and Anabaptism*. Scottdale, Pa.: Herald, 1979.

Kraybill, Donald B. *The Upside-Down Kingdom*. Scottdale, Pa.: Herald, 1978.

Perkins, John. *Let Justice Roll Down*. Ventura, Calif.: Regal, 1976.

Sider, Ronald J. *Christ and Violence*. Scottdale, Pa.: Herald, 1979.

————. *Rich Christians in an Age of Hunger: A Biblical Study*. Downers Grove, Ill.: InterVarsity, 1977.

————, ed. *Lifestyle in the Eighties: An Evangelical Commitment to Simple Lifestyle*. Philadelphia: Westminster, 1982.

Springer, Nelson P., and Klassen, A. J. *Mennonite Bibliography, 1631–1961*. 2 vols. Scottdale, Pa.: Herald, 1977.

Stayer, James M. *Anabaptists and the Sword*. Lawrence, Kan.: Coronado, 1976.

Wallis, Jim. *Call to Conversion*. San Francisco: Harper and Row, 1981.

Williams, George H. *The Radical Reformation*. Philadelphia: Westminster, 1962.

Yoder, John Howard. *The Christian Witness to the State*. Newton: Faith & Life, 1977.

————. *The Legacy of Michael Sattler*. Scottdale, Pa.: Herald, 1973.

————. *The Politics of Jesus*. Grand Rapids: Eerdmans, 1972.

Zablocki, Benjamin. *The Joyful Community*. Baltimore: Penguin, 1971.

V. THE PARADOX MODEL

Althaus, Paul. *The Ethics of Martin Luther*. Philadelphia: Fortress, 1972.

Ashaim, Ivar, ed. *Christ and Humanity*. Philadelphia: Fortress, 1970.

Aulen, Gustaf. *Church, Law, and Society*. New York: Scribner, 1948.

Bonhoeffer, Dietrich. *Ethics*. Ed. Eberhard Bethge. New York: Macmillan, 1955.

Bornkamm, Heinrich. *Luther's Doctrine of the Two Kingdoms*. Philadelphia: Fortress, 1966.

————. *Luther's World of Thought*. Trans. Martin H. Bertram. St. Louis: Concordia, 1958.

Braaten, Carl, and Jenson, Robert. *The Futurist Option*. New York: Newman, 1970.

Cranz, Ferdinand Edward. *An Essay on the Development of Luther's Thought on Justice, Law and Society*. Cambridge: Harvard University Press, 1959.

Duchrow, Ulrich. "The Confessing Church and the Ecumenical Movement." *Ecumenical Review* 33 (July 1981): 212–31.

————. "Identity of the Church and Its Service to the Whole Human Being: Interim Report on the Ecclesiology Study of the Lutheran World Federation Commission on Studies." *Lutheran World* 24:1 (1979): 93–99.

————, ed. *Christenheit und Weltverantwortung: Tradition-geschichte und systenatische Struktur der Zweireichelehre*. Stuttgart: Ernst Klatt Verlag, 1970.

————, ed. *Lutheran Churches–Salt or Mirror of Society? Case Studies on the Theory and Practice of the Two Kingdoms Doctrine*. Geneva: Lutheran World Federation, Department of Studies, 1977.

Duchrow, Ulrich, and Hoffman, Heiner. *Die Vorstellung von Zwei Reichen und Regimenten bis Luther*. Gutersloh: Gerd Mohn, 1972.

Duchrow, Ulrich, and Huber, Wolfgang. "The Church Facing Dependency Structures." *Dialog* 30 (Fall 1981): 269–73.

————. "The Doctrine of the Two Kingdoms as Resource for Our Time: Help or Hindrance?" Paper read at a convocation on "Luther and the Modern World," October 19–24, 1980, Lutheran School of Theology, Chicago.

————. "Studies and Actons on Root Causes of Social Injustice: Questions and Challenges for Lutheran Churches." *Lutheran World*, 24 (1976), no. 1:10–29.

————, eds. *Die Ambivalenz der Zweireichelehre in der lutherische Kirchen 20 Jahrhundert*. Gutersloh: Gerd Mohn, 1976.

Duchrow, Ulrich; Huber, Wolfgang; and Reith, Louis, eds. *Umdeutungen der Zweireichelehre in 19 Jahrhundert*. Gutersloh: Gerd Mohn, 1975.

Ebeling, Gerhard. *Luther: An Introduction to His Thought.* Trans. R. A. Wilson. Philadelphia: Fortress, 1970.

————. *Word and Faith.* Trans. James W. Leitch. Philadelphia: Fortress, 1963.

Eckehart, Lorenz, ed. *The Debate on* Status Confessionis: *Studies in Christian Political Theology.* Geneva: Lutheran World Federation Department of Studies, 1983.

Elert, Werner. *The Structure of Lutheranism.* Trans. Walter A. Hansen. St. Louis: Concordia, 1962.

Forell, George W. *Against the World, For the World: The Hartford Appeal and the Future of American Religion.* New York: Seabury, 1976.

————. *Christian Social Teachings.* Minneapolis: Augsburg, 1970.

————. *Ethics of Decision: An Introduction to Christian Ethics.* Philadelphia: Fortress, 1955.

————. *Faith Active in Love: An Investigation of the Principles Underlying Luther's Social Ethics.* Minneapolis: Augsburg, 1954.

————. *God and Caesar.* Minneapolis: Augsburg, 1969.

————. "Law and Gospel as a Problem of Politics." *Religion in Life,* 1962.

————. "Luther and Politics." In Forell et al, *Luther and Culture,* Martin Luther Lectures, vol. 4. Minneapolis: Augsburg, 1960.

————. "Luther's Conception of Natural Orders." *Lutheran Church Quarterly 18* (1945).

Forell, George W.; Grimm, Harold; and Hoelty-Nickel, Theodore. *Luther and Culture.* Decorah, Iowa: Luther College Press.

Hertz, Karl, ed. *Two Kingdoms and One World: A Sourcebook in Christian Social Ethics.* Minneapolis: Augsburg, 1976.

Holl, Karl. *The Cultural Significance of the Reformation.* Trans. Karl and Barbara Hertz and John H. Lichtblau. New York: Meridian, 1959.

Jenson, Robert. "The Kingdom of America's God" in *Religion and the Dilemmas of Nationhood: The 1976 Knubel-Miller-Greever Lectures.* Ed. Sidney Ahlstrom. Minneapolis: Lutheran Church in America, 1976.

Juhnke, James C. *A People of Two Kingdoms.* Newton, Kan.: Faith & Life Press, 1975.

Lazareth, William H. "Luther's 'Two Kingdoms' Ethic Reconsidered." In *Christian Social Ethics in a Changing World: An Ecumenical Theological Inquiry.* Ed. John C. Bennett. New York: Association, 1966.

Lutheran World 12:4 (1965).

Muehl, William. *Politics for Christians.* New York: Association, 1956.

Neuhaus, Richard John. *Christian Faith and Public Policies: Thinking and Acting in the Courage of Uncertainty.* Minneapolis: Augsburg, 1977.

Nygren, Anders. "Luther's Doctrine of the Two Kingdoms." *Christus Victor* 104 (March 1959).

————. "Luther's Doctrine of the Two Kingdoms," *The Ecumenical Review* 1:3 (Spring 1949): 301–10.

Pinomaa, Lennart. *Faith Victorious: An Introduction to Luther's Theology.* Trans. Walter J. Kukkonen. Philadelphia: Fortress, 1963.

Porter, J. M., ed. *Luther: Selected Political Writings.* Philadelphia: Fortress, 1957.

Rupp, E. Gordon. *The Righteousness of God: Luther Studies.* London: Hodder and Stoughton, and Naperville: Allenson, 1953.

Schroeder, Edward. "The Orders of Creation—Some Reflections on the History and Place of the Term in Systematic Theology." *Concordia Theological Monthly* 43:3 (March 1972): 165–78.

Sherman, Franklin. "The Christian in Secular Society: Insights from the Reformation." *Una Sancta* 25:2.

―――. "Christian Love and Public Policy Today." *Lutheran Quarterly* 13:3 (August 1961).

―――. "The Church as Advocate of Social Justice." *Lutheran World* 18:3 (1971).

―――. "The Church in the Modern World." *Dialog* (Summer 1966).

―――. *The Church in Social Welfare.* New York: Board of Social Ministry, Lutheran Church in America.

―――. *Corporation Ethics.* Philadelphia: Fortress, 1980.

―――. *The Left Hand of God.* Philadelphia: Fortress, 1976.

―――. "Secular Calling and Social Ethical Thinking." In *The Lutheran Church, Past and Present,* ed. Vilmos Vajta. Minneapolis: Augsburg, 1977.

―――. *Social Ministry: Biblical and Theological Perspectives.* New York: Lutheran Church in America.

―――. *A Theology of Politics.* New York: Board of Social Missions of the United Lutheran Church in America, 1960.

―――. *Work as Praise.* Philadelphia: Fortress, 1979.

Srisang, Kosong. *Perspectives on Political Ethics: An Ecumenical Inquiry.* Geneva: World Council of Churches Publications, 1983.

VI. THE TRANSFORMATION MODEL

Bieler, Andre. *The Social Humanism of Calvin.* Trans. Paul T. Fuhrmann. Richmond: John Knox, 1964.

Calvin, John. *Institutes of the Christian Religion.* Ed. Henry Beveridge. 2 vols. Grand Rapids: Eerdmans, 1953.

Dengerink, Jan. *The Idea of Justice in Christian Perspective.* Toronto: Wedge Publishing Foundation, 1978.

Figgis, John Neville. *The Political Aspects of St. Augustine's City of God.* Gloucester: Peter Smith, 1963.

Graham, Fred W. *The Constructive Revolutionary: John Calvin, His Socio-Economic Impact.* Richmond: John Knox, 1971.

Henry, Paul B. *Politics for Evangelicals.* Valley Forge, Pa.: Judson, 1974.

Hinchliff, Peter. *Holiness and Politics.* Grand Rapids: Eerdmans, 1982.

Holmes, Arthur F. *All Truth is God's Truth.* Grand Rapids: Eerdmans, 1977.

―――. *Faith Seeks Understanding.* Grand Rapids: Eerdmans, 1971.

Mouw, J. Richard. *Political Evangelism.* Grand Rapids: Eerdmans, 1973.

―――. *When the Kings Come Marching In.* Grand Rapids: Eerdmans, 1983.

Mueller, William A. *Church and State in Luther and Calvin.* Nashville: Broadman, 1954.

Ridderbos, Herman N. *The Coming of the Kingdom.* Philadelphia: Presbyterian and Reformed, 1962.

Van Til, Henry. *The Calvinistic Concept of Culture.* Philadelphia: Presbyterian and Reformed, 1959.

VII. HUMANISM

A Secular Humanist Declaration. Buffalo: Prometheus, 1981.

Blackham, Harold J., ed. *Objections to Humanism*. Westport, Conn.: Greenwood, 1974.

Breen, Quirinus. *Christianity and Humanism*. Grand Rapids: Eerdmans, 1968.

Brown, Colin. *Philosophy and the Christian Faith*. Wheaton: Tyndale, 1969.

Ehrenfeld, David. *The Arrogance of Humanism*. New York: Oxford University Press, 1978.

Hitchcock, James. *What Is Secular Humanism? Why Humanism Became Secular and How It Is Changing Our World*. Ann Arbor: Servant, 1982.

Humanist Manifesto I & II. Buffalo: Prometheus, 1973.

Johnson, Robert L. *Humanism and Beyond*. Philadelphia: United Church, 1973.

Kurtz, Paul, ed. *The Humanist Alternative*. Buffalo: Prometheus, 1973.

_____, ed. *Moral Problems in Contemporary Society*. Buffalo: Prometheus, 1973.

Maritain, Jacques. *Integral Humanism: Temporal and Spiritual Problems of a New Humanism*. Notre Dame, Ind.: University of Notre Dame Press, 1973.

_____. *True Humanism*. Westport, Conn.: Greenwood, 1970.

Martin, Janet-Kerr. *The Secular Promise: Christian Humanism Amid Contemporary Humanism*. Philadelphia: Westminster, 1964.

Molnar, Thomas. *Christian Humanism*. Chicago: Franciscan Herald, 1978.

Shinn, Roger L. *Man: The New Humanism*. Philadelphia: Westminster, 1968.

Storer, Morris B., ed. *Humanist Ethics*. Buffalo: Prometheus, 1980.

Strawson, William. *The Christian Approach to the Humanist*. London: Lutterworth, 1970.

Webber, Robert E. *Secular Humanism: Threat and Challenge*. Grand Rapids: Zondervan, 1982.

VII. LIBERATION

Armerding, Carl Edwin, ed. *Evangelicals and Liberation*. Philadelphia: Presbyterian and Reformed, 1977.

Bockmuehl, Klaus. *The Challenge of Marxism: A Christian Response*. Downers Grove, Ill.: InterVarsity, 1980.

Bonino, Jose Miguez. *Doing Theology in a Revolutionary Situation*. Philadelphia: Fortress, 1975.

Buhlmann, Walbert. *The Coming of the Third Church: An Analysis of the Present and Future*. Ed. Ralph and A. N. Woodhall. Maryknoll, N.Y.: Orbis, 1977.

Cone, James H. *Black Theology and Black Power*. New York: Seabury, 1969.

Costas, Orlando E. *The Church and Its Mission: A Shattering Critique From the Third World*. Wheaton; Tyndale, 1974.

Fierro, Alfredo. *The Militant Gospel and a Critical Introduction to Political Theologies*. New York: Orbis, 1977.

Freire, Paulo. *Pedagogy of the Oppressed*. Trans. Myra Bergman Ramos. New York: Seabury, 1970.

Gundry, Stanley N., and Johnson, Alan F. *Tensions in Contemporary Theology*. Chicago: Moody, 1976.

Gutierrez, Gustavo. *A Theology of Liberation*. Maryknoll, N.Y.: Orbis, 1973.

Kirk, Andrew J. *Liberation Theology: An Evangelical View from the Third World*. Richmond, Va.: John Knox, 1979.

Lawrentin, Rene. *Liberation, Development and Salvation.* Trans. Charles Underhill Quinn. Maryknoll, N.Y.: Orbis, 1972.

Soell, Dorothee. *Political Theology.* Philadelphia: Fortress, 1974.

Verkuyl, Johannes. *The Message of Liberation in Our Age.* Trans. Dale Cooper. Grand Rapids: Eerdmans, 1972.

IX. CHRIST AND AMERICA

Ahlstrom, Sydney. *A Religious History of the American People.* New Haven: Yale University Press, 1972.

Baldwin, Samuel D. *Armageddon: or the . . . Existence of the United States Foretold in the Bible, Its . . . expansion into the Millennial Republic, and Dominion over the Whole World.* Cincinnati: Applegate, 1854.

Beard, Charles A. *An Economic Interpretation of the Constitution of the United States.* New York: Free Press, 1914.

Bellah, Robert. *The Broken Covenant: American Civil Religion in Time of Trial.* New York: Winston, 1975.

_____. *The Broken Image.* New York: Seabury, 1975.

Benne, Robert, and Hefner, Philip. *Defining America: A Christian Critique of the American Dream.* Philadelphia: Fortress, 1974.

Cherry, Conrad, ed. *God's New Israel: Religious Interpretations of American Destiny.* Englewood Cliffs, N.J.: Prentice-Hall, 1971.

Cotham, Perry C. *Politics, Americanism, and Christianity.* Grand Rapids: Baker, 1976.

Davies, Samuel. *Religion and Patriotism, the Constitutents of a Good Soldier.* Philadelphia: James Chlattin, 1755.

Deloria, Vine, Jr. *God Is Red.* New York: Delta, 1979.

Fowler, Robert. *A New Engagement: Evangelical Political Thought 1966–1976.* Grand Rapids: Eerdmans, 1982.

Heimert, Alan E. *Religion and the American Mind: From the Great Awakening to the Revolution.* Cambridge: Harvard University Press, 1966.

Linder, Robert D., and Pierard, Richard V. *Twilight of the Saints: Biblical Christianity and Civil Religion in America.* Downers Grove, Ill.: InterVarsity, 1978.

Marty, Martin E. *The New Shape of American Religion.* New York: Harper, 1959.

_____. *The Pro & Con Book of Religious America.* Waco: Word, 1975.

_____. *Righteous Empire: The Protestant Experience in America.* New York: Dial, 1970.

Mead, Sidney E. *The Nation with the Soul of a Church.* New York: Harper and Row, 1975.

Monsma, Stephen. *The Unraveling of America: Wherein the Author Analyzes the Inadequacies of Current Political Options and Responds with a Christian Approach to Government.* Downers Grove, Ill.: InterVarsity, 1974.

Nagel, Paul C. *This Sacred Trust: American Nationality, 1798–1898.* New York: Oxford University Press, 1971.

Niebuhr, Richard. *The Kingdom of God in America.* Hamden, Conn.: Shoe String, 1956.

Novak, Michael, ed. *Democracy and Mediating Structures: A Theological Inquiry.* Washington, D.C.: American Enterprise Institute for Public Policy Research, 1980.

_____. *The Spirit of Democratic Capitalism.* New York: Simon & Shuster, 1982.

Perry, Ralph Barton. *Our Side Is Right*. Cambridge: Harvard University Press, 1942.

_____. *Puritanism and Democracy*. New York: Vanguard, 1944.

Richey, Russell and Donald Jones, eds. *American Civil Religion*. New York: Harper and Row, 1974.

Smith, Elwyn A., ed. *The Religion of the Republic*. Philadelphia: Fortress, 1971.

Strout, Cushing. *The New Heavens and New Earth: Political Religion in America*. New York: Harper and Row, 1974.

Tonks, A. Ronald, and Charles W. Deweese. *Faith, Stars, and Stripes: The Impact of Christianity on the Life History of America*. Nashville: Broadman, 1976.

Tuveson, Ernest Lee. *Redeemer Nation: The Idea of America's Millennial Role*. Chicago: University of Chicago Press, 1968.

Weber, Timothy P. *Living in the Shadow of the Second Coming: American Premillennialism, 1875–1925*. Grand Rapids: Zondervan, 1979.

Wilson, John F. *Public Religion in American Culture*. Philadelphia: Temple University Press, 1979.

X. CONTEMPORARY EVANGELICAL THOUGHT

Allen, Edgar L. *Christian Humanism: A Guide to the Thought of Jacques Maritain*. London: Hodder & Stoughton, 1950.

Barcus, Nancy B. *Developing a Christian Mind* Downers Grove, Ill.: Inter-Varsity, 1977.

Blamires, Harry. *The Christian Mind*. London: SPCK, 1966.

_____. *Where Do We Stand? An Examination of the Christian's Position in the Modern World*. Ann Arbor: Servant, 1980.

Bloesch, Donald G. *Wellsprings of Renewal: Promise in Christian Communal Life*. Grand Rapids: Eerdmans, 1974.

_____. *The Evangelical Renaissance*. Grand Rapids: Eerdmans, 1973.

Bockmuehl, Klaus. *Evangelicals and Social Action*. Trans. David T. Priestly. Downers Grove, Ill.: InterVarsity, 1979.

Cairns, Earle E. *Saints and Society*. Chicago: Moody, 1960.

Dennis, Lane R. *A Reason for Hope*. Old Tappan, N.J.: Revell, 1976.

Douglas, J. D. *Let the Earth Hear His Voice*. Minneapolis: World Wide Publications, 1975.

Eells, Robert and Bartel Nyberg. *Lonely Walk: The Life of Senator Mark Hatfield*. Chappaqua: Christian Herald, 1979.

Eidsmore, John. *God and Caesar: Christian Faith and Political Action*. Westchester, Ill.: Crossway, 1984.

Fackre, Gabriel. *The Religious Right and the Christian Faith*. Grand Rapids: Eerdmans, 1982.

Falwell, Jerry. *The Fundamental Phenomena*. New York: Doubleday, 1981.

_____. *Listen America*. New York: Doubleday, 1980.

Gladwin, John. *God's People in God's World: Biblical Motives for Social Involvement*. Downers Grove, Ill.: InterVarsity, 1979.

Hatfield, Mark O. *Between a Rock and a Hard Place*. Waco, Tex.: Word, 1977.

Helms, Jesse. *When Free Men Shall Stand*. Grand Rapids: Zondervan, 1976.

Henry, Carl F. H. *Aspects of Christian Social Ethics*. Grand Rapids: Baker Book House, 1971.

Henry, Paul B. *Politics for Evangelicals*. Valley Forge, Pa.: Judson, 1974.

Hollinger, Dennis. *Individualism and Social Ethics*. Washington: University Press of America, 1983.

Holmes, Arthur. *All Truth Is God's Truth*. Grand Rapids: Eerdmans, 1977.

Huyser, Joel. *The Whole Gospel for the Whole Person*. Denver: Evangelical Concern of Denver, 1978.

Jackson, Dave. *Coming Together: All Those Communities and What They're Up To*. Minneapolis: Bethany House, 1978.

Johnston, Arthur. *The Battle for World Evangelism*. Wheaton: Tyndale, 1978.

Jorstad, Erling. *The Politics of Doomsday: Fundamentalism of the Far Right*. New York: Abingdon, 1970.

Kraft, Charles H. *Christianity in Culture*. Maryknoll, N.Y.: Orbis, 1979.

Krass, Alfred C. *Five Lanterns at Sundown: Evangelism in a Chastened Mood*. Grand Rapids: Eerdmans, 1978.

Linder, Robert D., ed. *God and Caesar*. Longview, Tex.: Conference on Faith and History, 1971.

McLoughlin, William. *The American Evangelicals 1800–1900*. New York: Harper and Row, 1968.

Magnuson, Norris. *Salvation in the Slums: Evangelical Social Work, 1865–1920*. Metuchen, N.J.: Scarecrow, 1977.

Malik, Charles. *The Two Tasks*. Westchester, Ill.: Cornerstone, 1980.

Marshall, Peter, and Manuel, David. *The Light and the Glory*. Old Tappan, N.J.: Revell, 1977.

Moberg, David. *The Great Reversal: Evangelism Versus Social Concern*. Philadelphia: Lippincott, 1972.

Mooneyham, W. Stanley. *What Do You Say to a Hungry World?* Waco, Tex.: Word, 1974.

Mott, Stephen Charles. *Biblical Ethics and Social Change*. New York: Oxford, 1982.

Mouw, J. Richard. *Political Evangelism*. Grand Rapids: Eerdmans, 1973.

―――――. *Politics and the Biblical Drama*. Grand Rapids: Eerdmans, 1976.

Nicholls, Bruce J. *Contextualization: A Theology of Gospel and Culture*. Downers Grove, Ill.: InterVarsity, 1979.

Nida, Eugene A. *Customs and Cultures*. 2d ed. South Pasadena: William Carey Library, 1975.

―――――. *Message and Mission*. New York: Harper and Row, 1960.

Noll, Mark A. *Christians in the American Revolution*. Grand Rapids: Christian University Press, 1977.

Noll, Mark A.; Hatch, Nathan O.; and Marsden, George M. *The Search for Christian America*. Westchester, Ill.: Crossway, 1983.

Ortiz, Juan Carlos. *Disciple*. Carol Stream, Ill.: Creation House, 1974.

Padilla, C. Rene, ed. *The New Face of Evangelicalism*. Downers Grove, Ill.: InterVarsity, 1976.

Pierard, Richard U. *The Unequal Yoke*. Philadelphia: Lippincott, 1970.

Redekop, John H. *The American Far Right*. Grand Rapids: Eerdmans, 1968.

Robinson, James. *Save America to Save the World*. Wheaton, Ill.: Tyndale, 1980.

Schaeffer, Francis A. *A Christian Manifesto*. Westchester, Ill.: Crossway, 1981.

Schaeffer, Francis A., and Koop, C. Everett. *Whatever Happened to the Human Race?* Old Tappan, N.J.: Revell, 1979.

Scott, Waldren. *Bring Forth Justice*. Grand Rapids: Eerdmans, 1980.

Sider, Ronald, ed. *The Chicago Declaration*. Carol Stream, Ill.: Creation House, 1974.

Skillen, James W. *Christians Organizing for Political Service*. Washington, D.C.: Association for Public Justice, 1980.

Smith, Robert, ed. *Christ and the Modern Mind*. Downers Grove, Ill.: Inter-Varsity, 1972.

Stott, John R. W., and Coote, Robert T. *Christian Mission in the Modern World*. Downers Grove, Ill.: InterVarsity, 1975.

_____. *Gospel and Culture*. South Pasadena: William Carey Library, 1979; Grand Rapids: Eerdmans, 1980.

Tucker, Sterling. *Black Reflections on White Power*. Grand Rapids: Eerdmans, 1970.

Viguerie, Richard A. *The New Right: We're Ready to Lead*. Falls Church, Va.: Viguerie, 1980.

Wallis, James. *Agenda for Biblical People*. Grand Rapids: Eerdmans, 1972.

Walter, J. A. *Sacred Cows: Exploring Contemporary Idolatry*. Grand Rapids: Zondervan, 1979.

Webber, Robert E. *The Moral Majority: Right or Wrong?* Westchester, Ill.: Crossway, 1981.

_____. *The Secular Saint: The Role of the Christian in the Western World*. Grand Rapids: Zondervan, 1979.

Webster, Douglas D. *Christian Living in a Pagan Culture*. Wheaton: Tyndale, 1980.

Whitehead, John W. *The Second American Revolution* Elgin, Ill.: Cook, 1982.

Wirt, Sherwood. *The Social Conscience of the Evangelical*. New York: Harper and Row, 1968.

Woodbridge, John D.; Noll, Mark A.; and Hatch, Nathan O. *The Gospel in America: Themes in the Story of America's Evangelicals*. Grand Rapids: Eerdmans, 1979.

INDEXES

INDEX OF PERSONS

INDEX OF SUBJECTS

INDEX OF SCRIPTURE REFERENCES